TOP FUEL WORMHOLE

The Cole Coonce Drag Strip Reader, Volume 1

FIRST EDITION APRIL 2009
Copyright © 2009

All rights reserved under International and Pan-American Copyright Conventions.

Published in the United States by KeroseneBomb Publishing, a division of poverty and decrepidation, fueled by unsolicited amounts of whatever Takakjian brought over. Except for the parts that aren't, the information in this book is true & correct to the best of our knowledge & in no way conveys the intentions of the author. We just re-read one of Nick Tosches most memorable CREEM Magazine pieces, an interview with Patti Smith. It turns out he made the whole thing up. We think we like it even more now, than when we read it the first time, while in a High School Social Studies class. All recommendations are made without any guarantee on the part of the author or Publisher, who also disclaim any liability incurred in connection with the use of this data or specific details regarding secrets of the drag racing hyper-corporate complex.... We recognize that some words, model names & designations, mentioned herein are the property of the trademark holder. We use them indiscreetly and with abandon for identification purposes only. Originally conceived in a swirl of beer & bagels, half hits of blotter & noxious automotive exhaust fumes on the pavement. We're sorry about pissing off Jay Roach and Arley Langlo. On the other hand, they got it over it – we think. No part of this publication may be reproduced without prior written permission from the Publisher. With the exception of brief passages for the purpose of review. Or whatever.
    This publication is deemed inadmissable as evidence.

```
         Library Of Congress Cataloging-in-Publication Data
                      Coonce, Cole, 1961
                  Top Fuel Wormhole / Cole Coonce
                       ISBN 0-9719977-6-4
1.  Drag Racing in the Hyper-Corporate Age -- Meditations on. I Title
      Photographs by Cole Coonce, Dave Wallace(s), Forrest Bond & Ron Lewis
                      Postcard by Jack Logan
         Art direction, Design, Andy Takakjian, Cole Coonce
```

KeroseneBomb Publishing
Los Angeles, CA 90041
www.kerosenebomb.com
Manufactured in the United States of America

veni, vidi, creasy

A TIP OF THE CAN TO:

Andy Takakjian, Ron Lewis, Steve Collison, Dave Wallace, Dave Wallace. Sr, Sky Wallace, John Tottenham, Mendy Fry, Ro McGonegal. Richard Heath, Tom Hunnicutt, StOrMy ByRd, "Root Beer," Tom Slick, Walt Stevens, Wally Haynes, Jon Barrett, Kate Basic, Ikky Shivers, Bob Post, Chris Martin, Jeff Burk, Darr Hawthorne, Robin Richards, "Wild Bill" Alexander, "Techno Tim" Gibson, Forrest K. Bond, Phil Burgess, Dave Densmore, Champion Speed Shop, Sammy Hale, Craig Breedlove, "Nitro Neil" Bisciglia, Nitro Kitty Inc., Top Fuel Inc., Jack Logan and maybe Bob Frye. And Mike Bumbeck.

ILLUSTRATION: JACK LOGAN
ARLEY LANGLO PHOTO: RON LEWIS
SURFERS PHOTOS: FORREST K. BOND
SAN FERNANDO, "WILD BILL" ALEXANDER PHOTOS: DAVE WALLACE, SR.
SHEP GINZBURG PHOTO: SARAH CLAYTON
OTHER PHOTOS: COLE COONCE

PRAISE FOR COLE COONCE & TOP FUEL WORMHOLE

"Cole Coonce is a VTEC Tom Wolfe, a literary autojournalist tricked out with nitrous oxide and nightvision, writing for The Fast and the Furious generation."—Adam Fisher, Senior Editor, *Wired* magazine

"Tonight my butt's got a permanent ring around it after an extended stay in the library, reading Cole Coonce's '(Top Fuel) Wormhole.' Coonce is a Steinbeck/Kerouac/London banana split, and may just earn *HOT ROD* its first Pulitzer."—Larry Tolle, *HOT ROD* Magazine

"Cole is a writer that has expanded raceminds beyond jetting, performances, indexes and politics. His style has been to explore elements of the acceleration persona that transcend space available in mere magazines."—Phil Elliot, *draglist.com*

CONTENTS

PART ONE: THE HORIZON

FOREWORD by Robert C. Post	9
1. DEATH ON A SUNDAY AFTERNOON & THE WHINE OF BLOWERS OVER THE PACOIMA ARROYO	13
2. SMIRNOFF VODKA AND THE SPIRIT(S) OF THE 60s	16
3. BOOK REVIEW: HIGH PERFORMANCE	18
4. THE DRAG STRIP DIARIES, PART 1	20
5. WHO'S AFRAID OF ARLEY LANGLO?	25
6. THE DRAG STRIP DIARIES, PT. 2	30
7. TAYLOR STORMS TO 6.17	35
8. THE DRAG STRIP DIARIES, PT. 3	36
9. OVER, UNDER, SIDEWAYS, DOWN: THE STORY OF "WILD WILLIE" BORSCH	41
10. THE DRAG STRIP DIARIES, PT. 4	46
11. BAKERSFIELD BE HERE NOW	51
12. HAVE NITRO, WILL TRAVEL	59
13. SHIRLEY MULDOWNEY: ORIGINAL BLAST-OFF GIRL AND DRAG STRIP GRAND DAME	84
14. DUNLAP TASTES VICTORY	89
15. RITTER TURNS 5.98, 242 – WITH HIS EYES CLOSED!	93
16. BURY MY HEART AT EDWARDS AFB	95
17. BLAINE JOHNSON 1962-1996	106

PART TWO: THE CENTER OF THE SHADOW

18. HESITATION KILLS	111
19. MISHAP AT BLACK ROCK!	114
20. BISCIGLIA CRASHES '48 FIAT FUELER	118
21. TARGET SPEED: TWENTY NINE PALMS	119
22. THE UNIVERSE IS EXPANDING	128
23. THE EPIC SAGA OF THE SURFERS: THE SOUTHERN CALIFORNIA EXPLODING INEVITABLE	144
24. DRAG RACING IS MUCH MORE PUNK ROCK THAN ANY SLACKER GEN X SHITHEAD WITH AN OUT-OF-TUNE GUITAR	167
25. MURPHY MAKES MARCH MEET HISTORY	174
26. JIM HERBERT, R.I.P	177
27. W.W. TWO STARS IN BAKERSFIELD TEAR-JERKER	179
28. CHAMPION SPEED SHOP'S TOP FUEL WORMHOLE	182
29. THE CRASH, BURN AND RESURRECTION OF A WORKING CLASS HERO: THE "WILD BILL" ALEXANDER INTERVIEW	196
30. 1999: NOTES FROM THE HEART (LAND HOT ROD REUNION)	209
31. "SWINGIN' SAMMY" HALE EXITS COCKPIT	213
32. MIGRANT APES IN THE GASOLINE CRACK OF HISTORY	215
33. THE *MAD!* ROCKET SCIENTIST	217

PART THREE: COLLAPSE

34. THE PASSING OF STEVE COLLISON AND THE DEATH OF DRAG STRIP JOURNALISM	221
35. "VIVA LA NITRO!"	225
36. FRYING THE BALONEYS OFF OF DANICA PATRICK AT THE SMOG CUTTER	235
37. DRAG PRINCESS	238
38. BUCK OWENS, TOP FUEL AND THE DEATH OF THE BAKERSFIELD SOUND	243
39. TOMMY JOHNSON'S DIPPITY-DO AND A MODEST PROPOSAL TO SPIKE DRAG RACING'S BAD HAIR DAY	246
40. SMOKIN' DON SCHUMACHER'S, INTERNET WORM FOOD AND WHO KILLED MARK TWAIN?	249
41. THE DAY OF THE DELUGE AND SURVIVAL OF THE UNFITTEST	252

FOREWORD

by Robert C. Post

It's Valentine's Day, and the *Washington Post* lands on my doorstep with a hopeful forecast on the front page of the sports section—that NASCAR's "ailments" will be overcome in 2009 if a man who "wears a green-and-white racing suit and goes by the name of Dale Earnhardt Jr." wins or even contends for the Sprint Cup Championship. In a carefully crafted 700 words, *Post* staff-writer Liz Clarke leaves no doubt of her own hope that Jr. will deliver as NASCAR's personal "economic stimulus," that he will succeed in jump starting (has there ever, ever been a more overworked expression?) a spectacle that stalled out in 2008. This is the *Washington Post*, the epitome of effete liberalism, which, not so long ago, would never run one word of NASCAR results, and only print a story if someone died violently.

Now, ailing or not, their NASCAR exploits have put Jr. (and Jeff Gordon) on the Forbes Celebrity 100, not all that high up (37 and 52 respectively) but ahead of Jennifer Lopez, Reese Witherspoon, Nicole Kidman, and Rush Limbaugh, and way ahead of Wolfgang Puck and Tina Fey, who are down in the 90s.

Meantime we have drag racing, the main subject of Cole Coonce's anthology he calls *Top Fuel Wormhole*.

The Internet Encyclopedia of Science defines a wormhole as "a hypothetical 'tunnel' connecting two different points in spacetime in such a way that a trip through the wormhole could take much less time than a journey between the same starting and ending points in normal space." Fair enough. A trip through drag racing from its starting to ending points could take sixty years. Here, Cole takes us on a trip through compressed time in a few hours. It's a trip with moments of triumph, pathos, melodrama, and heartbreaking

top fuel wormhole

tragedy, and it is because drag racing has all this that I have started out with something about NASCAR. Which, though its fan-base may have dwindled, still has millions of them, still has a driver who ranks fourth among American athletes in endorsement income (that's Jr.), still has prime-time start-to-finish television, and still gets front-page writeups in the most respected newspapers. And what does drag racing get on that score? Almost nothing. As I wrote in *High Performance*, if it's lucky, in most places it gets a half-inch of results in agate type down there in the corner with football arena and duckpins.

If I were among the mandarins who control drag racing from their boardroom in Glendora, California, that would trouble me into life-threatening insomnia. But long ago they seem to have decided that the problem is insoluble, and recently they elected to pass the problem on to a new owner who, despite all, seemed ready to plunk down several hundred million dollars for control of drag racing's top performers. Well, that deal fell through in particularly embarrassing fashion, and yet embarrassments on a small scale are nothing at all unusual for drag racing:

Consider the money spent on Madison Avenue campaigns that were dead on arrival—remember "We Have Ignition" or what Cole called the "rather pushed comparison" between top fuel racing and the "extreme" amateur athletes who surf lava-flows? Consider the fiftieth-anniversary book that Cole and I wrote, *Life in the Fast Lane*, which had to be withdrawn from circulation because of the uproar when it was found to have been stripped of reference to important people not in favor in Glendora, in all likelihood by the sainted Wally Parks himself. Consider the continuing presence of a TV broadcast anchor, one Paul Page, whom Cole dubs "the mastadon of malapropism." Consider a leaker once dis-invited from national events but who was let back in the door in anticipation of a short field at the 2009 Pomona opener—and who showed thousands of appalled onlookers that his performances had sunk somewhere far below "an absurdist political statement."

And on more treacherous ground, consider that drag racing's all-time and forever hero, Don Garlits, has diverted his passions mostly to broadcasting vile racist pornography to his substantial e-mail list. Once unfairly nicknamed Don Garbage, Don really has become Don Garbage.

So, that's the downside. On the upside, we have Cole's wormhole. There are people from drag racing's Olympus, such as it is, like Shirley, like Jim Herbert, like Wild Bill and Wild Willie, like Mike Sorokin. With Mike, there is the ultimate tragedy, but there are others, Blaine Johnson and the poor forgotten young man who met his maker on the bridge over the Pacoima Arroyo. There are the clowns, tragic in their own way, like Arley Langlo (a friend of mine who knew Arley in high school in Santa Barbara remembers him as a bad-ass who was always getting in fights). At the other end of the spectrum, there are the boys of Black Rock.

Now, for the particular enjoyment of old-time enthusiasts who have washed their hands of the Full Throttle Series (or whatever it's called now)—Hall of Famer Dave Wallace comes particularly to mind—there is "nostalgia" racing. But as compelling as this is, nostalgia racing of course harbors the seeds of its own destruction. This is because people with "the desire to return to a former time" (that's what nostalgia means) will soon be gone, and one imagines that all the 1960s slingshot dragsters that have been lovingly restored or recreated will go through another cycle of consignment to the garage rafters. Perhaps most sadly, there will be nobody left who cares about sitting in one of these silent machines to go "vroom, vroom...."

All that will be left in the end is some sterling storytelling, much of it by Cole Coonce. That will have to be enough.

(Bob Post is the author of High Performance: The Culture and Technology of Drag Racing *(Johns Hopkins University Press, 2001), which, in a thoughtful moment, Don Garlits called "the bible of drag racing for future generations.")*

PART ONE: THE HORIZON

DEATH ON A SUNDAY AFTERNOON AND THE WHINE OF BLOWERS OVER THE PACOIMA ARROYO

I remember the whine and the zing of the Top Fuel cars. It was the sound of metallic machinery wound-up to the point of breaking into magnesium quarks and positrons. I'll never forget my Grandmother cursing the sound of the fuel cars on Sunday afternoons in the 1960s, hearing the blowers spin up into a glorious glissando and then the reverberation vaporizing instantaneously.

I remember playing in the street in San Fernando, catching footballs tossed by my grandfather, spryly huffing and puffing past parked cars and conifer trees, while abruptly pivoting on a buttonhook pattern and catching a spiral in the solar plexus or futilely extending my hands at the denouement of a post pattern in hopes of sticking the pigskin on my fingertips, and hearing the sounds of the nearby drag races— *WWWHHHHHHAAAAAHHHHH – UUNNNNDDTTT*—every few minutes while I ran back to huddle with my quarterback and we pretended he was Roman Gabriel and I was Jack Snow.

    Yes, I knew what all of the high-pitched racket was, the din my grandfather tried to ignore and my grandmother cursed. It took me years to marvel at the irony of my grandfather passing mute judgment on the noise pollution from San Fernando Raceway. He was one of Kelly Johnson's metallurgists at the Skunk Works adjunct at Lockheed in Burbank, and his role in the development and manufacture of various black-budget supersonic spy planes led to all the sliding glass door windows in the city of San Fernando rattling whenever one of Lockheed's Cold War babies did one of its faster-than-sound hole punches in the sky...

    (These sonic booms would rock the neighborhood fairly frequently... from the kitchen Grandma would curse at them as well as the sounds of the nearby drag races, not really grokking that this noise from above was symbolic of the family's meal ticket and Grandpa's employment on classified aircraft. It took her years to realize that some guys parked in the blue Ford sedan who appeared deeply engrossed in the front page section of the *L.A. Times* were actually G-men spooks whose surveillance was to ensure that Grandma wasn't one of them military industrial Rosenberg-types...)

    But I digress: even though I was younger than my underwear size, I had been to the drag strip enough to decipher the sound of a Top Fuel car under a load, making traction and attaining maximum velocity of 200 mph or so... We were a couple of *tacquerias* from San Fernando Raceway—say two or three miles from its entrance on Glenoaks and its "spin out area" beyond the Foothill Boulevard bridge over the Pacoima Arroyo.

    When my uncle was running his Jr. Gas dragster at "the Pond" (as Fernando was quaintly and derisively referred to, its moniker a diminution of Lions Drag Strip a/k/a "the Beach"), I would hear both fundamental tones of a nitro-burning motor as well as the overtones; the thundering grunt of the combustion chambers as well as the harmonic counterpoint of the blower spinning like a dervish eating serpents and hot coals and hell-bent upon breaking into ecstasy.

But away from the track you could only hear the whine of the blowers...

All of these years, I can't say I remember the day of the sound of the blower that just wouldn't quit. On June 16, 1968, Father's Day, Gary Allen Peterson was driving the *Beast From The East* Top Fuel dragster out at Fernando. While hauling ass down the drag strip, the throttle linkage hung and the fuel shut-off didn't seem to work and the damn thing just kept pulling and pulling and pulling and the parachute did not fully deploy.

As the car was still pulling, Peterson attempted to drive through the hole in the bridge; he struck a concrete barrier that catapulted and flipped his fueler into the bridge. The blown Chrysler engine somersaulted the distance of a football field into the so-called "Spin Out" area, wiping out its warning sign.

Seven or eight years ago I rode my bike to the arroyo and just kind of hung out among the remnants of the old San Fernando, the 1/4 mile drag strip that paralleled the wash.

There was a Jiffy Lube adjacent to where the drag strip's shutdown area used to be. And a coat of blue paint had been slathered on the bottom half of the bridge. But at the time, the tire tracks from Gary Allen Peterson's impact were still visible.

A couple of Sundays ago, I rode my bike back out there again. I thought of tossed footballs and the whine of blowers. City workers finally slapped another coat of fresh paint on the bridge over the Arroyo again. This time they managed to cover up most of the tire tracks.

While I took pictures, the homeless guys who sleep under the bridge packed up their tarps and their laundry and walked their beater bicycles up into the Sylmar Hills, seeking shade and shelter amidst the scrub brush.

(Originally published in Drag Racing Online*)*

SMIRNOFF VODKA AND THE SPIRIT(S) OF THE SIXTIES

I barely remember the days when Smirnoff vodka sponsored a AA/Fuel Dragster, and how gorgeous the car was in its original incarnation. But I do recall the car and that it was at one time shoed by the fabled dragster driver, Larry Dixon. What I really remember most is the stuff of family legend. Back in the day, my Uncle Phil drove a small-block Chevy Junior Gas dragster (*Connelly & Coonce*) at various strips in Southern California. In 1967 or '68, at one of Lions Drag Strip's "Professional Dragster Association" meets, my Uncle was suited-up and strapped in the car in the staging lanes, waiting his turn to make a qualifying pass.

As a myriad of dragsters thundered down Lions' 1/4 mile strip, my Uncle's car was methodically pushed closer and closer to the mechanical rolling "starters." At that moment, Larry Dixon Sr. (father of Larry Dixon, Jr., the guy who drives Don Prudhomme's modern Top Fuel car) was feeling no pain and got a little cheeky and prankster-ish. He stuck his mug in my Uncle's cockpit and foisted a bottle of hootch in his face.

"Hey Phil! Want any vodka?"

Phil responded with a muffled, "No thanks, Larry, not right now," his demure words garbled by his protective garb, but punctuated by the car rolling closer to the starting line. Dixon was having none of it however, and leaned in closer and repeated his offer of a pop or two of Smirnoff, a libation of which he was no doubt in ample supply.

"I'm a little busy, Larry."

The dragster was pushed even closer to the mechanical rollers, but my Uncle's muted plea for temporary temperance was met by befuddlement and shrugs. Dixon was nonplussed by the immediacy of the situation, and offered the bottle a third time.

"Larry! Leave me alone," Phil shouted through his asbestos suit. "I'm getting ready to qualify and we're the next pair up!"

"Hey listen!" Dixon warned, "You're not going out there alone, are you?"

(*Originally published on* Jalopnik)

BOOK REVIEW: *HIGH PERFORMANCE*

The Emperor wears no firesuit and Smithsonian curator-cum-*High Performance* author Robert C. Post is just the man to say so. Dropping the drawers on the National Hot Rod Association's supreme ruler, Wally Parks, is not the sole focus of Post's delicious and exhausting tome on the history, technology and culture of drag racing. The questioning of Park's policies on his concern for "hot rodding's image," "conservative influence," helping to "define bounds of legitimacy," "looking askance at jet dragsters," and his (hold on to your coffin nails, race fans) "making deals with R.J. Reynolds" is some serious bench-racing fodder you'll certainly never read in *National Dragster*.

Alas, children, before tobacco, McDonalds, and Budweiser were shoved down our throats via 300 mile-per-hour billboards, hot rodding was a bizarre and fascinating culture developed (almost exclusively) by teen denizens of Southern California in the 50s and 60s. Their concern was maximum horsepower, which they approached with raw ingenuity and wry aesthetics. Mr. Post encapsulates this period so evocatively that by reading his work I was sucked into the vacuum of a parallel universe and dropped back into reality only when I closed the book. Then I wondered: did Lions Drag Strip ever happen at all?

But Post doesn't stop at the closing of Lions; he follows the historical arc of the sport thoroughly—from the era of the rugged do-it-yourself individualist(s) building a slingshot dragster in somebody's backyard to the contemporary tableaux of a corporate shill masquerading as a race car driver while kissing Daddy Warbucks' flabby derriere and hoping for permission to go racing. Our intrepid author covers this transition including the "unholy marriage of tobacco and television" and the sport's monopolization by the NHRA (as well as the demise of the American Hot Rod Association, American

Drag Racing Association, United Drag Racing Association, et al.) with more than a whisper of sorrow.

It is, however, his conjuring of the zeitgeist of Southern California hot rodding—"T.V." Tommy Ivo, Gas Ronda, El Mirage, OCIR, Keith Black, Doris Herbert, John "the Zookeeper" Mulligan, *The Surfers* Top Fueler (to name but a few)—that rings the most profound and poignant. It will fill the hearts of those who were there with a warm nostalgia and perhaps the pangs of loss. For those who were not there, this is a crucial document about when the gestalt of drag racing meant speed, youth, chrome and rubber coming together where the desert heat is only tempered by the wind off of the Pacific Ocean.

(*Originally published in* Full Throttle News, *October, 1994*)

THE DRAG STRIP DIARIES (1994)

PART 1

February 3-6, NHRA Winternationals, Pomona CA—Parking was a hassle.

March 19-20, Goodguys' March Meet, Bakersfield Raceway—The Goodguys' virginal foray into the cool time-warp world of nitro 'n' nostalgia drag racing. This one was fraught with a lot of growing pains, unfortunately. Caz, Leah, Ikky and I made the trek from L.A. on Saturday morning in time to watch Top Fuel qualifying. Way too much down-time, and after interminable waits, very few fuelers ran in the second and third sessions. Everyone was cold and bored except me. We shined on Sunday's eliminations and went home Saturday night. The conversation was not exactly riveting on the way back to Los Angeles. Oh well.

April 5, El Segundo Tire, El Segundo CA—Cuz'n Roy Gittens was out visiting from Ranlo, North Carolina. We were cruising in a borrowed convertible, listening to a cassette of the great lost Beach Boys' masterpiece *Smile*. I took it upon myself to be a proper So Cal tour guide and show him the Foster Freeze on Hawthorne Boulevard that inspired Brian Wilson to compose the epic hot rod anthems "Shut Down" and "409" for the Beach Boys in '63. "Every time I heard those songs on my AM radio in Carolina, I knew something magical was going on somewhere else in this world," said Roy in a somber and reverent voice. Not knowing where Brian Wilson's house was, I suggested the next best thing: "Let's go talk racing with (Nostalgia Top Fuel driver) Jim Boyd at his shop in El Segundo," I said, hoping the sight of Boyd's lanky 1967-style AA/Fuel Dragster would conjure some of the same magic Brian Wilson ruminated about in early Beach Boys recordings. When we got to El Segundo Tire (where they keep the race car), Boyd was nowhere to be found. Ronny, his pit boss, was there, but did not seem to be in the mood to bench race. "No, we didn't run after the first session at Bakersfield because the tech guys were a pain in the poopshoot" and "No, we can't afford to run the ANRA race out in Palmdale next week," was about the extent of our "bench racing" session with Ronny. Out of the corner of my eye I noticed a copy of the "Premier Issue" of something calling itself *Full Throttle News* sitting on the counter of Ronny's shop. In reference to "Big Willie" Robinson's new drag strip out at Terminal Island, the headline screamed "The Beach is Back!" I took this as an omen: It seemed like a good time to go back and look for Brian Wilson's pad.

April 9, ANRA "Duel in the Desert," Los Angeles County Raceway, Palmdale, CA—Cuz'n Roy and I hauled ass through the back roads of Angeles Forest Highway in time for the first session of Top Fuel qualifying at 1:00. There were only four fuel cars, and nobody in the stands, which was kind of cool—it was like having a private matinee screening of front-motored fuelers, like I was King Farouk and Roy was Little Lord Fauntleroy or something. After enjoying the first session of Top Fuel, Junior Fuel and Nostalgia Eliminator, we sauntered down Pearblossom Highway to the Pines Cafe for a late breakfast worthy of royalty. We both enjoyed an "Oklahoma Tostada," which is the culinary manifestation of the Chaos Theory, but Boy Howdy! is it tasty. After this massive but sublime breakfast, we wobbled back to LACR for the second session of qualifying and eliminations. A few people were starting to congregate in the bleachers at this point, and we started chatting up a friendly couple from Little Rock, Robert and Donna Bent. After Bill "the Heartbreaker" Dunlap aced Top Fuel Eliminator with a string of 6-second E.T.s, the Bents invited us to their digs for some Pabst Blue Ribbons, but we had to demur. I opened my thermos, dispensed with some of the rocket-fuel-strength espresso I had brewed that morning, and we blazed down Soledad Canyon Road to Saugus Speedway for some yahoo-type roundy-round racing as a nightcap to the day's activities. Roundy-round is the kind of racing Roy would see on a given Saturday night in Carolina, but a style of racing that certainly was not endemic to Californians. It was a harsh contrast to the ANRA event—hellzapoppin' dense action and a full house of hell raisin' race fans. Maybe these roundy-round guys could teach the dragster associations a lick or two about the "gotta sing, gotta dance aspects" of show business. As a dyed-in-the-wool drag racing aficionado, I have to admit I was a little sad and a little ashamed by the disparity in attendance at the day's two racing events.

August 6, Brotherhood Raceway Park, Terminal Island, CA—I had missed all the racing action in the last couple of months due to scheduling and/or lifestyle conflicts (jobs, lack of jobs, non-race fan girlfriends, etc.), but Sean Vigle and I decided to go watch some drag racing this weekend come hell or high water. Neither of us had been to "Big Willie's" drag strip (aka Brotherhood Raceway Park) and somehow this seemed reason enough to hit the road. We listened to "White Lightning" by the Fall and some Bobby Fuller Four as we blazed down the Harbor Freeway—we were primed for anything, even disappointment.

As we crested the lofty Vincent Thomas Bridge, however, I noticed a sea of cars down below, a menagerie glittering in the setting California sun, transforming the once barren Terminal Island into the Magic Kingdom or something. As we began our descent down the bridge, I could see two doorslammers streaking down the drag strip. "Jesus," I said to Sean over the thundering din of "I Fought the Law," "there really is a drag strip in Los Angeles." We paid our admission ("Ten dollars—do you want to watch or race?"—"Uh, watch, I guess."—"Have a good time."—"Cool.") and joined the railbirds on the secondary guardwall. This was pure chaotic, anything-goes drag racing. The epic presence of "Big Willie" Robinson, however, was the glue that kept this spectacle from disintegrating into unmitigated anarchy. After awhile Sean and I joined the staff of *Full Throttle News*, Richard Heath, Tom Hunnicutt, Richard Morelock, and Holly Leather, in the bleachers. As the sun set over the Harbor we watched a potpourri of race cars—gas dragsters, super stockers, go-carts, roadsters, nitrous-assisted "rice rockets"—parade down the 1320. The diversity of the race cars, as well as the diversity of the patrons—it was a truly harmonious rainbow coalition—made me proud to be a denizen of the Pacific Rim. If anything could give me hope about the bleak future of humanity, this was it.

August 12, ANRA Points Race, Sacramento, CA—I left Los Angeles like a bullet at 2:OO Friday morning, bound for the Capital City under the cover of darkness. I took a sinuous, meandering, yet picturesque back route (Highway 49) through the Gold Country and Calaveras County en route to this drag race. The tight curves of this two-lane highway juxtaposed against the resplendent beauty of the Sierra Nevada Mountains, sent shivers of exultation down my spine. I actually ate granola at a turn-off in the mountains. It seemed like a good time to be alive. After all that nature I was definitely ready for a nice'n'noisy eye-watering drag race. I arrived at the track late Friday night, after having squandered my motel budget on some radiator repairs in Calaveras County. After a swim/shower in the Sacramento River, I was going to spend Friday night in my car which I parked behind the motor home of Nostalgia Eliminator racer Steve Warnicke. He had gotten to the track with his family a day early to test'n'tune the race car before Saturday's race. Warnicke and his friendly longhair pit boss Rick worked on his injected-on-nitro digger until 2a.m., but all the while we talked drag racing and drank Bud Sodas. Around midnight, his wife made some roast beef sandwiches. The conversation was good, the food was tasty, and the Warnicke's hospitality was extremely gracious.

On Saturday the San Joaquin Valley was hotter than a waffle iron. Despite the torrid temperatures Ted "the Bad Lieutenant" Taylor absolutely excoriated Top Fuel Eliminator with an epic 6.17 blast. There was a copious armada of injected-on-methanol, small block Junior Fuel diggers at this race, a phenomenon that never fails to fill my heart with glee. The final round seemed to be indicative of the tight, dramatic action that is a staple of Junior Fuel Eliminator, as a rampaging Bob McKray chased down the always cagey Stacy "the Femme Fatale" Paul, a 7.68 to her 7.76. In Nostalgia Eliminator the hospitable Warnicke went out in the semi-finals. Jim Scott, Jr. commandeered his old man's sleek, Ice Pak-blue slingshot to victory in N/E. In the final round Scotty was doused by an oil bath at 1000 feet out, but he kept his composure while hammering the throttle down, recording a right-on-time 7.51 (against the 7.50 index) that forced his opponent, the ever-daunting Bob Shearer in his badass '23 T blown-on-alcohol altered, to breakout with a 7.47. After sharing a victory brew with the "Team Scott" crew, I opened up the thermos, jammed a Link Wray cassette into the stereo and violated the I-5 speed limits all the way back to Los Angeles. Is it just me, or is a weekend like this what life is all about?

(Originally published in Full Throttle News*)*

WHO'S AFRAID OF ARLEY LANGLO?

Despite the inevitable encroachment of Corporate America into a once idiosyncratic sport, one man still burns the torch of individualism in contemporary Top Fuel drag racing.

I n the nether regions of the Pomona Fairplex (home of the NHRA World Finals), far beyond the cozy confines where the Fortune 500 park their 18-wheelers, one could find the seemingly innocuous, inconspicuous Arley Langlo, Jay Roach, and their *Titan Xpress* race team in their pit area. A ramshackle trailer, a 10-year old short (260-inch wheelbase) Top Fueler, an anti-matter black 1967 Dodge camper, and a race crew whose uniform consists of straw cowboy hats and stark white coffee-stained T-shirts, are the elements which define their existence, at least tangibly. Dwarfed by a phalanx of massive transporters, race teams with matching polyester uniforms, not to mention the copious off-the-shelf spare parts, all of which are *de rigueur* for modern day multi-million dollar operations, Langlo, Roach, and cohorts looked like they made a wrong turn on Fairplex Avenue in 1984, got lost in the Mojave Desert, mistakenly entered the vortex of the Twilight Zone, blinked, and somehow wandered back into Pomona, only to find ten years had elapsed. It was now 1994, but somehow the mayonnaise and the baloney in their Styrofoam cooler had not spoiled. In reality, no matter how anachronistic these guys were, their presence at the Winston Finals could not be ignored, nor swept under the carpet.

Sure, a lot of the hullabaloo was focused on the culmination of superstar Don "the Snake" Prudhomme's "Final Strike" tour, Shelly Anderson's dramatic 4.71 Low E.T., and Kenny Bernstein's shocking 314 mph blast in his indomitable *Budweiser King*. I maintain that all this was anticlimactic, however, compared to the incendiary, apocalyptic exploits of the *Titan Xpress* bunch. Indeed, among Arley Langlo's attempts to "qualify" into Top Fuel Eliminator at Pomona were a pair of the most curious, surreal meltdowns ever perpetrated on the ol' 1320.

Langlo and Roach probably had no hope of "getting into the show against these store-bought dragsters," as Arley put it, but the World Finals did provide an excuse for them to "test the new fuel pump." (This fuel pump, like virtually every piece of kit on their dragster, is homemade by Jay Roach in his hard-to-find J&S East Valley Garage, reclusively nestled in the hills of Santa Barbara County.) At the end of the weekend, whether the new fuel pump worked satisfactorily or not seemed entirely beside the point—although a point was made by the *Titan Xpress* at the NHRA Finals. What that point was, however, is subject to serious interpretation…

During Top Fuel qualifying on Thursday and Saturday, Langlo demonstrated some genuine human characteristics that are conspicuously absent from modern Top Fuel racing—specifically driving skills, i.e., how the driver responds to the nuances of an unrestrained technology gone gloriously amok. Traditionally, that is the drama of Top Fuel: It is about man and machine and their relationship to each other. Unfortunately, it is an increasingly rare occurrence for us—the gearheads and the punters—to feel overwhelmed or inspired by the exploits of the driver; when Bernstein goes 314, when Shelly runs 4.71, when Don Prudhomme feebly breaks traction and spins the tires on his "final strike," these runs were about the dynamics of technology—the drivers were merely passive. Anderson's clutch management system had been programmed brilliantly. Prudhomme's, on the other hand, had been set up erroneously—therefore the car overpowered the drag strip, the tires smoked ferociously but momentarily, and fluids puked out of the cylinder heads feverishly as the car shut itself off. That was it: *dragster interruptus*. Having been emasculated, Prudhomme limped impotently down the drag strip, naked and vulnerable. The shame of this "not with a bang but a whimper" finale, however, was the onus of Prudhomme's crew chief, the esteemed savant Wes Cerny, not the "Snake" himself. Likewise, the bravado and *chutzpah* requisite of a 314 mile-per-hour salvo are the machinations of *Budweiser King* crew-chief Dale Armstrong, not driver Kenny Bernstein who merely stomped on the go-faster, hung on, and then dumped the laundry before he ran out of real estate. Lowly Arley Langlo, however, laid down the gauntlet; this time, just once, it's gonna be about the driver.

On Thursday Arley fired what could only be interpreted as the first of two salvos of civil defiance. It started innocently enough with a nice smoky burnout—so far, so what. He gingerly and methodically staged the car, just another of 30 Top Fuel cars trying to qualify for Sunday's eliminations. As soon as the light goes green and he drops the hammer, however, something goes very wrong; the car lurches spastically, the sound of the motor changes pitch in an ill glissando, and a ball of flame the size of the Manhattan Project shoots out the back of the race car, scorching a big chunk of Parker Avenue. This is all within the first 60 feet of the run.

Arley feels the car nose over; he should shut 'er off, right? He should abort the run—something is amiss—cut his losses, see 'ya tomorrow, Mr. Amato. But *au contraire* and let the pyrotechnics begin. Arley kept the throttle nailed, even though the head gaskets hydraulicked as soon as he swapped pedals, allowing the billowing fuel and oil to feed an inferno that ballooned into a 30-foot mushroom cloud by half-track. Langlo stubbornly refused to void the run (even though he later acknowledged "it was a little on the rich side"), and he stopped the timers at 5.65 seconds—not bad for an experiment gone horribly awry—but the hijinks continue because this massive fireball burned off his parachutes. The ticket-holders are shaking their heads in disbelief, trying to come to terms with what they are witnessing, but ol' Arley methodically rides the hand brake, milking what is left out of the hydraulic brake fluid that has not been boiled to molasses by the inferno—he does not disengage the clutch lest the car pick up more velocity, preferring instead to let the torque of the motor slow the car down. The car decelerates under power, and Langlo swerves to avoid the catch net while wrestling the slightly yo-yoing fueler onto the border of the Fairplex parking lot. O-kay…

Come Friday the fuel pump is still "too rich." No boom-boom this time, and the car leaves hard, but Mr. Langlo shuts it off at half-track as it starts dropping cylinders, the hyperactive fuel pump frothing so voluminously that the spark plugs are being extinguished from the torrent of nitromethane. The next session ditto. There is one qualifying session left, and Jay and his acolytes are thrashing maniacally to rebuild the motor that has been stripped to the cylinder heads. Meanwhile, a bemused Langlo drawls, "We're progressively leanin' it out."

So it is last call for Top Fuel qualifying, newly crowned NHRA champion Scott Kalitta is clinging to the bubble with an eleventh hour go of 4.88 and who is strapped into the last dragster rolling into the staging lanes? None other than the Ayatollah of the Automotive Apocalypse hisself, Arley Langlo, replete with a new fourth-and-long "leaner" tune-up. He and his accompanying East Valley Garage Hezbollah are faced with the daunting challenge of trying to compete with the Uber-fuelers on their terms, not only bumping the NHRA champion out of The Show, but also sorting out this damn fuel pump. The quickest the *Titan Xpress* has run was a 5.28 at Palmdale; a potential 4.87 that would bum Kalitta's trip seemed highly unlikely, but who knows?

As soon as the tree flashed green, everyone in Pomona knew. An epiphany crystallized in the collective craniums of everyone assembled: bleacher bums, track officials, *National Dragster* paparazzi, the racers themselves (especially Scott Kalitta), and even the hot dog vendors—this was not about "qualifying." Once again, instantaneously, in a virtual doppelganger of Thursday's horrific absolute-zero flameout, Langlo kicked out the head gaskets as soon as he stomped on the throttle, creating another comet of fire that mushroomed exponentially as he rocketed down the quarter-mile. Amidst the terrified and confused looks of the spectators, Langlo once again ignored anything as banal as logic and refused to shut off this missile of the millennium, once more burning off his 'chutes and boiling his brake fluid into an ineffectual muck.

No, this was not about "getting into The Show." This was about the nobility of experimentation, freedom of expression, and the recapturing of the spirit of Zen anarchy vis-à-vis the manifestation of the Chaos Theory—which is what I thought Top Fuel is all about. It was a paean to all resourceful Americans everywhere who, if they can not afford a "store bought" fuel pump, will build it themselves, thus enabling the *Titan Xpresses* of this world to exist on their own terms, not Kenny Bernstein's. For these are the true beacons of "*Go! Fever*" in this wonderful sport, not some Stepford yuppie automaton for whom "driving ability" is a euphemism for how well they can splutter "I'd like to thank all my sponsors: Joy Jelly, Scientology, and the Trilateral Commission blah, blah, blah…" on TV—hey man, we see these names painted on the side of your car, we'll give all these people our money if you just shut up, okay?

Drag racing could stand to benefit from an influx of experimental, outside weirdos like Messrs. Langlo, Roach, and friends. And that was no mere oil fire, my friends. Arley Langlo was carrying the torch of freedom for all of us. Someday soon the drag strips will be ours again…

(Originally published in Super Stock & Drag Illustrated*)*

THE DRAG STRIP DIARIES (1994)

PART 2

August 20, the "Fox Hunt" LACR Palmdale, CA—I invited every L.A. chickee in my phone book who might appreciate drag racing to this event. I had not attended one of these "Fox Hunt" freak shows since Nixon was on Pennsylvania Avenue, but based on my memories of similar promotions during the mid-'70s at Irwindale Raceway and Orange County Int'l Raceway, I assured my assembled harem of hot rod honeys that this event was free for the femmes. Prior to the race Zukovic, Vigle, and I plied the ladies (Caz, Leah, and Clayton) with margaritas at a watering hole on Santiago Road outside of Acton. Even this fortification, however, did not prepare my guests and me for the preposterous Kafkaesque nightmare that awaited us at the LACR ticket booth.

If memory serves, back in the freewheelin' '70s the fairer sex was admitted *gratis* to the Fox Hunts. In the enlightened new wave '90s, however, the ladies have to fork over the dead presidents just like us menfolk. "Women in bikinis," the ticket marm told us, "are the only race fans allowed in free tonight." I rebutted that this was not the "Foxes in Bikinis Hunt," was it? She replied that a cabal of Do-Gooders and Supreme Court Justices concluded that allowing the *frauleins* in free was preferential, exclusionary, and discriminatory towards men. I countered that life is preferential, exclusionary, and discriminatory whether uptight, hotshot attorneys like Gloria Allred want to admit it or not—if you do not believe me, ask ol' Chuck Darwin—and that this is a basic law of nature and humanity.

Unfortunately, the more our society tries to subvert and shoehorn the laws of nature, albeit with the best intentions, the more our society ruins everyone's fun. The LACR promoters could skirt the court's arbitration by comping only the "foxes" who were willing to be exploited as swimsuit-clad sex objects under the guise of "providing entertainment," or some such Catch-22 pretzel logic. Whatever… all I know is that way back in the dark, misguided '70s, at OCIR's Fox Hunt my mom got in free. This is progress?

Yes, somehow the waves of liberation and freedom that swelled in the '60s and '70s have tsunamied the palisades of reason, even at something as absurd as this silly promotional gimmick. Although my posse was frustrated by the capricious decisions of an increasingly intolerant society, we opted to pay the admission with teeth clenched. Now we were in a foul temper, but I was hoping tonight's main attraction—a match race featuring Merlyn Johnson in the *Fatal Attraction* jet car facing off against Arley Langlo in Jay Roach's *Titan Xpress* Top Fuel dragster—would ease the political and sexual tension that had flared up after the L.A. chickees felt duped by my erroneous assumptions about "foxes get in free." Gratuitous displays of pyro generally soothe my psyche and make me feel better about life itself, and I know chicks dig the throbbing vibrations of the nitro dragsters. Certainly, the night could only get better. Top Gas West and the California Independent Funny Car Association also graced tonight's marquee, and after we quickly quaffed a few *brewkowskis* I was ready to enjoy some free-range drag racing with my friends.

Top Gas West is a particularly novel class, and on this night they were in superlative, provocative form. A strange parade of unorthodox dragsters propelled by a potpourri of experimental engine combinations loosely defines the TGW experience. Rear-engined dragsters using dual four-barrel carbs assisted by nitrous, or injected-with-nitrous, or blown-on-gasoline—it warmed my soul to observe a rear-engine dragster streak by sporting a couple of blue nitrous oxide bottles. Experimentation in drag racing has always aroused my rather delicate sensibilities, and now my veins were definitely dilated.

Indeed, to my way of thinking experimentation in drag racing has always been synonymous with what is noble about the human mind—the search for the better mouse-trap; the road less taken; nothing ventured, nothing gained—that sort of thing. Top Gas West certainly exemplified that spirit with their "run whatcha' brung" style of heads-up, no-index drag racing. Their only criterion for competition is that the digger must have petrol in the fuel tank—no nitro, no alcohol. Steve LaBurn took the event win with 6.60's at over 200 mph in a dragster that was powered by an injected small-block Donovan, assisted by a single stage of nitrous.

    The endeavors of CIFCA were also a joy to behold on the Day of the Fox. These machines are not as loud or quite as gnarsome as their high-dollar, nitro-burning NHRA counterparts, but what they lacked in bang they more than made up for in attitude. To wit: perpetual 660-foot burnouts, funky eclectic body styles (an '81 Corvette, a '74 Vega, even a friggin' Volkswagen) powered by a variety of combinations—the VW was even turbocharged. With such tangible diversity, these guys are perhaps the closest thing the West Coast has to a Pro Mod show like they run at podunk drag strips back east: cost effective and fun to watch, definitely a winning combination for spectator and racer alike.

    This generous helping of dragsters and funny cars, however, was a mere tease to the Fox Hunt's *piece de resistance*, the bizarre duel betwixt the *Titan Xpress* Top Fueler and the *Fatal Attraction* jet dragster. Most of our entourage had never seen a jet blaze down the 1320 before, and even the more experienced bleacher bums in our party had never seen one of these propulsion-propelled timebombs square off against a nitro-burning Top Fueler. Nobody was ready for this awesome juxtaposition of power. This was pure *Sturm und Drang*. Langlo's burnout was a shattering caterwaul of noize, as voluminous amber sheets of fire shot into the dark desert sky and simultaneously the jet car ritualistically purged its afterburners *BOOM... BOOM... BOOM...* as the staccato shards of hellfire cannonballed horizontally, the pitch of the jet's turbines ascending into a shrieking glissando. These were just the ceremonial gestures before the race itself—not unlike two Sumo wrestlers slinging salt at each other's feet. And after all this white hot foreplay, the noize and fire sent everyone's sense of anticipation into orbit, the collective tension reaching a frenzied peak, until the cars *f-i-n-a-l-l-y* crept into the staging beams. At the flash of the green light the moment of orgasm and release culminated with the weenie roaster succumbing to fuel control problems, meanwhile the Top Fueler fiercely smoked the tires at 500 feet, breaking traction violently until Langlo clicked it off just past halftrack and cruised to victory with a limping 7.09 at 119 mph; but who "won" and "lost" this freak show had very little to do with the impact of this spectacle.

This was a manifestation of chaos. The entire assembly was stunned into silence by this apocalyptic exhibition of sensory overload, everybody except Zukovic. He interpreted this outlandish Teutonic display of technology as a metaphor and conversely as an indictment and demonstration against the jaded, blasé consciousness of our time: "You can be cynical, you can be hip, and you can be kitsch—but ultimately you then become part of the problem. You can not nod and wink when confronted with the brutality of that jet car." Super Comp gas dragsters were doing burnouts, and Zukovic was also just getting warmed up: "Nor can you feel superior to this brazen showcase of power—these people have harnessed knowledge and sweat into something terrifying and that is not to be trivialized." Two more Super Comp cars whizzed by, but he was not distracted from his soliloquy: "When we as a culture are subjugated to pure, unadulterated, extreme horsepower we can not help but feel humbled. That is when the smarminess and insolence of our generation is not only moot, but also rather insufferable." All I know is that none of us asked for our money back, including the "foxes."

September 10, Brotherhood Raceway Park, Terminal Island, CA—Zukovic prides himself as being something of an authority on surf and hot rod music, but I know he never goes to the beach and the only drag strip he has actually ever patronized was LACR out in the Mojave Desert. Now that L.A. has a drag strip at the beach, I reckoned a trip to Brotherhood Raceway would fill the craters in his credibility gap. On the way to the strip, we stopped and ate a massive lunch at El Tepeyac in East L.A., where we both futilely tried to finish our "Manuel Specials" (imagine a 2 lb. splattering of every food group (including some otherwise unknown to mankind), haphazardly held together by a massive flour tortilla, prepared by a quaintly sclerotic leather-skinned *vaquero* decked out in a carnitas-stained smock and a cafeteria worker's hat emblazoned with "Manuel" across the front, who surreptitiously sploshed a couple of ounces of Cuervo Gold into his Orange Julius cup immediately after finishing our order). It was mighty fine dining.

After lunch we headed to the drag strip, cruising down Whittier Boulevard, admiring the lowered Malibus, Impalas, and Monte Carlos, et al.—nary a Ford or Mopar in sight along the entire stretch from El Tepeyac to the on-ramp onto the 605 Freeway. We grabbed the 605 South, then the 105 East, and as we listened to the Chantays "Pipeline," Zukovic began grilling me on my knowledge of surf music esoterica; no, I did not know Terry Melcher was one half of the Rip Chords, but yes, I did know that he was Doris Day's son... and yes, I did know that Melcher introduced Charles Manson to Beach Boys drummer Dennis Wilson, who not only lent Manson the use of his Rolls Royce, but also convinced Brian Wilson, the genius behind the Beach Boys, to produce some of Charlie's protest music. I also knew that Brian, who was becoming more schizophrenic by the day, had determined that Manson was a little too outside for even his state of mind and booted him out of Brian's beachfront studio. Concurrently, Melcher reneged on a promise to sign Manson to a recording contract. Shortly thereafter, several people were found savagely murdered at a Benedict Canyon house that motion picture director Roman Polanski had recently purchased from, yes, Terry Melcher. Surf music is a lot more complicated than most people realize...

Once we arrived at Brotherhood, our conversation became decidedly less macabre. Zukovic was in awe of the cool vibrations that permeated the drag strip. I told him that this was a 1990s correlation to the old Lions Drag Strip out on Alameda, a track shut down by government bureaucrat philistines. He seemed to understand. A blithe, carefree atmosphere enveloped the entire facility with smooth soul music wafting out of the p.a. simultaneous to Brotherhood President "Big Willie" Robinson's free-association color commentary. This created an incongruous sonic tapestry that served as a counterpoint to the rumble from the myriad of machines racing off into the distance. We were so smitten by the intoxicating environment that we decided to race my '71 Grand Prix down the 1320, only to be shut down three consecutive times. But so what if I got skunked?—Dennis Wilson was the only Beach Boy who actually surfed, and he drowned.

(*Originally published in* Full Throttle News)

TAYLOR STORMS TO 6.17

August 12, 1994, Sacramento Raceway – Borrowing a page ripped out of the "Stormin' Norman" Schwarzkopf playbook, Top Fuel driver Ted Taylor piloted the Jim Herbert-tuned *W.W. Two* front-motored dragster to a scud-like 6.17 elapsed time at 216 MPH, while qualifying for the American Nostalgia Racing Association's Sacramento meet. What made the record-breaking blast even more impressive is that it transpired in 103° mid-afternoon heat during the mother of all California heat waves.

    Taylor and Herbert's machine was seemingly oblivious to the arid heat as they later dusted Don Argee's *195* AA/Fuel Altered in the first round of eliminations. *195* was on a typically (for fuel altereds) banzai out-of-shape pass that Argee wisely aborted while Taylor slid to an off-pace but victorious 7.02.

    While Taylor strolled back to the pits the 67-year old Argee was jettisoned to the staging lanes and strapped into his dragster—yes, Argee drove two of the four Top Fuelers entered at Sacramento, but his stacking of the deck was nonetheless futile when his second race car broke on the starting line. Wally Giavia, meanwhile, drove Jesse Perkins *Cow Palace Shell* entry to a 7.81, 172 solo pass while Argee shimmied out of his hotter-than-coffee firesuit.

    The final was all Taylor. *W.W. Two* thundered to about the 1100 foot mark then clicked to a "mere" 6.23 at only 207 MPH. Admirably, Giavia gave chase but was never within four or five car lengths.

(*Originally published in* Full Throttle News)

THE DRAG STRIP DIARIES (1994)

PART 3

September 11, Southern California Timing Association Speed Meet, El Mirage, CA — I rendezvoused with Zukovic at the House of Pies on Franklin and Vermont in East Hollywood, and we made good time on Highway 14 out to Palmdale. This trip was just another aspect of my crusade to support, philosophically as well as financially, independent hot rodding in the Year of the Boomerang, 1994. Neither of us had experienced the endeavors of the SCTA before, but this could not be as outside as Brotherhood Raceway or Arley Langlo at LACR could it? It was.

At the El Mirage time trials there was a huge assortment of land-based lunar modules masquerading as race cars, including the nitro-burning streamliner of Joaquin Arnett and the Bean Bandits Car Club. Arnett has been campaigning his land-speed machines out at the dry lakebeds since about the time FDR enacted the New Deal, and here they were on the cusp of the new millennium, still going at it. As a relentless procession of lakesters, streamliners, modified Studebakers, and countless other experimental vehicles seemingly designed by NASA engineers with a raw sense of humor surged single file into the desert, Zukovic and I walked towards the timing tower at the top end of the dry lakebed. We knew the Bean Bandits were capable of turning some tremendous mile-per-hour clockings with their supercharged streamliner, which they reportedly ran on 50 percent nitromethane. (Folklore has it that Arnett has always run a 50/50 nitro-to-alcohol mixture: "It makes it easier," Joaquin has been quoted as saying, "a gallon of this, a gallon of that.")

In anticipation of Arnett's attempt to blast his way into the SCTA record books, we continued our pilgrimage to the big end for the optimum vantage point of what promised to be a maximum velocity horizontal rocket ride by a 70-year old man, out of his mind on nitro fumes. Speed machines continued to whiz by, interrupted only by sporadic sandstorms and ferocious dust devils that would whip and sting our legs, arms, and faces.

The desert heat was sweltering and we sought shelter under a canopy attached to a Winnebago that some elderly gearheads had rented for a home base for the duration of the speed meet. We struck up a conversation with our reluctant hosts and I offered them copies of the *Full Throttle News* with "Wild Willie" Borsch on the cover. It was an unspoken barter, but we all knew that the gratis copies of *FTN* bought Zukovic and me a reprieve from the heat and the sandstorms.

As we bench raced, our grizzled hosts mixed whiskey drinks and lounged in the shade in their lawn chairs. They had tuned a CB radio to the same frequency as the SCTA timing officials' walkie-talkies, and had run cable to a drive-in speaker that was duct-taped to one of the canopy supports. More race cars streaked by and we eavesdropped as their speeds were broadcast over the CB. I found it peculiar that our hosts would start talking amongst themselves as soon as the vehicles would pass our location, ignoring the cars as they reached the finish line. Intuitively, I felt that most of the action happened past the speed traps, the drama comprised of as to how the drivers managed to stop these contraptions on the desert floor.

A starting-line official announced that Arnett was slated to make his pass, and we all focused our attention on the racecourse. This should be good. Zukovic and I were within beer can-throwing distance of the speed traps, and by the time Arnett streaked by the Winnebago he was at warp speed.

"Hey, I don't think the Bean Bandits popped the chute," I theorized to the peanut gallery. "Aw, Joaquin does that shit every time they run," answered one of the whiskey drinkers. The CB lit up with this dispatch: "the *Bean Bandits*, 189.67 miles per hour." Our hosts stirred their drinks with swizzle sticks. "No, I'm serious, the parachute didn't open," I said. "Hey Slim, pass me a Budweiser," was the reply. Zukovic looked really concerned as the *Bean Bandits* streamliner continued to grind up the dry lakebed terrain, billowing clouds of dust and dirt occupying the void in space where his parachute should be. Meanwhile the CB radio/public address system was saturated with tinny transmissions of panic. "He's out the back door! He's out the back door!" screamed one finish-line official. "Roger that, the *Bean Bandits* are in trouble—no chute. No chute." The streamliner rocketed even further into the horizon, with no visible signs of abatement. This was an optical illusion, but it seemed to be gathering speed instead of slowing down. Our hosts offered Zukovic a drink—he passed. Eventually the rooster tail of dust disappeared beyond the shore of the dry lakebed, the combustion-driven land rocket still under power as it took to the rolling hills of the desert. Arnett finally came to a stop among the yucca trees, the streamliner on its side, fortunately not really any the worse for the wear. It was the most beautiful failure at a speed record since Chuck Yeager bailed out of an NF-104 fighter plane, 20 miles west of El Mirage at Edwards Air Force Base in the early 1960s. As we drove home on a dirt road leading back to civilization, I swore I could see the smoke from the embers of Yeager's plane, burning in the distance.

September 17, Goodguys Nitro'N'Nostalgia Bash, Bakersfield, CA—My racing sojourns were getting pretty frequent at this point, and I was really getting into a rhythm as far as attending a drag race damn near every weekend. I had worked late the night before as a sound technician on some bloated Hollywood film production, and I was really dismayed and appalled at the brazen displays of ego, pride, and megalomania on the set. Why smug, self-important schmendricks (otherwise known as "producer," "gaffer," "directors" etc.) insist on generating gratuitous tension at the workplace just because they are "creating some showbiz magic" never ceases to amaze me, but I suspect it has to do with people's inferiority complexes and their general unhappiness. Maybe subconsciously they know they are producing nothing of any real merit, and that disturbs them. Ultimately, these cretins are merely contributing to the Cultural Fascism that undermines the soul and spirit of our culture. Maybe these morons have no consciousness or self-awareness at all, they cannot fathom that producing another hackneyed motion picture means nothing in the universal scheme of things. Balding pony-tailed men in Armani suits, neurotic "production" women with cellular phones, and film school interns all work overtime to create crises that justify their sense of importance, as well as their feeble existence—and on this night their plume of anxiety was thicker than the tire smoke from a *Chi-Town Hustler* burnout circa 1972.

I overslept on Saturday morning, exhausted from the long hours and the claustrophobic hubris the night before. I was running late, but I was determined to make the opening session of Top Fuel qualifying at 11:00 AM. To compensate for my late start and my grogginess, I filled my coffee thermos with an especially potent batch of Cafe Bustello, checked all the fluids in the '71 Grand Prix, and blazed up the Grapevine, Bakersfield bound, headed north out of Los Angeles. If I was going to catch Top Fuel I really had to make time, and to pace this trip I inserted a Hank Williams cassette into the car stereo. Hank may have overdosed from amphetamines on New Year's Day, 1961, but I was still wiping sleep out of my eyes all the way up Interstate 5—even though I had the throttle wide open. Incidentally, today was Hank Williams' birthday. It was also mine.

I pulled into Famoso at 11 o'clock straight up, but the fuel cars were not even in the staging lanes yet. Apparently so many race cars made the trip, both track officials and the Goodguys were caught off guard by the sheer volume of participants. Many machines were still getting teched, so qualifying was postponed until noon. I took this hour of calm to catch my breath and score some breakfast. It turned out that I would need my nourishment, because it was a long hot day of vital, exciting drag racing and epic performances.

Indeed, by the time the smoke had cleared, Ted Taylor had terrorized Top Fuel Eliminator with a barrage of stunning elapsed times that had nitro aficionados absolutely agog. In qualifying, his E.T. of 6.17 tied a front-motored AA/Fuel Dragster record claimed 22 years ago by both "Kansas John" Wiebe and the legendary Don "the Snake" Prudhomme. In eliminations he upped the stakes, running a 6.11, a 6.10, and finally a 6.24 at an out-of-this-world 239 mph. Likewise, in Junior Fuel, Gene Adams tuned Ron Pratt to a sensational and sublime performance, eclipsing the 175-mph barrier by a methanol-burning small-block injected dragster for the first time in history.

Accomplishments like these are what drag racing is all about—to push the envelope, to debunk the laws of physics, to thumb one's nose at the nattering nabobs of negativism, to keep moving forward. I felt privileged to witness these peerless feats of bravado and gumption. It cleansed my soul, a spirit bruised by fallout and debris from the Hollywood hubris monsters, people who have deluded themselves into thinking they are providing the populace with escapist entertainment designed to brighten our dreary lives. They are providing nothing. Pardon me, but the accomplishments of Ted "the Bad Lieutenant" Taylor and Gene "the Injection Guru" Adams are much more noble than anything that Sid Sheinberg at Universal Pictures can muster. Sheinberg and his ilk could not draw Ted Taylor's bathwater.

I highly recommend people watch fewer films and television and go to more drag races. It might put Sheinberg out of a job (me too, come to think of it). Then maybe we can both get a job with real dignity, perhaps pouring grease-sweep for the Goodguys Safety Safari after a Top Fueler oils down the drag strip.

But on this night, my career in Hollywood did not even enter my thoughts. It was my birthday, I was alone in Bakersfield, and it was good.

(*Originally published in* Full Throttle News)

drive half a mile in order to go a quarter

OVER, UNDER, SIDEWAYS, DOWN!:

THE STORY OF "WILD WILLIE" BORSCH

I was roaming the Manufacturers' Midway at the '92 NHRA World Finals, separated from my friends, lost and slightly overwhelmed by the crowd and hullabaloo in this sideshow/Disneyland atmosphere. Off in the distance, out by where the econo-dragster guys pit, a huge white banner embossed with the phrase "Memory Lane" caught my attention. The pennant swayed in the wind, beckoning like a beacon. I weaseled my way through the throng of the midway, strains of "Nearer My God to Thee" echoing in mind as I bore my way through the multitude.

```
top fuel wormhole
```

It was here that I found a small cadre of slingshot AA/Fuel Dragsters, a couple of injected small-block junior fuelers, a dry-lakes streamliner, and other quaint relics from the days of yore. Inside this outdoor pavilion a smattering of hard-core nitro hounds had come to pay their respects at this impromptu memorial to the men and machines that mattered, this shrine to the legends and luminaries of drag racing. I was by myself, eavesdropping on the chatter and the bench racing. The conversation was good. In the center of this display was a restoration-in-progress that had the assembled cruster gearheads and nitro hounds all agog.

The source of their excitement: the *Winged Express* '23 T AA/Fuel Altered, replete with what looked like one of the countless trophies it had won resting in the drivers seat. Yes, the legendary, record-breaking machine that had been masterminded and crafted by Alvin "Mousie" Marcellus and driven by his soul mate "Wild Willie" Borsch would soon drag race again. I knew that Borsch had passed on to the great taco stand in the sky, succumbing to cancer in October of 1991. This restoration project was a tribute to the skill and genius of a fallen hero. (It was too ironic: the man who cheated death every time he climbed into his asbestos fire suit, the man who drove his race car in a style entirely too ornery for pregnant women or the faint of heart to observe, the man who held the grim reaper hisself in a chokehold, claimed by something as banal as cancer. It seemed a cruel, sick joke.)

The men and women gathered in a semi-circle around the half-finished *Winged Express*, alternately laughing and listening in reverent silence to the yarns spun by Mousie. Marcellus was "in the house," as they say, working the room with the grace and panache of Swifty Lazar at Spago on Oscar night. He regaled his minions with the story of when Willie flipped and rolled the altered at Martin, Michigan in '70, one of the few times the machine got away from him. Marcellus and the crew arrived at the scene to find Borsch had become rabid with fear and anxiety. Willie was wailing and bellowing, "I'm blind, I'm blind," only to be answered by roars of laughter from his crew. After all the howling had subsided, Mousey patiently explained to Willie that he could not see because his head was wrapped and intertwined in the parachute.

Marcellus then launched into another anecdote about Borsch, and in the meanwhile I started chatting up nostalgia Top Fuel scenester Tom Hunnicutt. Hunnicutt asked me if I had said, "Hello to Willie?" I told Tom I went over and tipped my hat to the newly restored *Winged Express* but no, Willie Borsch was dead, what do you mean did I go over and say hello to him? Hunnicutt then asked me to examine more closely the "trophy" sitting in the driver's seat of the *Winged Express*. I walked back over and looked more discriminately at the cockpit of the roadster. That was no trophy—it was an urn... containing the ashes of William Bowen Borsch. He had come home.

...Yes, even in death, the exploits of "Wild Willie" continue to be stranger than fiction. But it was his displays of bravado and fearlessness on Planet Earth for which he will be most remembered. Consider the time he banged the car off the guardrail, crossed the centerline, bounced off the other guardrail, crossed the centerline again (to get back into his own lane), and caught and passed the guy he was racing. The fact that he denied to Mousie that he was driving the altered with one hand—Marcellus had to show Borsch photographs of him in action to prove it. Or the night at Lions Drag Strip when Willie stabbed the throttle and the entire machine leaped into the air, it landed, Willie whapped it again, she became airborne once more, it came down facing the guardrail, Willie punched the throttle anyway, straightened 'er out and consummated the run. The crowd went apeshit.

Marcellus tells of Borsch's affliction with narcolepsy. Because of which, people mistook his drowsiness for a laconic obstinacy. On more than one occasion, moments before a typical over-under-sideways-down pass "Wild Willie" would nod out while strapped into the altered in the staging lanes. Marcellus would nudge the race car with the push truck, rousing Willie from his slumber. And the time the *Winged Express* qualified for Top Fuel Eliminator at the '69 Winternationals, bumping "Big Daddy" Don Garlits out of the show. Before eliminations the remaining 31 dragster shoes called an impromptu drivers' meeting, threatening to boycott the event if they had to race next to Willie. Garlits was reinstated.

Yes, 32 dragster drivers could not be wrong. They knew that the practicality of running a AA/Fuel Altered is really an exercise in the "square-peg-in-a-round-hole" theorem, with a co-efficient of the "bigger hammer" principle. In other words, when you shoehorn a nitro-guzzling supercharged Chrysler motor betwixt a few pieces of exhaust tubing masquerading as a chassis, especially one with a real short wheelbase, you are asking for trouble. There are some basic laws of torque and Newtonian physics that must at least be acknowledged—regardless of the mounting of a giant airfoil in hopes of pile-driving enough downforce to make this monstrosity go straight. Due to the short wheelbase, there is a whole lot of horsepower with no place to go—except approximately 45 degrees stage right. Then you add a stiff-necked Borsch to the equation, which is definitely tantamount to throwing gasoline into the fire. In fact, the popular platitude murmured in the cheap seats (in those days they were all cheap seats) to describe one of his stereotypical, non-linear excursions down the 1320 was this: "Willie has to drive half a mile in order to go a quarter."

It was his uncompromising bullheadedness, however, that contributed to the conquering of the "Lions" share of Marcellus and Borsch's competition, as well as their procurement of many AA/FA performance plateaus; the first in the 8's, the first in the 7's, and the first to eclipse 200 mph in one of these highly unpredictable suicide machines.

Ironically, this same attitude that garnered these men all of the accolades (Willie was voted *Car Craft Magazine's* Competition Eliminator Driver of the Year in 1973; he did not even compete in that class that year) also severed a friendship and an inspired collaboration, a creative partnership worthy of Weill and Brecht, or Lennon and McCartney. After Marcellus had procured some dough from Revell Models, the duo seemed to be on their way to Easy Money, U.S.A. Before the ink was dry on the contract Borsch insisted on propelling their new Dodge funny car with a big-block Chevrolet, apropos of nothing. They had always run Chrysler hemis, Mousie insisted, why sabotage a winning combination? Unfortunately, these creative differences began to swell. They detonated when Borsch refused to put on his shirt at a photo shoot for the Revell people. Marcellus in effect handed Willie the keys to the tow vehicle, telling Willie he had become too headstrong to work with. The Revell deal lasted a few months for Borsch, but without Mousie the combination never gelled. Their friendship was shattered, a friendship that began at a South Central Los Angeles elementary school in the 1930s, not to be reconciled until the waning years of Willie's life.

Yes, let us applaud and bow to the spirit and zeal of Marcellus and Borsch. It was the yin and yang exemplified. But we must remember this: Neither man was the same without the other. And because of Borsch's stubborn independence, many race fans never got a chance to appreciate his genius, a brilliance he showcased every time they ran their race car. When it comes to the art of drag racing I think corporate America can go fuck themselves too, Mr. Borsch. But if you had only put that shirt on, Willie…

(*Originally published in* Super Stock & Drag Illustrated)

THE DRAG STRIP DIARIES (1994)

PART 4

September 24-25, Governor's Cup, Sacramento Raceway—Cuz'n Roy telephoned from Chattanooga, saying he was in transit to Cali from Ranlo, North Carolina. We mulled over a rendezvous in Sacramento as I mentioned my plans to attend the Governor's Cup. Jet cars, "Outlaw" front-motored Top Fuel dragsters, CIFCA funny cars, Pro Mod doorslammers—the cup seemed to runneth over with unorthodox drag racing machines.

We blew off our Sacto trip, however, when our gal pals Caz and Leah hinted that they would accompany us to Saugus Speedway but not to Sacramento. Roy hooked up with the three of us at the Speedway to watch the roundy-rounds race Figure 8 style. It was the season finale for the local stock car racing scene, and the bleachers were packed tighter than Linda Vaughn's jeans.

The evening's festivities concluded with a good old-fashioned demolition derby, a spectacle foreign to us drag racing fans, except Cuz'n Roy. This was a curious exhibition: junker cars bashing the shit out of each other until nothing is left. We interpreted the demo derby as a metaphor for the proletariat deconstruction of the mass-production paradigm. Ironically, most of the participating vehicles looked pretty demolished before the event even started, which made the contest itself rather redundant and anticlimactic. This car-bashing ritual seemed a little tired, a little effete, even for the stock car faithful. At this stage, I felt a more refreshing and reactionary gesture would be to enact a demolition derby stocked only with new Honda Accords, Nissans, Suzuki Samurais, or any other soulless modern vehicle—domestic or imported—that comes off the assembly line with either a car phone or one of those mechanical devices that fascistically yanks and harnesses the driver into his seat, whether he wants to submit to somebody else's concept of safety or not. (Every time I climb into one of these vehicles those mechanical shoulder straps either spills the coffee out of my hand, or knocks my AHRA hat off my head—who's responsible for these engineering brainfarts? Why do today's engineers—technical and social—insist on trying to make my life better for me? In these times, must the tail always wag the dog?)

At this point, motor vehicles equipped with robotics and cellular communications systems cease to be automobiles, anymore than HAL in Stanley Kubrick's *2001* was just a computer on a spaceship. No, it is no longer an automobile; it is now a symbol of oppression that must be smashed into scrap carbon fiber, in my humble opinion. Next year, unless the mavens of Saugus Speedway promise to destroy some automobiles whose essence is relevant to the human condition as mankind enters the 21st century, Roy and I will motor all the way to the Governor's Cup in my '71 Grand Prix, instead of across town to some feeble demolition derby freak show, I swear. Regardless of what the womenfolk want to do.

October 1, ANRA Finals, LACR, Palmdale, CA—Caz, Cuz'n Roy, and I arrived in time for Top Fuel qualifying, no small feat considering what it takes to motivate Roy into action on a Saturday morning...

This event was emblematic of the joys and disappointments of attending old-style drag races. Although most of the classes were pretty well represented, the Top Fuel turnout was rather paltry. I did not regret the drive, however, because this might have been the farewell racing appearance of Top Fuel hero "Wild Bill" Alexander.

Alexander was one of the first Top Fuel shoes on the West Coast to break through the 200-mph barrier, a feat he pulled off—if my memory serves me correctly—at San Fernando Raceway *w-a-y* back in 1964. Those were heady times; the Southern California renaissance was in full effect, the proliferation of ideas, diggers, and drag strips seemingly inexhaustible. In those years Alexander stood tall among a constituency of Top Fuel pilots that numbered over 100 in California alone.

On this day in 1994, however, "Wild Bill" was but one of three—yes, only three—Top Fuel drivers entered at the Season Final out here in the Mojave Desert. Many things have changed since Alexander's epic groundbreaking assault on the San Fernando asphalt 30 years ago. To enumerate and catalogue on paper these social, technological, and political changes would require the clear-cutting of the entire state of Oregon. But suffice it to say, in 1964 the Beach Boys were selling more records worldwide than the Beatles.

In 1994, unfortunately, two Beach Boys, Brian Wilson and Mike Love—who, incidentally, are cousins—were suing each other over disputed royalty payments from the song "Good Vibrations." In between their long journey from the console to the courtroom, America absorbed JFK, Vietnam, LBJ, MLK, RFK, Woodstock, Apollo 9, Altamont, the Last Drag Races (San Fernando, Lions, Irwindale, OCIR, etc.), Watergate, Iran, disco, MTV, AOL, NAFTA, and Microsoft into the sponge we call our collective consciousness.

By 1994 most of us had figured out that Camelot was a mirage, and that the Beach Boys had reduced themselves to bickering magpies, surf music mercenaries devoid of passion and inspiration. The presence and persona of Alexander, however, remained a constant—just transpose San Fernando, 1964 for Palmdale, 1994. Obviously this was not about money for Alexander, this was about something much purer. If speed is a metaphor for freedom, then the exploits of "Wild Bill" must be considered pure poetry.

In Top Fuel eliminations, Alexander was paired off against Bill "the Heartbreaker" Dunlap. It was just before sunset when crew members for both race cars primed the injectors with gasoline, and then applied aircraft starters to the blower pulleys, enabling both nitro-huffing machines to roar to life, each motor sounding extremely stout, loud, and potent. Each driver coaxed nice and gnarly, smoky burnouts out of their front-motored dragsters, as acrid nitro fumes melded with the copious tire smoke, creating a pungent perfume that soaked everyone near the starting line.

As the dragsters cackled at maximum decibels, each driver eased his machine into the staging beams. Alexander staged first, then Dunlap. As the Xmas tree flashed "go!" both men left simultaneously, their dragsters streaking down the 1320 like a pair of chrome-moly bullets. It was either man's race, until about 800 feet down track Alexander's digger began to drift. His tires suddenly broke traction, the car immediately hooked left, "Wild Bill" boldly fought to correct the now disobedient and insubordinate machine, never lifting off the throttle, never relinquishing control, virtually out-muscling this stubborn, deafening 2000 horsepower missile, keeping it between the guardrail and the centerline, not to mention out of the path of the hard charging Dunlap (who was feeling pretty darn anxious when he noticed that for one moment Alexander's dragster was basically aimed at him). Be that as it may, Dunlap was in no mood to get off the throttle either, so both drivers kept the hammer down in a brazen display of chutzpah and bravado. When the clutch dust settled, the win light was revolving in Dunlap's lane, his 7.13 defeating Alexander's epic-but-futile 7.18.

Nobody realized it at the time, but due to finances and parts attrition, this may have been the swan song to "Wild Bill" Alexander's drag racing career. For a curtain call, this man hit the high notes—even in defeat. What a pity more of his constituents were not there to hear them.

October 15, FTN's "Thunder Island," Brotherhood Raceway Park, Terminal Island, CA—At about 3 p.m. two carloads of race fans rendezvoused at my house in Silver Lake. Once on the Harbor Freeway we formed a compact convoy, snaking our way through traffic in unison, blasting loud punk rock music on our car stereos, high on the anticipation of an extremely cool drag racing show.

Eight front-motored "Outlaw" Top Fuel dragsters had been booked into this invitational "Chicago Style" meet, and this was the first time nitromethane would penetrate the cool ocean air of the South Bay since that dark day in 1972 when the Harbor Commission Coyote Gods bulldozed our sacred sanctum of speed, Lions Drag Strip.

But that was then, this is now... And on this warm Autumn night, the cadre of "Nitro Outlaws" united with the usual plethora of racers that congregate at BRP every Saturday night—"space age cowboys," experimental econo dragsters, LAPD muscle cars, nitrous-assisted street machines, etc.

This was a highly incongruous marriage—the front-motored Top Fuel crowd in concert with the Brotherhood regulars—but somehow it made karmic sense. I do not think a lot of the BRP posse had ever witnessed a Top Fueler rocket down a drag strip before, especially one with the motor in front à la 1967. During the first session of Top Fuel, a lot of the uninitiated seemed to regard the nitro cars with a cautious curiosity—by the second session they understood the appeal of Top Fuel racing's *sturm und drang*. And conversely, this was the first time I ever heard a dragster crowd cheer and whistle for doorslammers, but they did...

Yes, this was a weird, surreal mutual admiration society that peacefully convened on some enchanted evening, a mere tossed blower belt from the old Lions Drag Strip. Contrary to the wisdom of ol' Tommy Wolfe, it seems that, at least for one night, you could go home again.

And on that note I must conclude my ruminations on free-range drag racing in 1994, the Year of the Boomerang. I am running out of real estate, so to speak, even though there was a lot more really cool drag racing at the end of '94. All of these trips to the various drag strips have taught me something, but it is now March, 1995—I cannot keep writing about last year's drag races, no matter how much those endeavors informed my philosophy of the world, or how much these travels gave my life meaning. 1994 was the year that I rediscovered the joys of the exciting and existentially correct world of "free range" independent drag racing. Something I learned in these travels is that, like anything else in life, the journey has to be its own payoff, an end unto itself, never mind the event itself. In other words, the drive to the drag strip has as much relevance and resonance as the drag race itself.

(*Originally published in* Full Throttle News)

THE 1994 CALIFORNIA HOT ROD REUNION
BAKERSFIELD BE HERE NOW

Don't call it a reunion, call it a festival; the third running of the California Hot Rod Reunion was the roundup that smoked 'em all. Making the haul to this hot rodder's hootenanny was a cavalcade of car clubbers, nitro dirgehounds, and hepcats and kittens all hell-bent on a romper-stomper good time. Joining this *hoi polloi* was a convoy of front-motored "outlaw" drag racers and exhibitionists who seemingly crawled out of the cracks and crevices of drag racing's past, loaded with a three-pronged agenda: to respectfully tip their hats to the sport's here and gone; to tip the barkeep at the local honky tonk 'till Johnny Law says it is time to go home; and to tip the can at Famoso Raceway the next morning so's to nurture some preternatural performances out of their race cars.

Yep, in addition to the hoopla of the festivities and the good-natured hell raising, this was one gnarsome, powerful drag race. It was also a venue to showcase what the burgeoning phenomenon known as "Nostalgia Drag Racing" is all about. Perhaps the sport's best kept secret, and with over a dozen old-style events staged in California alone—between the American Nostalgia Racing Association, the Goodguys' VRA Series, the West Coast Timing Association, and the occasional "Outlaw Dragster" events promoted by *Full Throttle News*, these retro renegades keep their plate pretty full. The only event sanctioned by the National Hot Rod Association is the California Hot Rod Reunion itself, and they do a bang-up job promoting and organizing this extravaganza. In fact, this two-day event drew 15,000 to Bakersfield. The irony however is that the Coyote Gods of the NHRA are confused by the fact that some people seem to prefer drag racing 1967-style to the NHRA's own highly publicized, arguably fascistic, mondo-enormo racing events.

In fact, one question seemed to resurrect itself in Bakersfield repeatedly: Why are the NHRA Coyote Gods afraid to promote this thing as a "real" race? Does this competition represent the uncouth days when maverick, unkempt men piloted sleek but unpredictable machines? Men who used to get dirty with grease, oil, sweat, blood—substances that appear unsavory to television executives and millionaires in luxury boxes. But back in those days there were no corporate suites at the drag strip. It was an era defined by the random, the gonzo, and the beautiful chaos that is a byproduct of intrepid technological forays into the unknown. Obviously, if any age was worthy of nostalgia, it was these halcyon days of hot rodding—but if this nostalgia is necessary, what does this imply about our sport's status quo? These philosophical issues were dealt with extensively by motorheads, dragster drivers, and pundits alike at the CHRR3—in the bleachers, in the pits, and in the watering holes of Bakersfield.

The Hot Rod Reunion is the only "nostalgia" event that the Coyote Gods are directly involved with, but the NHRA propaganda machine really downplays the actual competition between the dragsters—in fact *National Dragster*, their house organ, gives as much ink to the Reunion's BBQ as it does the race itself. Yes, the chow was tasty, and yes, the conversation was good—but there was a drag race going on, replete with sensational displays of driving and tuning *chutzpah*, not to mention a continuous battering of the "nostalgia" Top Fuel and Junior Fuel E.T. and MPH records. All of which could have happened on another planet as far as the NHRA is concerned. ("Hello! Is this thing on?")

Perhaps the competition is innocuous and insignificant compared to any given drag race on the "Million Dollar NHRA Winston Drag Race Series." Or maybe the powers-that-be are unnerved and disturbed by the insouciant attitude the "nostalgia" brigade seems to relish and thrive on—and that this attitude strikes a chord for a growing number of folks who feel left out by big-time corporate drag racing.

This is not to suggest that this relatively rag-tag bunch of misfits pose any real threat to the Men in the Gilded Towers. They possess neither the wherewithal, ammunition, or desire to topple the sophisticated and precise machine that is today's NHRA. Indeed, the old-style crowd is quite content to race on their own terms, albeit where the venture capital, the risks, and the payoffs are relatively diminutive—especially compared to the outrageous expenses incurred in today's Fortune 500 drag racing. These guys are "outlaws" only in the sense that they exist on a different plane—that is, a parallel universe where the arbitrations of the NHRA have no resonance or relevance. This attitude was encapsulated by Frank Pettinato, the tuner and owner of the icy blue *Rat Poison* front-motored Top Fueler, who suggested that he was not impressed with watching contemporary Top Fuel racing because "every time I reach into my ice chest for a beer, I've missed an entire run."

According to the laws of quantum physics and the "Butterfly Effect," you cannot harness chaos but the NHRA figures they can at least contain it. The NHRA will be in concert with the Goodguys for the Vintage Racing Association Points Series in '95. As further evidence of the NHRA's clueless meddling, there is some not-so-subtle pressure to restrict these unwieldy yahoos and their machines to 1/8th-mile drag racing in this series. At the very least, in

top fuel wormhole

June '95 these new bedfellows will stage a 1/8th-mile front-motored exhibition at Indianapolis Raceway Park. The Goodguys were in agreement on this proposal—especially since the NHRA dangled a carrot promising television exposure as well as column space in each week's *National Dragster* devoted to 1/8th-mile "nostalgia" E.T. and MPH records—all the racers have to do is agree to race on a 660-foot course instead of the traditional 1320.

To the California "outlaws," however, this is an ugly precedent. To them 1/8th-mile drag racing is like listening to Van Cliburn play only the white keys, or like having the Packers and Steelers play arena football, or like telling Merle Haggard he can't sing about prison—the entire dynamic is changed and it just ain't as exciting. One anonymous correspondent put it in these rather parochial terms: "I grew up writing race coverage at San Fernando, Orange County, and Bakersfield in the '60s—this isn't Podunk, North Carolina, for Christ's sake, this is California, where drag racing was born. The whole thought of '1/8th-mile nostalgia' is oxymoronic because these guys have never raced that way in their lives. They aren't some rolling exhibit out of a museum—these guys are real drag racers. None of them can relate to a 3.89 E.T. on their time slip—what the hell is that? To them racing to 660 feet is like making love to a woman, but only using half of your manhood."

At an impromptu meeting in the pits on Saturday, the 1/8th-mile brainfart was vetoed by the fuel racers almost *en masse*, in a show of solidarity worthy of Gdansk, Poland, circa 1980. They threatened to boycott the entire VRA Series, television be damned. Whether they maintain their united front or succumb to division in the ranks is anybody's guess—look for the turnout at IRP as a barometer of their integrity. As if to prove the validity and excitement of 1320-foot drag racing, the second session of Top Fuel qualifying at CHRR3 featured a few fearless, run-it-through-the-back-door type exhibitions of bravado that would have made a cup of coffee nervous.

Three of the most intrepid assaults on the asphalt were perpetrated in subsequent qualifying runs by Sam "Eight Miles High" Chastain, Gerry "Panzer Man" Steiner, and Kenosha, Wisconsin's "Nitro Neil" Bisciglia. Neil was first, blasting out a 6.73 second, 195 mph run that was nullified when he crossed the center line twice—which to him was a mere technicality. At this point Bisciglia was barely "in the show," and he must have figured that the only way to rectify his vulnerability was to keep the injector's butterflies wide open—even if he coincidentally happened to end up in his competition's lane. So despite having the *Foothill Flyer* shake violently and get out of shape, Bisciglia kept his shoe nailed to the throttle in what amounted to an epic exercise in futility. After Neil, Steiner ripped a 6.74/216 shot that was also voided. At 1000 feet the car hooked left without warning, the "Panzer Man" corrected—maybe overcorrected—at maximum velocity, and the *Welty & Steiner* dragster poached into Mike Boyd's lane at the 1320 mark, scattering the timing cones into the heavens ala the monkey throwing the bone in Stanley Kubrick's *2001*. Boyd, meanwhile, had the front wheels in the air, using them as a rudder to guide the *Nitro Warrior* AA/Fuel Dragster into the 7th qualifying position inches ahead of a rampaging Steiner. Finally, Chastain, who was not qualified into the show, got a chance to showcase his improvisational skills as he wrestled the *Chastain & Hedge* digger from the 660 feet mark all the way to the top end, also knocking the styrofoam timing reflectors into the ozone while powering his machine through the turbulence at maximum velocity in a maneuver worthy of Chuck Yeager as he approached Mach 1 in the *X-1*.

Moments after watching these fearless displays of raw nerve and insanity from Steiner, Chastain, and Bisciglia, newly retired drag racing legend Don "the Snake" Prudhomme, who has not shoed a front-motored dragster since 1971, was broached about the possibility of hittin' the "nostalgia" circuit—y'know, dust off his formidable yellow '69 *Wynn's Winder* AA/FD in which he won the U.S. Nationals twice consecutively, maybe coax fellow legend "Big Daddy" Don Garlits out of retirement and have him yank his old *Swamp Rat XX* slingshot out of his museum, have 'em both barnstorm the "outlaw" Top Fuel shows in California, maybe '94 wasn't Prudhomme's "Final Strike" after all... Whaddya say, Mr. Snake? "Not on your life," muttered Prudhomme, visibly shaking his head in disbelief as he wandered off towards the BBQ tent.

So "the Snake" was not interested in shedding his skin, and the racing resumed on Sunday morning. It was then that Top Fuel ace Ted "the Bad Lieutenant" Taylor, in the Jim Herbert-tuned *W.W. Two* slingshot, absolutely *banzai'd* his way into the CHRR3 winner's circle, leaving behind a wasteland of carnage that had spectators mumbling about Sunday's Top Fuel Eliminator being "a day that will live in infamy." Taylor had laid down the gauntlet in qualifying on Saturday with a 6.07/217, good for the #1 slot. Taylor shot down Bisciglia in Sunday's first round, a 6.21 to "Nitro Neil's" valiant 6.63. "The Bad Lieutenant's" semifinal opponent, the fresh-faced Fritz Kaiser, shut-off after his ride shook violently, while Taylor blithely reeled off an absolutely apocalyptic 6.04/221 mph blast. This shot lowered the front-motored Top Fuel record that Taylor already held at 6.10, but the vibes permeating Bakersfield Raceway suggested he was just getting warmed up. Taylor's opponent for Top Eliminator was young Dan Horan, Jr., aka "the Irish Intimidator." Horan seized a tenth of a second advantage out of the gate, but Taylor rocketed past him at the big end, 6.05 to 6.20. It was Jim Herbert's tune-up, however, that enabled Taylor to snatch the victory—the *W.W. Two* machine recorded an outrageous 247 mph top end speed, another benchmark claimed by "the Bad Lieutenant" for the dragsters that time forgot. (There was no truth to the rumor that following this *blitzkrieg* Taylor whispered to Herbert, his comrade-in-arms, that "We had to destroy the village in order to save it.")

Parenthetical to Taylor's torrid performance is the fact that he is accomplishing these feats in a class that is governed not so much by nostalgia as it is by the concept of limited performance. Don Prudhomme and "Kansas John" Wiebe both extricated E.T.s of 6.17 out of their front-motored fuelers in the early '70s, but Taylor and Herbert are handicapped even more than slingshots of yore. "Taylor going 247 was as newsworthy as Bernstein running 314," explained Gerry Steiner. "No electronics, no computers, no big wings, none of that high-tech shit. Small tires, a small fuel pump, one magneto, only 18% overdrive on the blower, a 3.90 gear ratio compared to the NHRA guys running a 3.20 rear end gear ratio. All these limitations are designed to keep the costs down, but with Taylor running those numbers it's not really nostalgia anymore."

Also contrary to the notion of nostalgia is the age of the drivers themselves: Bisciglia, Horan, Kaiser, Scott Hesselgrave, and Dan Pettinato are among the drivers who were born around the time the Beatles broke up. In fact, of the 18 or so active "old school" Top Fuel slingshot drivers in California, only Taylor, Steiner, and maybe Jim Boyd are old enough to share their rheumatism medicine with '94 NHRA U.S. Nationals Top Fuel finalists Connie Kalitta and Eddie Hill. Most of the competitors in nostalgia racing are probably younger than John Force.

"Nitro Neil" tried to explain the attraction of front-motored fuel cars to Generation X as well as the paradoxical discrepancy of the wet-behind-the-ears nostalgia Top Fuel pilots in a free-association rap worthy of Dean Moriarty in *On the Road*: "What is so neat about this deal is that almost everybody here is in it for the racing end of it—I don't think there is any real big sponsorship in any of the nostalgia cars. These people are in it because there is this nitro sickness and this has given us a way to deal with it. A lot of these guys had put it on the back shelf for a lot of years, but my sickness is hot and new." So for Neil this is a fevered quest for purity of tone then, a vehicle for free expression unencumbered by the trappings of Madison Avenue. Just drag racing because you couldn't *not* drag race. Or as Neil's tuner Pete Jensen puts it: "This is all free-style shit. Take it to the outside, you're not hurting anybody." Jensen really starts to salivate when the "outlaw" Top Fuel moniker is tossed around: "I fought the IRS and I won—the NHRA cannot throw me out of their club because I am not a member." W-h-o-a. Sam Chastain reiterates this Zen libertarianism: "Very frankly, we are out there because it is not the NHRA. There is a refreshing lack of their Mickey Mouse politics. And a lot of us won't be out there as the NHRA gets more involved."

The CHRR3 created a window for the drag racing culture to peer into itself. This whole phenomenon is a manifestation of a collective consciousness—a consciousness whose soul has little to do with the notion of "nostalgia." Nostalgia is, after all, ultimately synonymous with the banalization of history. The resurrection of the hula hoop, water bongs, and John Travolta's dreary acting career is trivial and superfluous. The concept of nostalgia lacks soul, it is fraught with either kitsch irony or schmaltzy sentimentality—it is not real. Two deafening nitro-burning dragsters—even with the motor in front à la 1967—roaring side-by-side down the ol' 1320 is not however a mere affectation of nostalgia. Front-motored or no, the acrid fumes still make your eyes water, therefore this is very real, this is definitely of the moment. When the "Bad Lieutenant" rockets to 247 mph you realize that history is an abstraction, but this is happening NOW.

Listen to the ruminations of Robert Post, Curator of Technological Installation at the Smithsonian Institution and the erudite author of a comprehensive historical overview entitled *High Performance: The Culture and Technology of Drag Racing 1950-1990*, who was at CHRR3 signing copies of his book. He summed up his theories of Paradise Lost and Paradise Regained vis-à-vis the front-motored dragster phenomena this way: "I really like what these cars represent, an era when the sport was more of the people. I mean, it was a nice universe and I'm glad it found its way back, because this is a lot better scene for a lot of people. You can see smoke and fire for a reasonable cost—you can make smoke and fire for a reasonable cost, for that matter. That's a winning combination, any way you look at it. Besides, this is the way dragsters are supposed to look."

This "outlaw" drag racing movement is happening for a reason. A collective of misfits, malcontents, and dropouts whose common bond is that they are quite comfortable with their karma, have reconvened at what is left of California's drag strips to put on their own go. Or as Tom Hunnicutt, pit boss of the *Nitro Warrior* AA/FD and co-editor of SoCal racing rag *Full Throttle News*, so eloquently put it: "I guess a lot of these guys realized that the real world isn't that exciting after all. Unless you've spent the last 20 years locked in a motel room doin' two blondes, you're gonna want to go drag racing again."

No, this is not exactly Family Values Drag Racing, but as long as this free-form forum is allowed to survive on its own terms, it will serve as a crucial reminder to all of us that there are different schools of thought besides the one officially sanctioned by the NHRA. But if the NHRA increases their involvement with a subculture they do not really understand, they will asphyxiate this movement, mark my words. They will be the ones destroying the village in order to save it. In fact, Sam Chastain announced he was walking away from drag racing after the Hot Rod Reunion. To Chastain, the Goodguys/NHRA alliance already reeks of a hostile takeover. He told me, "Those guys don't know which end the big tires go on. This is horseshit—and I'm not going to put up with it." Ironically, that is why nostalgia racing started in the first place.

(*Originally published in* Super Stock & Drag Illustrated)

These women want to mount those race cars.

HAVE NITRO, WILL TRAVEL

PART ONE

"The only thing about traveling with Frank Madieros is this: we can't listen to the radio. Or the tape player. Madieros hates music. And he's too big to argue with." It was the voice of Pete Jensen, calling long-distance from the shop where he stores his dragster in Gold Country, CA. He was trying to convince me to carpool with him and his pal Madieros to a drag race at Thunder Valley Raceway Park in Noble, Oklahoma.

"Oh, that's no problem—with a few exceptions I hate music too," I said. "For all practical purposes music died on either the day Ernest Tubb allowed snare drums on the Grand Ol' Opry in 1955, or when the Beatles charted 1, 2, and 3 on the American Top 40 in 1964. I'm really not sure which."

top fuel wormhole

"You and Frank Madieros will get along swimmingly," Jensen said.

Jensen runs a front-motored Top Fuel dragster out of Calaveras County, in the foothills of the serene Sierra Nevada Mountains, where the ghosts of eccentric malcontents Mark Twain and John Sutter peacefully co-exist. Madieros, a part-time oil-pan magnate and blown-on-gas altered driver out of Sacramento, is what the mountain-types derisively refer to as a "flatlander." But because Frank is approximately a half-foot taller than God, and could pass for Sonny Barger's hippie bodyguard, nobody would say this to his face.

"Listen Pete," I said, "I have to admit that this is one of the more interesting phone solicitations I've ever heard. But why would I want to drive all the way from L.A. to Oklahoma just for another drag race?"

"Well," he said, "it's gonna be a helluva' show. Between the American Nostalgia Racing Association and the local Okie track promoter, they've booked in 8 front-motored Top Fuel cars, plus some gassers and altereds, not to mention a match race between Don Garlits and Shirley Muldowney. They're calling this thing the ANRA Nitro Nationals. Frank and I have to deliver some oil pans and a new blower to "Nitro Neil" Bisciglia, who is towing his dragster down to this race from Kenosha, Wisconsin. After the race is over, we are going to 180 it back to California to get ready for the Goodguys race in Sacramento the next weekend, and Neil's gonna follow us back to our shop in the Sierras so he can run his car at the California Hot Rod Reunion. He says if you ride back to the West Coast with him and keep him company, we'll let you climb into the cockpit of the dragster. Y'know, we'll let you be the test monkey while we fire it up outside our shop. But if you don't think you can make it, that's cool."

"So you're gonna strap me in your fuel car?"

"Only if you can make the trip."

"Uh, I think I can make it."

Jensen and Madieros swung by my house in Los Angeles at 8 p.m. Wednesday night. This was pretty cool: I was being escorted and chauffeured to Oklahoma by two charter member of the "Juggers Race Team." The "Juggers" are a loose consortium of Bay Area, San Joaquin Valley, and High Sierra non-conformist gearheads, most of whom are a little too outside, a little too loose, and certainly too crazed to fit into mainstream drag racing in 1995. And for the next week or so, I felt like an honorary "Jugger."

Yep, Jensen and Madieros belong to the same hot rod car club—and their bond does not stop there: both are big-rig truck drivers during the week. And both funnel the discretionary cash from their "straight jobs" as Kenworth cowboys toward their insatiable addictions to speed, nitromethane, and clutch dust. Ironically, their respective truck drivin' routes had never taken either man east of Phoenix or Reno.

So there I was, motoring out of L.A. at night, in tow with two forty-something forty-niners, a couple of hippie/hillbilly nitro-freaks who had practically never been outside the state of California in their lives. Jensen told me in our earlier phone conversation that he had been "watching a lot of 'reality based' documentary cop shows on teevee," and he wanted to know "is that what America is really like?" I assured him it was not an accurate representation. I sensed that both men were, in all actuality, ultimately afraid of America. Madieros's Beta-cam-fueled paranoia ran particularly deep: He insisted that we follow the speed limit, and absolutely no left-handed cigarettes would be consumed for the duration of our trip. Though not entirely unfounded, Madieros's theories of an American Society's ever-tightening sphincter and whose intolerance is enforced by video-camera technology were a little irrational. These fears had to be dealt with. So I plotted an itinerary that would take us through some of the more exotic locations that the Deserts of the Southwestern USA had to offer. We would avoid driving the Interstates. No billboards, no McDonalds, no Burger King, and no television camera crews from "Real Stories of the Highway Patrol." None of that shit. There would be nothing generic or oppressive about this expedition. This mission was all about the search for what is cool and weird about America; it was about the search for purity of tone—both on and off the drag strip. I knew it was still out there somewhere. It was incumbent upon us to find it...

I calculated that we would arrive in Phoenix sometime a few hours before daybreak, and that would give us ample opportunity to admire the breathtaking scenery of the Mescal Mountains and the splendiferous landscape of the adjoining Fort Apache Indian Reservation. My calculations were based on Madieros's insistence that we would observe the posted speed limits at all times. These calculations were tossed out the window, however, because

Jensen—not Madieros—was driving the first leg of our trip. We arrived in Phoenix almost three hours ahead of schedule. Yes, I had neglected to calculate into our itinerary the intangibles, such as the fact that I was traveling with two hippie Zen-anarchist-drag racer-truck drivers, one of whom was unafraid of barreling down Old West Highway at 90 mph in Apache Country, USA. To hell with camera crews and "Real Stories of the Highway Patrol"—Jensen tasted freedom, and this feeling of liberation manifested itself every time he stepped on the throttle pedal of the rent-a-car. Geronimo hisself would have been quite proud.

And there we were: blazing across the Fort Apache Indian Reservation under the cover of darkness. Listening to the radio was verboten—Madieros's Law, y'understand—so we resorted to conversation. While Jensen dodged the wild elk grazing on the highway, we talked about thermodynamics and the atomization principles of nitromethane, the anti-cavitational characteristics of dry sump oil pumps, and why my ex-girlfriend hates drag racing so much...

"Y'know, guys," I said from the back seat, "I have a friend named Zukovic who developed a rather Freudian theory about Top Fuel cars. He had never been drag racing before, so in '92 I took him to Pomona for the Winternationals. He was totally in awe of the whole scene: the crowd, the noise, the vibrations, the California race track chickees in hot pants and halter tops. We were discussing the physical quivering the drivers must experience in a Top Fuel car, when I told him that a lot of these drivers were virtually senior citizens and at their age, this might be the most sensual physical sensation they experience. We were hanging on the fence at about half-track, next to a couple of sultry blondes, and we could totally feel the palpitations of the fuelers as they whizzed past us. I mean you could really feel the ground shake—y'know every time a pair of dragsters went by 'the earth moved,' if you will. So anyway, two fuelers went by, coincidentally driven by two sixty year-old drivers, and the two chickees next to us absolutely squealed with pleasure as the earth finally stopped vibrating. So Zukovic leans over to me and he says, 'These women don't want to mount those race car drivers. These women want to mount those race cars.' In fact, he referred to the dragsters as '20-foot penis rockets' as I recall."

"Your pal Zukovic seems to have tapped into a big part of the psychology of Top Fuel racing," Jensen acknowledged.

"Well, that's what I thought. So the next day I decided to take my girlfriend—who also had never been to a drag race, but was extremely bored every time I would watch it on teevee—to Pomona. I was keeping Zukovic's Theory in mind, figuring this would be good for our relationship. She was really dubious about the whole thing, so my plan was to situate her on the fence right next to the starting line—y'know give her maximum bang per buck, if you know what I mean. So there we were, waiting for the show to start and Connie Kalitta pulls up and stages against Eddie Hill. Smoke and rubber from the burnout is swirling in our faces, both cars are just spewing massive amounts of raw fuel out of the pipes, our eyes are watering, the whole thing is deafening, and my ex-girlfriend is looking very confused and very afraid. Finally, the Xmas tree flashes green, Kalitta and Hill drop the hammer, there is this primal roar, the ground is shaking, the fence is shaking, our teeth are shaking, our eardrums are shaking, everything is shaking, right? Four seconds later the shaking stops and she is still clenching onto the chain-link fence, and I'm thinking: 'Instant orgasm, just add nitro,' y'know? She looks at me with the meanest case of stink-eye and says to me, 'This is the most anti-sexual thing I have ever seen in my life.' That moment marked the beginning of the end of our relationship."

Jensen seemed to understand. "For all the hullabaloo about Family Values Drag Racing that I read about in National Dragster," he said, "I've seen this stuff break up more families than unite them."

Madieros nodded in agreement. "Hell, my ex-old lady was what you might call the perfect wife," he said. "Loved to go drag racing. Maybe too much. We finally had to split up, though."

"Why the hell would you want to deep-six a marriage like that?" I asked. "It sounds perfect." "Well, for awhile it was," Madieros replied. "Until we had a helluva fight one day. We had squirreled away some extra cash and we were trying to decide what to spend it on. I wanted to get some new drapes for the house, and she wanted to buy a new blower for the race car. I knew right then it was best we went our separate ways."

It got quiet in the rent-a-car for a while. I was about to suggest we turn on the radio, but....

top fuel wormhole

The sun was coming up directly in front of us, creating a gnarly glare that made it kind of hard to drive, especially at the speed we were traveling. After nearly harpooning an elk that was taller than Madieros, we decided it would be prudent to stop in the next town for breakfast. We stopped in Pie Town (I'm not making this up, I swear), New Mexico for gas and grub.

"Where y'all boys headed?" the waitress asked.

"We are traveling across America, searching for purity of tone," I replied. "We've been told it still exists at a drag strip in Noble, Oklahoma, so that is our final destination."

"That's nice. Can I get y'all some more coffee? Or some pie?"

As we paid for our petrol and pie I asked the cashier what would be the most direct route from these here parts to Amarillo. He recommended that we continue to traverse Highway 60 past the White Sands Missile Range, and through something he quixotically called the Valley of Fires. Once we pass the lava rocks, he said, we then need to grab Highway 380 through Lincoln, where Billy the Kid fought his last gun battle, and from there mosey on into Roswell, sight of the infamous UFO crash of '47, on Highway 70. I thanked the man for his guidance and we motored on. This route proved to be both epic and enlightening...

"Pete, you guys think you blow shit up when you bang the blower on your Top Fuel car?" I asked rhetorically. "Right over that mountain range is the White Sands Missile Range, a/k/a the Alamogordo Bombing Range." I was pointing to a hermetically fenced-off area to our right, replete with a phalanx of satellite dishes at the foot of the mountains. The juxtaposition of the space age radio transmitters against the multi-hued, Neapolitan rock formations, a geological work-in-progress that was first sculpted in the Paleozoic Age, was a little surreal and unsettling.

"Fifty years ago, that's where Oppenheimer and his pals detonated the first A-bomb in what used to be Apache Country. In fact," I gurgled, "the explosion was so massive the local yokels and the Injuns thought the Valley of Fires volcanic craters were reigniting."

"Lucky for them it was just an Atom Bomb going off."

"Didn't the military brass call that Operation Arley Langlo?"

We continued to gain altitude and the desert tableaux commenced to darken. Indeed, there was something primal and humbling about the Valley of Fires itself. At an elevation of approximately one mile above sea level, this is where big chunks of molten lava had baked into charred rock formations after 15,000 years of exposure to the slow burn of the high desert sun. I pulled the rent-a-car off the highway and onto some sandstone. We all got out and kicked some boulders. Jensen, Madieros, and myself were merely passing through the Valley of Fires; but after beholding the effects of a cruel, fiery series of detonations on an unsuspecting landscape, we knew that we were merely passing through in more ways than one...

Jensen got behind the wheel once more and we blazed out of the Valley of Fires and began gaining altitude once again, climbing into the dark forest of Lincoln County, site of some seriously bloody range wars, including the last cattle-ranch battle of Billy the Kid. Once again, we got out and kicked some boulders.

"Man, this state has a lot of weird karma," Jensen said softly, as dark, threatening storm clouds continued to blanket the sky.

We then descended out of the Lincoln National Forest into the flatlands of Chaves County. I then proceeded to share with my traveling companions a little folklore about Roswell, the next town we would encounter.

"According to my sources, the military captured some extraterrestrial life forms who had crashed their flying saucer on the outskirts of Roswell in July, 1947. Legend has it that the remains of both the spacecraft and the space creatures were whisked off to Hangar 13 at the Wright Patterson Air Force Base in Dayton, Ohio."

"Hey, I think I saw that whole thing on the teevee show 'Sightings,'" Madieros blurted out. "Roswell's where the government recovered a flying saucer, and they took it apart and now they can't figure out how to put it back together. I remember watching this and thinking to myself, 'what kind of oil pumps do they use in outer space?' The show never did say."

"Well, according to these ufologists, musicologists, and historians I know back in Los Angeles," I continued, "it was simultaneous to all this weirdness that notorious Country & Western legend Lefty Frizzell was thrown

top fuel wormhole

in the Roswell slammer on statutory rape charges. Y'see Lefty, who was playing at a local honky tonk called the Cactus Garden at the time of his arrest, insisted until the day he died a mean, miserable drunk that the spiritual life-force of the captured aliens visited him in jail and invited him and his jailbait girlfriend to come live with them in outer space."

"No shit. I wouldn't mind listening to some of his music," Madieros chimed in enthusiastically.

Jensen, on the other hand, was confused. "Was all of this before or after you said country music died because Ernest Tubb allowed snare drums on the Grand Ol' Opry?" "A few years before. But regardless of the state of country music, anytime an itinerant oil-field worker cum honky-tonk hero starts writing love songs to UFOs from a jail cell in Roswell, I think it's safe to say that there is an artist worth listening to," I replied. Once we arrived in Roswell, we all intuitively understood why Lefty was yearning to be taken to another planet, county jail or no county jail. This town was flat, dreary, and weird. Indeed, it was the epicenter of the dark collision of science, nature, and the cosmos—in the guise of A-bombs, volcanoes, and flying saucers.

"This is the creepiest city in America," Jensen intoned.

"I think if God administered an enema to the U.S. of A, he'd stick the hose in Roswell," Madieros belched.

Jensen agreed: "Well, aesthetically speaking, I think the architectural highpoint of Roswell would have to be the Wal-Mart."

As we hit the outskirts of town Jensen put the hammer down, and we motored at maximum velocity toward the Lone Star State. Nightfall was imminent and I suggested that a hefty dinner at the "Big Texan Steak Ranch" in Amarillo would give us ample opportunity to catalog, process, and inventory the day's events. It had been a hard day's traveling, and we were past due for nourishment and sleep. 90 miles-an-hour seemed like a decent speed for cruising.

Once we crossed the border into Texas, however, Madieros was having none of this. He freaked "I recall an episode of *Real Stories of the Highway Patrol*, when they were on location in the Texas Panhandle, and the officers beat the bejeesus out of some longhairs because they spit on the sidewalk. Pete,

I suggest we slow down to the posted speed limit." I was incredulous: "We have just hauled ass through where the military-industrial complex is back-engineering UFOs, where primordial volcanic explosions had covered the entire topography with molten tar and ooze, where the friggin' Manhattan Project blew up and radiated an entire desert, including the last place where Billy the Kid indiscriminately cut people in half with a shotgun, and based on what you saw on *Real Stories of the Highway Patrol,* or something, you trying to tell me the real danger is ahead of us?"

Apparently Jensen had seen the same episode. "Hey, that's how it starts nowadays," he said. "When honest American citizens let their guard down."

The point was well taken. We were in the Texas Panhandle. It was time to Obey The Law. A few hours later, well after dark, we arrived at the "Big Texas Steak Ranch," where Old West Highway meets Route 66, and we proceeded to order some whiskey drinks and slabs of charred animal tissue. As we chowed down in a most prodigious manner we were approached by two strolling cowboy troubadours, replete with gee-tar and a stand-up bass, who felt compelled to share their love for music with us. Knowing how Madieros felt about the art of music, I was preparing myself for the worst—this could get seriously ugly…

"Do you guys know any Lefty Frizzell songs?" Madieros asked.

> *"We'll travel far*
> *To some shining star*
> *Just you and my guitar*
> *I want to be with you always."*

The steaks were tasty, the music was euphonious, and we tipped the waiter and the musicians generously. We had found purity of tone and we were still hours away from the drag strip in Noble, Oklahoma. We were in Amarillo and we were exhausted. It was the time and the place for sleep.

The next morning, after a night of sawing enough logs to clear-cut the state of Oregon, we jammed down to Oklahoma on I-40. As we motored through downtown Oklahoma City, the conversation stopped and the three of us gawked at the nifty architecture that graced the city's folksy, yet urbane landscape. We were just passing through, but my impression of Oklahoma City was that, judging by the architecture, this was a town whose collective consciousness seemed a lot more karmically correct than say, San Francisco, Los Angeles, or New York, i.e., a refreshing lack of those oppressive glass towers that are so in vogue in most major metropolitan areas. We were appalled and bewildered at the notion of anybody wanting to destroy such a cool city. Fortunately for our psyches we were less than a half-hour from the drag strip, where, when people blow shit up at least they do it righteously. We pulled up to Thunder Valley Raceway Park in Noble, and the three of us were all pleasantly blown away by what we saw. Situated way out in the boondocks, the Thunder Valley facility was a drag racer's dream, a veritable ivory tower in the heart of Sooner Country. Far off any real beaten path and surrounded by wilderness, the track seemed to contain the best elements of the modern uber-motorplex combined with the folksiness of a humble backwoods drag strip. It reminded me of the now-defunct Orange County International Raceway, back when it was buffeted by orange groves, well before it was consumed by techno-industrial strip malls and the accompanying California real estate wars. Pardon the parochialism, but it immediately conjured images of drag racing back when it mattered, and back where it mattered—i.e., Southern California in the '60s. And as some sort of sick, redundant correlative to all this, as we pulled up to the pit gate the track operators blasted "Surfin' U.S.A" by Hawthorne, CA's finest, the Beach Boys. It was the eeriest of deja vus. Even Madieros appreciated this impromptu soundtrack to our reconnaissance mission. (Maybe he didn't hate music after all—maybe he just hated what has happened to music in the last thirty years...)

And Beach Boys or no Beach Boys, a casual observer might assume that Oklahoma's Big Go was happening in California, what with all the Left Coast license plates in the pits. Yep, a whole lotta' California race teams made the trek through the deserts of the Southwestern U.S. in order to participate in this positively boffo drag race in the twilight zone. (Motorists gawking at the caravan of tow vehicles and race car trailers traversing I-40 must have thought they were witnessing a rerun of *The Grapes of Wrath*—this time, however, instead of a migration of Dustbowlers heading towards the Mecca of California, it was now a buncha' Golden State-types heading due east on what used to be Route 66, to test their mettle in Okieville, USA.) And it was a real who's who of West Coast front-motor dragster types that made this pilgrimage: Fuller & Dunlap, Ty "Thumper" Norton, Hallock & Hedge, Dan Horan Sr., Brendan Murry, and the father-and-daughter Jr. Fuel tag-team of Jim & Stacy Paul.

The appropriate bookend to this entire time warp was the presence of perhaps the most outside and fearless California drag racers of the Golden Age, the team of Marcellus & Borsch with their *Winged Express* AA/Fuel Altered. And yes, both "Mousie" Marcellus and "Wild Willie" Borsch were on the premises, never mind the fact that Borsch did technically pass on to the next dimension in 1991. But just because he is dead, that doesn't mean he couldn't party with his pals, does it?

"Mousie" towed out to Oklahoma with "Wild Willie's" cremated remains in an urn which was secured to the passenger seat of their early model Dodge pick-'em-up truck. Mousie insists that traveling with Willie, who was narcoleptic, was just like old times, since Willie slept all the time anyway. So once again, as the two men barnstormed across America, "Mousie" did all of the talking and all of the driving. And we thought Lefty Frizzell was strange...

Surf music was still blaring over the tinny public address system when "Nitro Neil" and his crew pulled into Thunder Valley. He and his boys had pulled an all-nighter from Kenosha, WI, but arrived looking no worse for the wear, perhaps due to the excitement, joy, and enthusiasm of being in one's element will definitely overshadow something as trivial and insignificant as no sleep whatsoever...

PART TWO

It had been an epic, yet surreal, last couple of days. I had been shanghaied by two members of the notoriously crazed "Juggers Race Team," Pete Jensen and Frank Madeiros, to tag along on a mission to a remote drag strip in Noble, Oklahoma, ostensibly to deliver oil pans and blowers. But that was all a smokescreen: This mission was really all about getting out on the highways and searching for what is cool and weird about America; it was about the quest for purity of tone—both on and off the drag strip...

But the nobility and soul of the Continental U.S.A. is not all we found while en route to the ANRA Nitro Nationals at Thunder Valley Raceway Park. It was on this trip that we also tapped into the dark side of the American psyche, for the three of us encountered the fallout from A-bombs, volcanic cinder cones, the back-engineering of UFOs, cattle-range wars, and assorted other weirdness. But all of that was forgotten once we finally arrived at our destination...

In Noble, Oklahoma we soaked up the ambience of a totally chill drag race; an event whose consciousness was an exemplum of 100%, undiluted purity of tone. Indeed, it had all the elements: diggers, altereds, and radical torque-twistin' doorslammers, all of whom loudly matched wheels, fossil fuels, and header flames under the phosphorescent lights which seemed to glow transparently in the clear Oklahoma sky at night. And it wasn't just the race cars that made this event so spiritually correct. It was also the hospitality of the hosts (local Okies Wally Hanes, Todd Stevens, and Jon Barrett) and the cordiality of the racers themselves (everyone from nitro-huffing legends like Shirley Muldowney, Don Garlits, and Alvin "Mousie" Marcellus to not-quite-as-famous quarter-mile fanatics like 31-year-old "Nitro Neil" Bisciglia and his rag-tag team from Wisconsin). And it was more than apparent to everybody here that for a weekend in the fall of 1995, they were all tapped into, privy to, and part of something truly special—it was a righteous and noble gathering. Everybody felt at home in Noble, because, well, because they were at home. Even if you were from California. Or Kenosha, Wisconsin...

So, the ANRA "Nitro Nationals" was now history, and with this half of our mission accomplished, the blowers and oil pans delivered and installed into nitro-burning race cars, we were to hightail it back to California. It was to be a convoy: Jensen and Madieros in the rent-a-car, Neil and I tagging along in his 1970 Dodge pick-em-up, with his vintage 150" *Firepower Flyer* Top Fuel Dragster (which is even earlier-modeled than the tow vehicle) in tow. Once we reached the Sterling Racing Service's shop in the Sierras (where Jensen's fueler is stored) there would be serious work ahead, tuning and prepping the Castagnino & Jensen *Foothill Flyer* AA/Fuel Dragster for a race the following weekend in Sacramento... Bisciglia, who shoes the *Foothill Flyer* in addition to piloting his own railjob, would be assisting in the tune-up of the Castagnino & Jensen machine. Since Neil could not simultaneously adjust the barrel valve and engage the clutch, the "Foothill Flyers" needed somebody pushin' the pedals in the cockpit. This would be me. I was to be the stunt monkey while they monitored the tone and pitch of the motor, as well as examined the color and consistency of the header flames, reading them like an organic oscilloscope—all to determine how fat or lean the fuel volume should be, what percentage of nitro should be coursing through the fuel pumps, and whether to advance or retard the spark of the magneto, etc. But meanwhile, back in Oklahoma: "Nitro Neil" and I motored towards the Texas Panhandle on I-40, headed due west, California bound. Gas fumes were wafting through a corrugated floorboard—indeed a lot of the structural integrity of his truck was severely compromised by all the salt on the roads in Kenosha, WI—and it was kinda' hard to breathe. But Neil was oblivious to the whanging toxicity of the petrol seeping into the cockpit. He was mulling over the play-by-play of the "Nitro Nationals" in his head, while chain-smoking ciggies and extemporaneously blathering about the drag race...

Neil, who had qualified on the pole with a seesawing 6.62 at 218 mph, was slightly bummin' from a sense of lack of closure at the Nitro Nationals. He was one of the two finalists for the Top Fuel Title. Bill "the Heartbreaker" Dunlap, the shoe for the high-dollar, state-of-the-art "nostalgia" fueler of Mike Fuller, was the other contender. The conclusion of the event was thwarted due to a power failure moments before the final round of eliminations. So the two teams split the purse equally, a compromise that was not to either man's satisfaction. And, despite the disparity in "cubic dollars," Neil was pretty confident he could have taken out "the Heartbreaker." More importantly, he needed the dough...

"I'm not all that hurtin' for money," he said as we rumbled into the Lone Star State, "but sometimes, like if there is a fire or somethin', I kinda' ride the fire out just a little bit, to see if it will put itself out, because if I pull the fire bottles that's $300 worth of foam, meanwhile my phone bill back home is at least $400—so I think about those kind of things when the flames first creep under the firewall. Y'know, don't pull the fire bottle, that's $300."

We then discussed how cool the Oklahoma experience was; particularly the lush, verdant, and beautiful terrain and topography. It was nothing like what one would associate with Oklahoma from reading John Steinbeck—it is awe-inspiring scenery. And we agreed that the Noble drag strip itself was as cool and as scenic as any race track we had ever visited on our travels—or had read about in drag racing magazines when we were kids—be it Great Lakes Dragaway, U.S. 30, or Englishtown for Neil; or Lions, OCIR, San Fernando Raceway, Sonoma, or Spokane for moi. In fact, although it hurt my sense of civic pride, I said that all told the track surface, accommodations, and amenities of TVRP surpass the conditions at virtually any drag strip left in California—especially when one factors in affordability and track-operator attitude. This is a fact that is sad, humbling and true, unfortunately, for California racers and bleacher bums, I added. I also told Neil about the recent closings of Brotherhood Raceway Park and Norton AFB, two ideal locations for a positive drag scene in the So Cal area—and more importantly, two economically-depressed areas (the South Bay and San Berdoo) that would flourish with activity (social and financial) if certain imbecilic bureaucrats and politicians spent a fraction of their energies trying to help create something as opposed to destroying some phenomenon that is truly happening. And, I continued, while Neil furrowed his brow, that after passing through a town recently ravaged by domestic terrorists, while visiting the beautiful countryside of Oklahoma (with its hospitable people and immaculate drag strip), and then to confront the sorrow and disappointment from another pair of race track closures in the L.A. Basin (again!), I have come to the conclusion that those militia-types are blowing the wrong places up. Forget the Alfred Murrah Building in Okieville—give it to the Harbor Commission in La-La Land.

Neil nodded in agreement, and then began apologizing profusely for the petrol fumes and the ciggie smoke, but I was nonplussed and not disturbed by either offense to the olfactory. (Personally, I do not smoke, but I do encourage it in others.)

I noticed that Neil had a Radio Shack cassette player that was mounted rather haphazardly into the dashboard; Bisciglia asked if I wanted to listen to some music.

"Only if it was recorded before the Beatles killed rock and roll," I said. "I don't mind the gas fumes or the fact that this truck is one big, rolling burnout box, but I refuse to listen to anything recorded in the last 30 years."

"Wow, relax," he replied. "How about some of this? I scored it at that last truck stop in Elk City. I thought it would make a nice road tape for the ride out to California."

In his hand was a crude bootleg cassette of the "Greatest Hits of the 1960s."

I scanned the cover art and noticed there were no Beatles songs on the tape. "Perfect," I uttered.

"Surfer Girl" came blaring out of the stereo's speakers, sonically competing with the roar of the wind rushing through the holes on the truck's floorboard. It was kinda' nice to hear some music for a change, and it did take my mind off the gas fumes seeping through the floorboards.

"So you really think the vibe at this race was like California in the old days?" he asked. I shared with Neil my memories about various drag strips in Southern California that I frequented with my family as I grew up. Bisciglia was all ears as I rhapsodized about the Southern California Experience, climbing into the cockpit of my Uncle Phil's Junior Gas dragster at the PDA Race at Lions Drag Strip, being pushed down the return road by an Impala station wagon, the cool ocean air brushing by my face in a smooth, exhilarating stream that I could still feel to this day.

Neil asked me when was the last time I sat in the cockpit of a dragster. I told him that had been the last time. Soon after that fabled PDA race at "the Beach" my uncle was racing on a Sunday afternoon out at "the Pond" (San Fernando) and a u-joint came apart in the drive shaft and violently ripped through his foot, temporarily incapacitating him, but the seriousness of the injury kept him out of the police action in Vietnam.

"Whoa," Neil whispered.

It was kinda' quiet in the truck, so I quickly changed the subject.

"Hey man," I said, "you were skatin' around last night real good. What was the traction like on the track?"

top fuel wormhole

All of a sudden Neil lit up like Chrondek timers. He became real animated and excited—it was like he turned into the spiritual stepchild of beatnik-poet-gearhead Neal Cassady, or if crazed funny car driver John Force was shoeing the converted school bus in *The Electric Kool-Aid Acid Test* (say, instead of Cassady). Indeed, vis-à-vis a stream of barely linear thoughts, sentiments, and philosophical tangents, Neil captured the essence of the Oklahoma Thunder Valley Experience, and rather poetically...

"Holy Mackerel, that whole deal was a fuckin' total wild card 'who can do this here?' y'know? And plus th-the slippery track thing was too cool, that's what really made it, to me, that makes it a little bit more of a, of, uh, it also combines that driver's game and every... I thought everybody there was, y'know, there was, not that there isn't a lot of the times where there isn't a driver y'know, like it isn't, couldn't be a driver's game, y'know? But I thought it was just slippery enough, and cooling off enough at night, where um, where it was going to be real interesting—especially for the guys that had a lot of horsepower and that were, that knew, that you knew uh... I didn't think anybody was going to back their motor down just because of the track—because they would rather just say 'let the driver deal with it.' And I like that. It was a skating rink, but it was a smooth skating rink, y' know what I mean?" (Uh... sure, Neil.)

The conversation then segued into a discussion about the Shirley Muldowney versus *Swamp Rat 34* (with "Big Daddy" Don Garlits wrenching and Richard Langson shoeing) Top Fuel match race at TVRP, which Shirley swept with a best of 4.95 at 291 mph. Neil rationalized "I guess Rahn Tobler and Shirley really showed that it wasn't that much of a skating rink, if you really knew how to manage your clutch and managed the amount of horsepower you have. They did show us that, but then again they got a little bit better tires than us..."

That morning I had observed Shirley, Rahn Tobler, and their minions demurely enjoying breakfast, while the more unruly nostalgia nitro guys loudly consumed their meal. It was a sharp contrast, Shirley's team was polite, well-groomed, and refined, while the front-motored guys seemed a little more unkempt, uncouth, and boisterous. Indeed, as Shirley watched the hijinks and shenanigans of the other crews during the breakfast buffet, it looked like Shirley was examining an apparition of her past, which had come to life at a coffee shop in Norman, Oklahoma. But she certainly did not seem to miss the low-buck lifestyle... So we were chugging down the highway and I mentioned to Bisciglia that I thought Shirley Muldowney was checking out the demeanor of the *Firepower Flyer* race team in the motel coffee shop. I asked Neil what was the common bond between himself and Ms. Muldowney. "She's got the sickness, man," he said. "Tell me she don't have the sickness. Anybody who can bounce back from as many things as she did has got to have the sickness. And "Big Daddy," he's got it too."

"You think Garlits is envious of what you guys are doing?" I asked.

"Well, it's weird—for a long time he really bashed front-motored cars big time. The last U.S. Nationals I was at as a spectator, they were displaying some front-motored cars and Garlits was on the p.a. saying something like, 'these people boggle my mind,' y'know? and 'why would anybody drive one of these things in this day and age?' He was pretty much comin' across like 'this is utter stupidity.' And at that time I was getting a lot of flack from a lot of established Super Comp and Super Gas racers that I knew—they thought the iron-block Chrysler Hemi I use was nothing but a boat anchor—and they told me 'well, "Big Daddy" says you're stupid too.' I was crushed."

"Well," I said, "I think he kinda' changed his mind about you guys. I saw Garlits checkin' you guys out yesterday, and the look on his face was one of admiration, not contempt. I think he knows you guys would not be doing what you are doing without his trailblazing, and it was probably kinda' neat for him to see the scene come back full circle, at least for a weekend in Oklahoma. And," I added, "Shirley told me you guys are much closer to the spirit of what drag racing is all about, than what it has become in the big leagues." "Whoa."

I then told Neil that in Oklahoma, I felt blessed, charmed, and honored to witness the existential throughline of these two talented legends of the drag strip, Garlits and Muldowney. And although their careers are still flourishing at IHRA shows and at match races, their lifeworks—for all practical purposes—may be in its autumn. This being the case, it was neat to watch these heroes of the 1320 reflect on their pasts in both a coffee shop and in the staging lanes, and to watch them become somewhat philosophical while peering into the humble shadows of their achievements.

Neil seemed to grasp what I was rambling about, and then he got philosophical. "Oklahoma was a good one for us," he said. "It makes you feel good and proud for what you do. I look at it and go 'wow,' I'm not reading about someone else in a hot rod book this time, this is actually happening—it's real and we're part of this deal. It just blows me away."

And so it went as we journeyed through the Southwestern United States. It never got real quiet in the cabin of the truck, the hum of the 318 cubic inch Dodge motor providing a perpetual *om*-like drone, the valves and the combustion chamber belying the wear and tear of a quarter of a million miles worth of service and rumbling like a mantra, creating a sonic wash that was interrupted and punctuated only by some surf music and Neil's peppery, rambling monologues about his last blast down the ol' 1320. Indeed, he would ruminate for as much as an hour about a six-second run. The beauty of it was that this never got tedious. On the contrary, it was inspiring to hear a man systematically chart, catalogue, and diagram the progress of the pursuit of his dream—a dream that is cost prohibitive to damn near all of us—which is to run a fuel car on the blue-collar salary of an O'Hare Airport airline mechanic (his day gig) in this, the Year of the Maximum Stock Dividend, 1995.

PART THREE

Neil is somehow cheating the economics of life in post-industrial America. There is nothing more daunting than running a fuel car—a) it is one big exercise in what economists call "negative cash flow" and b) it is also extremely labor intensive—much more so than running relatively-benign (and inexpensive) fuels like alcohol or gasoline through the cylinder heads of an internal combustion engine. The incendiary, volatile, explosive nature of nitromethane corrodes, corrupts, contorts, chars, blackens, and disintegrates anything and everything in the loop: rings, pistons, rocker arms, the heads themselves, connecting rods, $3,000 crankshafts, superchargers, etc. Not much escapes its awesome, destructive wrath. And when something breaks, it has to be replaced. Again, this is both time-consuming and expensive...

"When you are ready to light $100 bills on fire and not flinch, then you are ready to be a drag racer." Bob Sanders of Titan Engineering told me that once, describing the financial drain of running a Top Fuel car, but he only clued me in on one half of the equation—the other half being an acute lack of sleep because, due to the absurd parts attrition inherent in running a fuel car, you are continually working on the race car until the cows come home...

But nothing as trivial as finances and sleep deprivation is going to keep someone like Mr. Bisciglia from showcasing his tuning prowess and his natural aptitude for wrestling with an alligator (formally known as a AA/Fuel Dragster) down the drag strip. And thank the heavens he chooses to do so, because... Neil is necessary. He has a function in our ever-increasingly stuffed-up sewer line of a society—an uptight society where the pursuit of pleasure is a crime, an oppressive society that thrives on hammering into us exactly what we can not do, as opposed to liberating and enabling us toward what we can do. So, no, it is not just "Nitro Neil's" function to entertain us with his uncanny talent of harnessing and finessing an uncontrollable suicide machine, it is also his function to show us that anything is possible—especially if one is naive enough to believe that with mere talent, perseverance and chutzpah one can accomplish his or her goals and aspirations; all this despite the deck being stacked quite heavily in the dealer's favor.

And Bisciglia has made quite a reputation for himself driving 'er out the back door, but, logically speaking, that is the only way he could possibly drive 'er is out the back door because that is the way he lives—with the butterflies wide open.

Sometime around midnight, somewhere between Kingman, AZ and Needles, CA on I-40, I came to another realization as Neil delivered some color commentary about a match race he won against a blown fuel altered at Great Lakes Dragaway, which was this: It isn't that nobody told this guy he couldn't be Don Prudhomme in 1969, or that rolling down the highway with a race car in tow à la the 1973 road picture *Funny Car Summer* has no bearing whatsoever on life in the Age of the Information Superhighway—nope, a whole lotta' folks back home told Neil his decision to barnstorm a 1960's vintage Top Fuel dragster across America in 1995 was impractical, insane, and foolish (which is the beauty of his whole operation)—and it is not that he didn't listen to these nattering nabobs of negativism, it's just that he didn't really hear them. He was nodding his head like he heard the naysayers and was processing the logic of their arguments, but really his cranial activity was consumed by notions of the Bernoulli effect as applied to Enderle injectors or something.

So yeah, Neil is necessary and we, the railbirds and the wannabees, project ourselves on Neil's exploits and heroics. And because he is not somebody we see on teevee, but someone we are more likely to encounter pumping his own gas at a truck stop, then maybe Neil is the favorite stepchild of German philosopher Frederick Nietzsche—that is to say, Neil may not be the archetype for Nietzsche's Uber mensch (translation: Superman), but he most certainly is Uber Every Mensch. The man is the embodiment of the do-it-yourself ethic—y'know: "Conceive, Believe, Achieve"—but the truth of the matter is that few of us are as obsessed and consumed by our desires as this chain-smoking cheesehead driving a dilapidated pick-'em-up truck—soaked with gasoline fumes that had permeated the salt-corrugated floorboards—across America. In other words, most of us lack the necessary *cojones* and zeal to actually live the dream. This guy has to do it for us.

Eventually we hit Needles. Jensen, Madieros, and I persuaded Neil, who wanted to motor on to the Sierras, into pulling over and spending the night in a motel. (This no-sleep lifestyle is no longer out of necessity for Bisciglia—it is more like the man thrives on it. I think his metabolism is now permanently tweaked and damaged from barnstorming across America with a fuel dragster.)

The next afternoon we reach the flatlands of Sacramento, and dumpster Madieros (who had to crank out some more oil pans before the big race this weekend). We bid our fellow "Jugger" adieu, and then begin our ascension into Calaveras County, the final leg of this long, strange trip.

Once we finally arrive in the Sierras and park Neil's rig, everyone gets crackin' on the Castagnino & Jensen digger, prepping 'er for the big go this weekend. Jensen is in the shop mixing a batch of fuel (82% nitro, the rest methanol), Ken Castagnino has got the valve covers off the engine and is torqueing the cylinder heads, and Neil is jacking the ass end of the race car up while explaining to me what my duties will be once they turn the motor over.

Ah yes, soon I will be tasting nitro—the most mystical and mythical of explosives...To explain the essence and mythical qualities of nitromethane to somebody who has never had it burn their eyes and olfactories, who has never had it rock their sandbox, is almost impossible. It is tantamount to having quantum physicist Stephen Hawking explain how quarks and other subatomic particles are the essence of the universe to a crackbaby. Good luck—because to the uninitiated, both quarks and nitro are abstractions at best.

But I am assuming the demographic of this here drag racing magazine is not the uninitiated, that you, the reader, have at least caught a whiff of this mystical nectar of the gods as it propels a fueler down the quarter mile and therefore nitro is not an abstraction. You can relate to the sensory properties of nitromethane—the smell, the sound, and the flames—that make it so gloriously addictive.

Be that as it may, allow me to explain my prior experience with "liquid horsepower": on many occasions I have been graced with the opportunity to stand five feet behind someone like fuel Funny Car ace John Force when he stomped on the loud pedal, and have felt the brutality of the sheer nitro-induced propulsion: the pressure waves stinging my ribs, the exhaust and raw un-burnt fuel melting my eyes, and the roar of the motor hammering my eardrums like a piledriver pulverizing Play-Doh.

But none of this prepared me for my experience behind the bellhousing of a AA/Fuel Dragster, however...

And indeed, on this night I am contemplating the raw power of a Top Fueler as I climb onto the slicks, straddle the rollcage, plant my feet in front of the rear axle and slither into the cockpit. Once inside, I begin to acclimate myself to the ergonomics of the *Foothill Flyer* cockpit: getting a feel for the throttle, the clutch pedal, the handbrake, the parachute lever, as well as locating the magneto switch and the fuel shut-off. The fit inside the rollcage is quite snug, verging on claustrophobic. The feeling of being hemmed in becomes even more acute when I tightly wrap the firemask around my face, and then slip the goggles over the eyeholes in the mask. Even though nothing has really happened yet my heartbeat is somewhat accelerated, and the intensity of the situation is exacerbated by the tightness of the synthetic aluminized facemask. I could hear heavy breathing—it sounded more like Leatherface in the *Texas Chainsaw*

Massacre than Marilyn Chambers in *Behind the Green Door*—and I realized that it was my heavy breathing, but somehow the dynamic was all wrong; that is, despite the mask, I wasn't the Leatherface-figure... no, in fact the scary id-monster was actually not even human, it was the supercharged Chrysler hemi lying dormant at my feet. But yes, I was in bondage, a point highlighted by the mask: I was the slave, and nitromethane was the master.

"The psychology of this whole situation is really absurd," I say, but nobody listens. So the mummification is complete, and Pete Jensen, Ken Castagnino, and "Nitro Neil" Bisciglia are ready to turn the motor over. The first task is to warm the engine, so the initial blast of activity will be on alcohol, fed into the fuel lines from a gravity valve perched on top of the injector hat.

"Mag switch off?" Jensen asked.

"Mag switch off!" I shouted back, my decibel level muted considerably by the fireproof material wrapped around my face.

Castagnino mounts the aircraft starter onto the blower pulley, hits a switch that propels the pulley and subsequently the blower belt. Simultaneously, the blower drive, the camshaft, and the crankshaft spin in unison, Jensen primes the injector hat with alcohol spritzing out of an old mustard dispenser, nods his head in the affirmative—which is my cue to flick the mag switch, which I do—and *voila! The Foothill Flyer* roars to life.

With the motor running on alcohol, the sensation inside the cockpit is somewhat soothing, the syncopated firing order of the spark plugs creating palpitations in an almost tranquilizing rhythm. It is rather hypnotic. And as the motor continues to run I get cozy. It's strange—what was once claustrophobic is now comfortably womb-like. I like this.

The three men listen solemnly and reverently to the pitch of the engine as it continues to sing. Occasionally, Ken will point to something on the motor, Pete will nod, and Neil will do nothing but rest his hand on his cheek, deeply engrossed in thought, not unlike Plato contemplating *The Allegory of the Cave* or something. After awhile, as per instruction (via hand gestures from Jensen), I release the clutch and the hand brake and the massive slicks on either side of me begin to spin. This makes the rollcage vibrations more palpable, but it is still a pleasant and comforting experience. After more analysis from the three "Juggers" I am told in sign language to engage the clutch and the brake, the slicks stop spinning and Jensen hits the external fuel shut-off. The motor dies as everything stops spinning, and I pull the mag switch into the "off" position. Everything is quiet, serene, and quite copasetic in the darkness of the Sierras' foothills.

Off come the valve covers, and I keep the clutch pedal engaged as Ken, who wants to set the valves, rotates the camshaft via a ratchet. He and Neil discuss matters over the exposed cylinder heads while Jensen tells me they are about to run 'er on fuel.

"Okay mister hot shot drag strip journalist, you've just played with Hot Wheels," Jensen says. "Are you finally ready to lose your cherry?"

"Hit me with your best shot," I shout back, but the smarminess was muted and diluted considerably by the fire mask muffling the volume of my reply.

"Mag switch off?"

"Mag switch off!" This is it. Top fucking fuel.

They rotate the blower drive, camshaft, and crank with the aircraft starter, they squirt the injector hat with alcohol, I flip the mag switch as instructed, the motor rumbles back to life and starts sucking alcohol out of the gravity valve, the cage rocks a little bit, the three "Juggers" look for fluid leaks and other anomalies, everything checks out okey-dokey, and the moment of truth is imminent.

Jensen nods at me and smiles, flips a lever on the gravity valve, and with the transformation from alcohol to good ol' CH_3NO_2 complete all hell breaks loose. No longer is alcohol gurgling down from the gravity valve, all of a sudden blasts of 82% nitromethane are gushing through the veins, arteries, lungs, and heart of this primal beast that moments before was almost a pussycat of a reciprocating internal combustion engine. Instantaneously, the whole rollcage is shaking, rattling, and threatening to bounce off the jack-stands. Fire is now shooting out of the headers, licking at either side of the cage, inches from my head. It is fucking l-o-u-d, as this whole contraption has mutated into the most savage of wild, untamed beasts. Immense, tremendous heat waves, billowing from both the motor and its exhaust, invade the once cool confines of the cockpit and warm my flesh. But despite the cacophony and pyrotechnics I am cool, calm, and collected. At least on the surface... Neil is completely fixated on the fire jumping out of the pipes, like the pattern and the color of this arpeggiated torch contains the key to the mysteries of the universe. The motor continues barking out its brutal sequential cadence as Ken aims a timing light towards the blower belt. Jensen points at me and twirls his forefinger. I release the brake and the clutch, allowing the M&Hs to rotate most prodigiously and the chassis vibrations increase commensurately. My body is shaking in sympathy with the revolutions of the tires as I hang on to both the steering yoke and the hand brake, bracing myself as my eyes begin to water, the seal between the goggles and the fire mask not as airtight as I had assumed. Eventually there are more gesticulations, and accordingly I step down on the clutch pedal, firmly engage the brakes and the slicks stop their spin cycle. I am high on fumes and drunk on the blood of an iron-block hemi, but I am totally sent into orbit when Jensen reaches over and tweaks the throttle linkage and *WHOMP! WHOMP!* the whole 220" machine contorts and jumps, the flames subside for a nanosecond, then leap even further into the darkness and lick at the underbelly of the moon. As the beast returns to an idle it is still louder than a fleet of Concordes.

It is *h-o-t* in the cockpit, my ears hurt, my eyes hurt, my heart is beating like a wild go-rilla, my brain is racing like an Osterizer set on pulverize, and my veins are dilated and pumping like those of a werewolf. And I am diggin' it big time. For I am Danny Kaye in *The Secret Life of Walter Mitty*, I am George Plimpton in *Paper Lion*, but beyond that I am Ho Chi Minh fornicating with a pile of bleached bones in Cambodia and barking at the moon. Goddamn, it's great to be alive.

And on this night, with the roar and cackle of a nitro-burning blown hemi reverberating into the mountains of Calaveras County, I am at one with my universe.

So we repeat this whole scenario a few times, more adjustments are made to the barrel valve, fuel nozzles, and the magneto, but all that stuff is of little interest to the stunt monkey. I am wired on sheer sensory overload—the kind you only feel from nitromethane. Nitromethane—the holy water for the soul of a drag racer. And drag racing—a sacrament that is both cool and weird and uniquely American. Be it in Wisconsin. Be it in Oklahoma. Be it the memory of Lions Drag Strip. Or be it in Mark Twain Country a/k/a Calaveras County, California on a cool autumn night.

When Madieros, Jensen, and I embarked on our sojourn to Oklahoma, our unstated goal was to find what was cool and weird about America—or more to the point, to see if there was anything out there left to discover. But by the time I got back to California I realized I had been riding shotgun with what was left of the nobility of America the whole time. And then I climbed in the driver's seat.

(*Originally published in* Super Stock & Drag Illustrated)

top fuel wormhole

the feminine archetype of drag race culture

SHIRLEY MULDOWNEY:

ORIGINAL BLAST OFF GIRL AND DRAG-STRIP GRAND DAME

The sound of a dragster is nothing if not the sound of destruction. Every time a valve opens in the combustion chamber of a supercharged Top Fuel motor—an action that takes place as many as 80 times a second *per valve*—it allows a highly volatile mixture of oxygen and nitromethane (a fuel developed for use not only as a fertilizer (!), but also by both Allied Power and Third Reich scientists as a rocket propellant during WWII) to penetrate the cylinder. This incendiary mixture then awaits a high-amperage spark so it can EXPLODE. Not burn like the gasoline in yer grocery-getter, but detonate like the Manhattan Project in minutia. This series of (barely) controlled explosions in the motor's cylinder heads is what propels these contraptions down the racetrack at speeds in the 300 mile-per-hour range. This whole experience is somewhere between an orgasm and a glimpse of Armageddon. It is *l-o-u-d*. It is primal. It is ferocious.

I have been fascinated with the machinations of nitromethane and its incumbent pyromania for quite some time. I am also fascinated with women who harness, finesse, dominate, and control the fierce, unwieldy machines of drag racing. That is to say, women who drive dragsters. Recently in Oklahoma City I had the honor of meeting the feminine archetype of drag race culture: Shirley Muldowney.

That's right, Ms. Shirley Muldowney, the High Priestess of Top Fuel and the driver formerly known as "Cha Cha," was "in the house" as the Main Attraction of the Thunder Valley show, a best 2-out-of-3 match race against her longtime nemesis, the Grand Ol' Man of Drag Racing, "Big Daddy" Don Garlits. Inarguably the two most epic figures in the sport of drag racing, Shirley and Garlits were facing off for bragging rights.

Shirley Muldowney versus "Big Daddy" Don Garlits. (Wo)Mano-a-mano. The Grand Dame of "Go! Fever" facing off against the man who once eschewed anesthetics after getting half of his right foot blown off by an exploding transmission in 1970. Garlits and Shirley have had an on-again, off-again love/hate relationship that dates back to the early '70s, but here in Oklahoma, on the cusp of the new millennium, their once-adversarial relationship had mellowed into a more good-natured grudge match. Indeed, "Big Daddy" was not even driving his black-as-a-subatomic-particle dragster known as the *Swamp Rat*. He had recently relinquished the steering yoke to his pal Richard Langson. (After doctors predicted "Big" would eventually go blind, Garlits climbed out of the cockpit. He suffered a series of detached retinas from the negative 5g impact after deploying the parachutes used to stop his dragster.) But none of this was important to the gathered bleacher bums in Oklahoma: It was still, for all practical purposes, the Shirley Vs. Garlits Show, a marquee match-up worthy of Ali Vs. Frazier.

But to understand the relevance of boxing's "Thrilla in Manila" metaphor, one must follow the arc of Shirley's exalted racing career: From street racing with her high school snookums, Jack Muldowney, in the Teenage Badlands of Schenectady, NY, to driving a supercharged, twin-engined Top Gas Dragster in the late '60s, to driving a nitro-burning Funny Car in the early '70s, known as the *Bounty Huntress*. (Speaking of the notoriously fiery and unstable Funny Cars and the accompanying danger of gnarly and potentially fatal oil fires, she said, "I drove 'em when they were really bad machines." She still bears the scars.)

No, Ms. Muldowney is no ordinary drag-strip girl. Indeed, she has become its suffragette. Once marketed by the drag-culture Svengalis as a feisty feminist temptress—part Gloria Steinem, part sexploitation. Indeed, Shirley allowed herself to be photographed in hot pants, go-go boots, and a halter-top that left little to the imagination, moments before donning an asbestos firesuit and climbing into the fire-breathing *Bounty Huntress* flopper. She was a pretty girl driving a he-man's race car, but something clicked in Shirley's psyche back then that told her this image rang hollow. And after a particularly brutal Funny Car fire in 1973, she changed. Shirley was now no longer "Cha Cha." In fact, she later uttered this pearl of wisdom in denigration of a bleach-blond female Top Fuel driver, "There is no room for bimboism in drag racing." As a coda to this anecdote it should be noted that the shoe (that's dragster parlance for "driver") she was dissin' has since retired due to a lack of funds. Shirley, despite likewise suffering from a lack of Other People's Money, continues to burn down the quarter-mile on her own dime.

Shirley spews that, "I am grouped in this women's drivers group that could not find serious funding if their lives depended on it, and it just pisses me off." Shirley is nothing if not candid. The truth is that professional drag racing today is a billionaires boys and girls club that depends on corporate financing for its existence. Shirley, with the able assistance of her husband (and pit boss) Rahn Tobler, generates a positive cash flow without the help of Fortune 500 patronage, thank you. No less a source than "Big Daddy" Garlits himself has been quoted as saying, "Theirs (Tobler's & Muldowney's) may be the only Top Fuel team in the country that still makes a living drag racing."

Yes, Shirley is ignored by the Movers & Shakers of the Corporate Drag Racing Establishment despite accomplishments such as being crowned the NHRA Top Fuel World Champion 3 times (a feat matched only by Garlits and "Joltin' Joe" Amato). Currently, there are a few other female Top Fuel shoes gettin' fat off of Daddy Warbucks' bankroll, but Shirley agrees that most of 'em are "glorified trophy girls." She says, "They are a product of their crew chief."

Which leads us back to Oklahoma, the Fall of 1995, and the setting for a Battle Betwixt the Sexes, specifically Shirley and "Big Daddy": In the first session Langson, Garlits' driver, was disqualified for red-lighting, the dragstrip equivalent of premature ejaculation, while Shirley smoked the tires and overpowered the race track with too much horsepower—sort of like *coitus interruptus* or something. So, despite a less than stellar performance, Shirley was the winner of this round due to Langson's foul start. In the second heat it was "Big Daddy" who dialed in too much horsepower for his driver Langson, while in the other lane Shirley expertly rocketed down the drag strip in victory, covering the quarter-mile track in a scintillating 4.95 seconds, with a terminal velocity of 291 miles-per-hour. Final results from the OK Corral: Shirley 2, Big Daddy 0. Wow.

After Ms. Muldowney disposed of her long-time rival in two straight contests of horsepower, she found time to riff and ruminate on the trajectory of her life. Your humble reporter was then granted a private audience with a living legend, drag racing's Queen Bee. There was something Freudian and cool about chatting with Shirley Muldowney, 55 years old, in the privacy of her trailer. I felt like I was in the same room with greatness, like I was allowed to peer into the soul of a woman I had admired tremendously from a grandstand. And that is to say, a woman I consider to be every bit as epic as any Matron of Nobility that has honored Western Civilization with her aura in the last 100 years: Sylvia Plath, Amelia Earhart, Marlene Dietrich, Emma Goldman, Simone de Beauvoir, Shirley Chisholm, Barbara Stanwyck, or even Grace Slick.

In the confines of her trailer Shirley was gracious, existential, and open with her thoughts. Her state of mind in 1995? "I have changed," she said. "I have mellowed. It's not the fight that it was in the early days. Not that I've relaxed myself at all—I still want to win as much, I want to kick butt as much, because that is my competitive instincts, I want to show them the way home. That's normal with all drag racers."

Her station in life? "It would be nice to have someone pay your dress shop receipts every month, but that has not ever been the case for me. I've been at this a long time, I've worked hard at it, I'm disappointed that it hasn't done anything to secure my future. I'm pretty sure that once I am out of the race car there will not be a place for me in this sport."

So is there, in fact, life after drag racing? "When this is done I will probably go get a job at Hudson's in the Store Decoration Department or something," she said facetiously. "I am a driver, and I do not make a good spectator." When she does hang up the firesuit will there be a lot of fanfare? "No, I would quit before I would retire." Talk about bowing out with grace and dignity...

What are her thoughts toward the state of the female condition in 1995? "It's ideal," she says, "because the door is wide open now. If you want to do something bad enough there are ways in which you can do it. But you gotta stand your ground—if not they will walk on you like an old shoe."

Regrets? *Nyet*. "Without drag racing, I can only imagine where I would be today. I only pray that I have done as much for this sport as it has done for me. A lot of people are aware that the early years were really hard..."

The moral of today's drag-strip history lesson seems to be this: In life, either you conquer the circumstances or the circumstances conquer you. In Shirley's case, it was the former. But what is Shirley's rationale for her accomplishments? How did she do what she did? "It's because I'm a tough old broad," she said.

Yes, drag racing gave her a sense of purpose. And who amongst us isn't searching for a sense of purpose? Who amongst us isn't looking for a reason for being, a sense of fulfillment?

In Oklahoma, I felt blessed, charmed, and honored to witness the existential throughline of the sport's original "blast-off girl." Though still flourishing, Ms. Muldowney's lifework may be in its autumn. And as I reflect on what I have been privy to, I feel kinda' warm about humanity and the nobility of achievement, especially as exemplified by the spirit of this inspiring drag strip legend. Drag racing can be enlightening like that, y'know what I mean?

(Originally published in BIKINI*)*

DUNLAP TASTES VICTORY AT SONOMA
TEDFORD CRASHES, IS UNHURT!

Goodguys Jim Davis Nitro Nationals, Sears Point Int'l Raceway, April 13-14, 1996 – After a winter of discontent, fueler guys Fuller & Dunlap have begun to flourish and bloom like the wildflowers that grace the hillsides of Napa Valley in the springtime. Indeed, after the clutch dust from another gonzo/lost weekend of drag racing finally settled, everything smelled like roses in the Mike Fuller Motorsports pit area. For they drank from the cup of victory there, soothing the pain from previous disappointments in Top Fuel Eliminator earlier this year. These memories included a faulty fuel pump raining on their keg-boogie during the final round at the ANRA Winter Classic in February, and an uncharacteristically sour tune-up flattening their mimosas at the Goodguys March Meet. If you ask owner/tuner Mike Fuller or shoe Bill "the Heartbreaker" Dunlap, they'll tell you victory never tasted so good as it did out here in Wine Country, CA.

Ah, but the road to the chalice of bubbly can be paved with the glass from broken Night Train bottles… In the first session of qualifying Dunlap reeled off a 6.43, a number which resulted in an unenviable #5 qualifying position. This slotted Dunlap against pole-sitter Denver Schutz, who qualified with a 6.24 at a stout 235 mph—Top Speed of the Meet—in the awesome *Ground Zero* machine. Schutz has been the Preparation H on Dunlap's toothbrush recently, Denver having defeated Bill in the final round of the Winter Classic (where Schutz smoked the tires and Dunlap broke on the burnout), as well as the opening stanza of the March Meet (where Denver flat out whupped up on 'im).

But qualifying position was actually the least of Fuller & Dunlap's folly. For on the 6.43 run they torched five pistons. After thrashing to repair the damage and potentially improve their station on the qualifying ladder (and avoid Schutz), they warmed 'er up in the pits, as is standard operating procedure. What was out of the ordinary, unfortunately, was spark retardation from a loose magneto that forced the blower to sneeze, popping the burst panel. Collectively, the Fuller folks took a deep breath, exhaled and shined on the last session of qualifying as they triaged the damage to the only wind machine in their inventory.

This set the stage for their encounter with Schutz in the 1st round. To reflect the feelings of Fuller & Dunlap after this heat, one might paraphrase Chuck Dickens, something like, "It was the best of drag races, and it was the worst of drag races." Dunlap beat Schutz out of the gate—perhaps to compensate for the two-tenths disparity in their qualifying E.T.s—but nobody on the premises expected the massive burst of horsepower out of the Mike Fuller-tuned digger. The slicks smoothly black-tracked the pavement for the first 330 feet as it marched towards the top-end eyes. At 1100 feet, however, a *b-i-g* cloud of smoke billowed out of Dunlap's motor, as more than a few connecting rods rammed through the oil pan in mutiny. Despite the destruction, Dunlap won the race, recording a bodacious, Low E.T. 6.05 at a stomping 233 mph. Schutz tripped the timers in defeat with a 6.33 at 229 mph.

In the semi-finals Fuller & Dunlap, who crammed a fresh, untested bullet between the framerails, squared off against "Nitro Neil" Bisciglia. Dunlap, who later said of his tune-up, "We were kind of lost, actually," caught a break when Bisciglia red-lighted—leaving too early to even register an e.t on the clocks, thus allowing Dunlap to coast into the finals uncontested. "We were experimenting with Neil leaving the line with the rpms way up," confessed *Foothill Flyer* team captain Pete Jensen during a *mea culpa*. "Neil did what I wanted, it just pulled him through the staging beams, unfortunately." Nothing ventured, nothing gained, eh?

So the *Foothill Flyer* lost in the semi-finals, therefore Dunlap's opponent in the final round was... the *Foothill Flyer*. This was due to the Goodguys enlightened use of the break rule ("thank you, thank you, thank you," sayeth the bleacher bums.) According to the scorecard, Dunlap was supposed to face Gary Ritter in the *W.W. Two* fueler, but this Jim Herbert-tuned creation succumbed to engine damage in its semi-final victory by virtue of a 6.27 e.t to David Tedford's losing 6.36. So technically this would make Tedford low E.T. loser and therefore *he* was the beneficiary of the break rule, not Bisciglia, right? On paper this is an accurate assumption, but what the box scores don't tell you is that Tedford's ride was in more pieces than Humpty Dumpty after his great fall.

Tedford's semi-final sleigh ride was perhaps the most frightening excursion in California since dragster driver Paul Gommi cannonballed into the guardrail at Bakersfield a couple of years back. Tedford, a low-buck crusader who was having a career weekend (howz' about a 6.27 in their first round defeat of *Pure Hell* for chutzpah?), was on another sizzling run against Ritter when the motor discombobulated in the lights. A huge puff of smoke and a flash of flame overwhelmed the cockpit after the valve cover gaskets melted, Tedford was completely oiled in, the car drifted and veered right mere paces behind Ritter (who already had the chute out). The dragster smacked a concrete abutment at a 45-degree angle, crumpling as it catapulted over the embankment, the whole mess snapping and breaking as it *w-r-a-p-p-e-d* itself around a support pole, the 5-point cage (and Tedford's noggin) coming to a sudden stop against the pole itself and facing China.

It was pretty quiet for a while, with no one in the stands or in the staging lanes certain about Tedford's well being. Unbeknownst to the racers and the peanut gallery, the '72 Tuttle chassis was in pieces and the left side of the cage somewhat caved-in. Tedford was conscious the whole time, barking, "Get me out of here," like a mantra. (So yeah, it didn't appear he would make the next round...) Later, after a high-speed jaunt to the hospital, Tedford was spotted back at the race track with his arm in a sling, a couple of purple bruises on his forehead and his eyelashes singed, drinking a lite beer and extolling the virtues of SPIR track operator Georgia Seipel and her crackerjack crew of Safety honchos.

So pinch-hitter "Nitro Neil" suited up against the "Heartbreaker" for the title, and ironically these were the two cars on the premises with no real baseline for a tune-up. Like they say in Vegas, "It was a pick-'em."

After the burnouts, Bisciglia brought the r's up—although not to the soprano pitch of the run before—and staged first, with Dunlap following suit. Bisciglia left first with a sharp-as-muenster cheese .414 reaction time, Dunlap commenced to chasing and then overtook Bisciglia in the mid-range. As they approached the eyes with the butterflies horizontal Dunlap recalled it this way, "I went by him and I thought I had him covered pretty well. That's why I didn't hesitate in clicking off just before the first mile-an-hour light, but man, he was right there. He came streaking by me and I thought, 'Uh oh, did I shut off too soon?' I had some header flame coming out of the left bank and I was losing pistons. I shut if off because I didn't want to go down in flames." Dunlap recorded a victorious 6.43 at 198 mph, while a determined Bisciglia turned a 6.56 at a never-say-die 221 mph. Factoring in the reaction times, the margin of victory was *two-hundredths of a second*. Now that's drag racing...

(Excerpted from Full Throttle News*)*

RITTER TURNS 5.98, 242 – WITH HIS EYES CLOSED!

May 5, 1996, Sacramento Raceway – The plot lines of the Left Coast "Prostalgia" fueler wars continue to twist, turn, and implode. The latest tangle? Two weeks after Hoosier "carpetbagger" Paul Romine made history in Indiana as the first front-motored Top Fuel shoe to smash through the 5-second barrier—and simultaneously putting a dagger through the hearts of the Bear Republic fueler guys who have been shooting at that target for a few years now—Gary Ritter and the California race team of *W.W. Two* returned fire with a 5.98 shot at 242 mph. By Braille.

"I couldn't see," said "Blood, Sweat & Nitro" Ritter as he described what local nitromaniacs consider a retaliation volley. For his historic run, Ritter had borrowed partner (and retired shoe) Ted "the Bad Lieutenant" Taylor's old-school helmet and firemask. "It was okay with Ted's mask until the air caught it and it was about to choke me to death," he laughed. "And then the helmet went up and so did the eyeholes."

Not only did Ritter join the 5-second club with his vision blocked, he joined it *because* his vision was blocked. Indeed, Ritter was under explicit instruction from pit boss Jim Herbert to click 'er off at 1100 feet in order to avoid winding the crank too high (Herbert is notoriously frugal and savvy that way and in the nostalgia AA/FD society parts attrition is still considered somewhat "uncool"), but Ritter was merely guessing where the speed traps were. "I could see a little bit, then it completely went away so I said, '1-2-that's enough.'"

Taylor, who literally came within a millisecond (!) of claiming the 5-second grail himself last November in Bakersfield, greeted his replacement at the turn-off at the far end of the drag strip with this admonishment after the momentous run: "You drove it too far." For the rest of the race Ritter used his own modern-type helmet, and, not surprisingly, annihilated the competition and claimed Top Fuel Eliminator as well as Low E.T. and Top Speed. His last conquest was of Gerry "the Panzer Man" Steiner, with Ritter clocking a 6.20 at a mere 193 mph—one assumes the diminutive speed is probably indicative of Ritter's clear vision—to Steiner's 6.27, 228.

(Originally published in Full Throttle News*)*

BURY MY HEART AT EDWARDS AFB

Or... the sands will come again.

"We did it all, and we'll never see times like these again."—Dean Batchelor, *The American Hot Rod.*

At first I thought it was a mirage. Or an apparition. I was suffering from an acute lack of sleep, my disorientation and sensory deprivation amplified by a lack of proper coffee as well as the blinding reflection of the morning sun as it bounced off of the milky-white, crystallized floor of the dry lakebed. I shook my head, threw back the dregs of the caffeine, and blinked. It was no hallucination. There I was at Edwards AFB, deep in the heart of the cruel and unforgiving Mojave Desert, a landscape that a French philosopher once called a "slow catastrophe," and three paces from my bones was the man who organized hot rodding after WWII on this very same uninhabitable desert. That's right: Wally Parks, President of the Southern California Timing Association in 1946. Editor of Petersen Publishing's *Hot Rod Magazine* in 1948.

top fuel wormhole

President of the National Hot Rod Association during its birthin' in 1951, until Dallas Gardner stepped in during the Reagan Years. And probably the first man to call the linear pursuit of horsepower a "drag race," way back in 1939 in the *Racing News*.

I was stunned and I was silent. I did not know how to approach the man. Or, closer to the heart of the matter, maybe I did not know how to approach the myth and the legend that is Wally Parks as he stood there larger-than-life, towering over the proceedings at the most mystical and legendary plot of real estate in these here United States of America.

Ah yes, the mythology. There has been more history, folklore, and mythology concocted at the Muroc Dry Lake than anywhere else on the planet since the days of Apollo and Aphrodite making noise on Mt. Olympus. For it was at this wasteland where the Muroc Racing Association, predecessor to the SCTA, predecessor to the Russetta Timing Association, predecessor to the NHRA, etc., etc., etc., began in 1932, hosting competition between renegade hot rodders from the far side of the San Gabriel Mountains, men who would test their mettle, bravado and mechanical acumen by racing hari-kari across the lakebed, sometimes four or five abreast, kicking up such a furious tempest of dust and debris in their wake that only the leader of the pack could actually see where he was going. The other drivers? Well, crashing into your colleagues and barrel-rolling, hobbling into the nearest hospital in Palmdale, 30 miles away via an undulating washboard of a dirt road, only to find upon your return—assuming you survived—what was left of your race car had been scavenged and stripped down to the frame rails, that was the price one paid for inferior horsepower out there in the Mojave Desert during the years of Herbert Hoover and FDR. This, race fans, was the true genesis of drag racing.

Beyond the isolation of this primeval racing on the lakebeds and just when we thought America had already made the world safe for democracy, a funny thing happened beyond either pond that flanks these here Continental United States—the Second World War. And not to trivialize the battles Iwo Jima or Normandy, but the SoCal hot rodding community also suffered a loss in the War. By virtue of eminent domain, the Muroc Dry Lake, the birth place of drag racing, was claimed by Uncle Sam as a "proving ground" for military aerospace research and development. The pangs of this loss were mitigated by a couple of factors: The dry lakes racers and the car clubbers were migrating to other lakebeds, among them El Mirage, Harper, and Rosamond where they continued "cuttin' the crystals" during single-file "speed trials" (side-by-side competition was now deemed entirely too unsafe at the dry lakes) nearly every weekend; as well as the fact that at night the lakester guys and the car clubbers were matching wheels at either say, Slauson Avenue or Lincoln Boulevard or Glenoaks out in the Valley; or, as early as 1950, they wuz' changing rear tires and gear ratios, pouring increasingly generous helpings of nitromethane into the combustion chambers of their flathead Ford V-8s and "draggin'" down at CJ Hart's chunk of airstrip known as the Santa Ana Drags out in Orange County where, for once, they didn't have to worry about outrunning the fuzz as well as the competition.

And as Chuck Yeager banged through the palpitating turbulence of the Speed of Sound over the hallowed ground of Edwards AFB (nee Muroc Field) in October '47, teenagers continued racing across the alkali crystals of the Mojave, or down the concrete banks of the arid, withered L.A. River bed. Soon after Yeager's scrotal-squeezing supersonic gonzo sleigh ride, President Eisenhower unleashed the clandestine ramjet-propelled SR-71 spy planes, which would rocket through the heavens over Muroc—50,000 feet high!—at speeds in excess of 2,000 miles per hour, subsequently blaze over the bleached bones of the coyotes in Death Valley, and ultimately descend, minutes later, 300 miles away into Nevada's notorious Area 51. At Muroc in 1959, NASA unveiled its team of astronauts destined for the moon, the Mercury Seven.

Through all of this, there was Wally, always astute and alert as per the trends of speed-addled youth, be it time trials at the dry lakes, rumbles at the malt shop, or draggin' at the strip. A man of epic scope and vision, he was deftly plotting the co-option, development and commodification of America's horniness for horsepower into what Parks called in a April 1950 *Hot Rod* feature "Controlled Drag Racing," as administered by his yet to be unveiled NHRA. (The birth of the NHRA itself is part and parcel emblematic of how much mythology is intrinsic to the history of hot rodding. To wit, in 1951 Parks asked Lee O. Ryan, Petersen Publishing's GM, to compose a fictitious "letter to the editor" expressing concern over the lack of direction in hot rodding. In rebuttal, Parks proposed an organization "dedicated to safety," while providing the gearhead with a place to race, thus decreeing the formation of the NHRA whilst simultaneously inviting everyone to join.)

Suffice it to say, what made Wally Parks' presence out at Muroc 1996 interesting was how the NHRA, which began as a nationwide extension of the ethos of the MRA and the SCTA—y'know, bitchin' trophies for the industrious back yard tinkerer—has metamorphosed into an organization that became a player and a schmoozer in the Multi-National Corridors of Power in America. There are no luxury suites out in the desert. There isn't even any running water. But as I stood there blinking my eyes, there was Wally...

So the paradox is this: out of the ashes of the Dry Lakes rose the multi-headed Phoenix which is *Hot Rod Magazine*, the NHRA, *National Dragster*, the Winston $1,000,000 series, and the "members only" glass-tower corporate suites that lease for $30,000 per event so's High Society-types can watch the races on closed-circuit monitors while sipping snifters of Napoleon Brandy and eating weenies on a stick. That entire reality is of no concern to the lakebed Bedouins, however. This is because the SCTA and the whole culture of the dry lakes have continued to exist on their own terms for all those years since WWII, albeit with a low profile. In fact, it has been flourishing out at El Mirage with dyed-in-the-wool lake guys supplemented by refugees from the drag-strip wars, veterans of the 1320 who could no longer abide the rampant parts attrition as well as the exorbitant costs of contemporary drag racing. 13,000 gearheads descended upon Muroc on Saturday April 27th 1996, to symbolically reclaim Muroc, ironically a happening that never would have come to pass without the clout, sociopolitical machinations and handshaking ability of Wally Parks.

And like I say, while wiping the sleep out of my eyes, I stood in the shadow of the exalted hot rodder who embodies the duality of man, the avuncular and towering Wally Parks. I thrust a micro-cassette recorder in his mug, and lofted a softball of a question like, "How does it feel to be back on the dry lakes?" and away he went...

"We're all absolutely delighted," sez Wally, "that we've had a chance to come back here, because it's been 55 years since the SCTA ran here. I think having access to this place has got as much value for historic reasons as it has for the satisfaction of running down the course. But the thing we like most is the people who have returned here, who were once up here, and the newcomers who come in to see it. We just think we've got 100 percent success and we are very grateful to the Air Base here and the commander for letting us be here.

"Our presence here," he continued reciting, his towering, lean torso magnificently framed against blue skies and Jet Propulsion Laboratories' rocket launchers burrowed into the nearby Rosamond Hills, "ties in with research and development programs and their technology and so forth, which is the spirit of Edwards AFB, the test center, which is what this is all about: people testing new ideas. It may not apply to aircraft but it all comes out of the same box."

Aahh, the Mojave Desert is the perfect backdrop for a powerful oratory, and at 83 years of age, Wally Parks was showcasing his rhetorical skills. But something was a little too perfect about this sermonizing. I wasn't sure if I was interviewing the man who is not only the driving force behind the SCTA's wistful return to its Mecca, but also the embodiment of laissez-faire capitalism, or if I was merely on the ass-end of a feedback-generated tape loop fed into a 10" speaker implanted into a cryogenically-enhanced human body, not unlike, say, the walking-talking Mr. Lincoln Exhibit at Disneyland. It was weird—I've been dying to bench race with the Man, the Myth, the Legend that is Wally Parks, a complex man, a man who personifies the dichotomy of everything that is virtuous, controversial, banal, and perhaps even disturbing about the Master Capitalists of America, be it Henry Ford, Walt Disney, Dick Clark or Bill Gates. As sandstorms started to kick up and pelt my face with sharp crystals of fossilized mud, Wally continued riffing about America and "the pioneering spirit." Despite the dust devils he never stopped talking. I have to confess at some point I began to tune out Parks' monologue about the nobility of Muroc, as the repetitive read-only memory functions of his speech were kicking into high gear. I began to free-associate about Mr. Parks' pivotal role in the SCTA "taking back Muroc" (at least for one weekend), and I began to wonder if this gesture was not unlike a long-in-the-tusk mastodon going home to his elephant's graveyard. The speechifying continued, and as I dutifully held my micro-cassette aloft I thought, "Who is this guy? Who am I really interviewing?

Machiavelli? Dwight D. Eisenhower? Charles Keating? Charles Foster Kane?" As I write this, I am still not sure...

As the interview with Wally continued, I was overcome by the swirling dust and the heat. As the temperature was climbing into the triple-digit range, the sweat and the sand and the sun block coagulated into this afterbirth-ish goop which seemed to gravitate from my brow into the recesses of my eyes. I tried closing one, then the other, but to no avail. I couldn't see anything beyond vague forms perpendicular to the earth's curvature—one of which was talking non-stop (Wally)—all of this tableaux more surreal and bizarre than your typical mirage. Wally was either oblivious or just nonplussed by my fevered perspiring and blinking, the loop tape continuing unabated. I knew this was my only chance to heave a curve ball at the most legendary figure in the NHRA. So as I wiped my eyes, I asked him, "Did you derive more pleasure from your tenure at the SCTA or shaping the NHRA into what it is today?" He answered, "Both, although it's apples and oranges. One is a non-profit dedication and the other one is trying to keep a big thing going..."

At that moment, with the loop tape mechanism finally disengaged, I felt Wally and I were on the verge of a meaningful dialogue. I was poised to ask him if he felt the longevity of the SCTA was perhaps due to a reaction to the politics and fiscal policies of the NHRA. Fate intervened, however. A senior member of Wally's entourage (I think it was his sister-in-law) sought relief from the heat and the sand and the noise, and Wally, who had been extremely gracious and accommodating with me, begged off further questions, and chivalrously went to assist the member of his party in distress. I was that close to the truth.

*****

Before, during, and after Wally's discourse on the nobility of the pioneering spirit, various lakesters, nitrous-oxide powered coupes, land-speed streamliners, and blown Studebakers began their procession across the desert, hurtling across the lakebed towards the timing beams, over a 1.3 mile course marked by scores of pylons. There were hundreds of drivers in pursuit of various Muroc speed records in machines encompassing a multitude of engine, body, and chemical combinations. Among them was Al Teague, windin' out his *Spirit of*

76 streamliner in second gear at well over 200 mph—this same combustion-engined contraption clocked a Wheel-driven land-speed record 432 mph out at Bonneville a few years back. Joaquin Arnett, who has been tippin' the can since the late 40s, also showcased the home-built *Bean Bandits* nitro-burning streamliner. There were a few vintage "belly tank" lakesters—speed machines crafted out of fuel tanks from P-38 Lightning fighter planes that were liberated out of aerospace surplus yards. There was even a land speed entry from Guam.

*****

All told, before the dust settled, fourteen drivers were initiated into the Muroc 200 MPH Club. This included SCTA v.p. Mike Cook, who raced across the desert in his blown Ford T-bird at 227 mph. While the eclectic assembly of speed machines continued kicking up gigantic rooster tails of dust, their clockings were announced over Channel 1 on citizen's band radios, which were employed in lieu of a public address system. It was an interesting counterpoint, the juxtaposition of low-fidelity c.b. radios against the various satellite communication systems and megawatt transmitters deployed by the Air Force. Out of earshot of the "p.a." and beyond the pylons, I encountered a messianic figure trekking across the desert in flip-flops. It was Robert "Jocko" Johnson, inventor, bohemian sculptor, and mechanical visionary. (In 1959 at Riverside, CA, Jocko stunned the world of hot rodding with an 8.35 E.T. in drag racing's first full-bodied streamliner, a clocking 3/10ths of a second quicker than any other Top Fuel dragster. Before he could improve on this outrageous performance, the streamliner subsequently self-destructed at Lions Drag Strip.) Out at Muroc, Jocko was on a mission whose dual agenda was thus: a) to show Alex Xydias (proprietor of the "So-Cal Speed Shop" in Burbank) a brand new pocket-sized centrifugal force-powered supercharger, a device Jocko designed to replace the relatively bulky and inefficient GMC "roots" design; and b) to get a sno-cone and beat the desert heat. He invited me over to his tent for tacos later that evening and I graciously accepted.

That night, after consuming more than a few of "Jocko's tacos" and discussing Jocko's plan to unveil a streamliner propelled by an 18-cylinder, 25 cubic inch radial motor—capable of 400 horsepower(!)—out on the salt flats, it was time to explore the "proving grounds," as it were. As the racers put their exotic machines to bed, the campfires, the Coleman lanterns and the barbecues provided the sole source of illumination, besides the constellations and the orbiting satellites (which, out in the Mojave Desert, are visible to the naked eye). I wandered through the pits, blown away by the massive proportions of this congregation of motorheads who had migrated to this uninhabitable air strip in the Mojave Desert. And as I waded through the nomads camping in the barren flats of the Seventh Circle of Hell, I overheard a campfire conversation about Project Mercury ace Gordo Cooper's appearance on a "reality-based" teevee docudrama about the Paranormal, riffing about his brushes with alien spacecraft while in astronaut training. The winds began to howl, I looked up at the stars and the satellite space stations and continued walking.

I heard music over at another campsite and I followed its call. Dusty Springfield was singing "Son of a Preacher Man" over a car stereo ratcheted into the door panels of a not-exactly-cherry flamed '52 Chevy sedan, while a couple of "Go Cat Wild!" retro-rockabilly greaser-types, twenty-somethings who had complete and utter distaste for contemporary fashion and values, were engaged in a high-octane bench race session. At that moment I knew the Muroc Reunion was a metaphor. I stood off in the shadows, eavesdropping as these reactionary rodders debated the fall and debasement of the late Dean Moon's legendary speed emporium, "Moon Special Equipment," recently rechristened "Mooneyes" by its new Japanese proprietors, and which may or may not be a bastardization of the translation of "Moon." At this point, I piped in from the darkness and suggested there was still a decent cam-grinder in the employ of "Mooneyes."

"The issue is just because one good cam-grinder still works there," said one lanky car clubber with a thick Cockney accent, "doesn't mean that it isn't the biggest sell-out in the history of (*expletive*) hot rodding, man."

"Dean Moon was a genius," his friend burped, "but it makes me want to puke that people are trying to make money off all that dashboard crap they sell behind the counters of these so-called speed shops."

"What people are building today holds absolutely no interest to me," returned the Brit, spilling his can of libation. "I came from (*expletive*) millions of miles away to live in this country because I'm a (*expletive*) hot rod freak, right? And when I got to this country I was so (*expletive*) disappointed because the entire (*expletive*) place had sold out. And everybody is driving Japanese (*expletive*) cars.

"I came to (*expletive*) America and I came to Muroc today because I thought it was the last bastion of hot rodding," the émigré gearhead was gathering steam now, double-clutching his soliloquy into overdrive, "and I think that this is (*expletive*) great today because shit like this rolled up (points to a '32 Model A D/Gas lakester) and made me a believer that hot rodding is still alive. (*Screw*) all that painted chrome and shit, this is a proper hot rod (*points to the '52 Chevy sedan*). You know what? I hate all this 'family values' and wearing shorts with flames on it, like 'blar, blar, blar' and 'blar, blar, blar' and 'Excuse me, you can't have no beer on that site.' 'Ex-cuse me?' y'know-what-I-mean? I ain't got no kids, I don't want no (*expletive*) kids, I don't want to be in an environment where I have to watch my (*expletive*) behavior because there might be kids present, I want to go and hang out where the is some old (*expletive*) proper hot rods, man."

"Our ancestors," his pal extrapolated, "much like him, left Europe to do what we wanted to do, when we wanted to do it. He came over here, and he found he can't do what he wants to do, when he wants to do it."

"It's not a case of that exactly," the Brit resumed. "It's a case of indoctrination. It's a case of the asses who run the magazines these days—the writers are getting paid wages by the suits who run the magazine to say what's trendy because the advertisers tell them to. So he has to say what is trendy, and it's like 'new-(*expletive*)-stalgia!'. What the (*expletive*) does that mean?

"Street rodding, as far as I'm concerned, means conforming to the rules the magazines have put down. Y'know: it's easy to have a 350 Chevy with this person's steering column, and this person's (*expletive*) tie-rod, and this person's (*expletive*) blah-blah-blah. That's not, as far as I'm concerned, what hot rodding is all about, which is hauling shee-it out of a (*expletive*) junkyard and building a car on the *jeeg*."

top fuel wormhole

"Real hot rods don't have tan interiors," one of his pals summed up.

"You can build an old-looking car out of new pieces, but that doesn't make it an old hot rod. Old hot rodding, truly, has disappeared. I think an article, really a lament, on the decline of true hot rodding would be a cool thing because nobody wants to do it—they're scared to do it, they don't want to put that in a magazine because they are supported by the people who are selling the parts."

I reckoned he was correct, no magazine would publish those sentiments. I also told these adrenaline-addled hell raisers that most of their heroes—Alex Xydias, Stu Hilborn, Joaquin Arnett, etc. were in their seventies nowadays, and were probably trying to catch some shut-eye. The most reverent yet politic gesture these hep cats could make would be to turn down their stereo, put out their campfire and go to sleep...

The next morning, after a handful of test runs down the parched mud where NASA, the JPL, and the Southern California Timing Association pulled off their bizarre romantic visions (indeed the only place that could not only tolerate but actually nurture their dreams), the winds kicked in with a ferocity that rendered further speed-record attempts futile. As the mother of all sandstorms blew fiercer and more torrentially, the desert rats collapsed their tents and loaded their belongings into their motor homes, trailers, and deuce coupes and began their journey home. But for one weekend this procession of the Timelords of the Apocalypse, a gathering of tribes seriously in touch with the soul of the Universe, got to play in their Garden of Eden—never mind that the only foliage in this Garden were a few sandblasted Joshua trees out by the rocket launchers.

As the timing officials announced the cancellation of the speed trials over the c.b. radio, I closed my eyes. I could see the plume of thick, charcoal-black death smoke, emanating off of the horizon on the desert floor. And I got the chills as the stinging pricks of the torrential sands continued to dig into my face. Aerospace. Jocko Johnson. Wally Parks. Project Mercury. Rockabilly Anarchists. Sonic Booms. The SCTA. Jet Propulsion Laboratories. Drag Racing. Mach One. The Bean Bandits. They were all the same thing, big chunks of the Southern California Experience, just expressed in different ways out at Muroc. It was all a twisted, glorious manifestation of what the Mercury Seven called "*Go! Fever*," a sickness that starts out innocently enough as an intellectual exercise to debunk physics via downforce (with a co-efficient of drag) or propulsion or torque, anything man, just hit the throttle!, a fever so mesmerizing that its victim becomes caught up in his quest for speed, speed, and more speed, until the rational and linear thought processes have been superseded by raw desire, damn the torpedoes and damn the consequences, I want to live man!, even if it means dying, so turn up the boost and gimme some nitro! Jocko Johnson spit out the quote that defined the existence of these veterans of the dry lake sandstorms. Over turkey meat tacos the night before he said, "The more creative you are, the closer you are to God."

Anybody who tells you that soulless corporations are a necessary ingredient to the pursuit of horsepower has never stepped foot on the fossilized dry lakebeds of the Mojave Desert. Those who have seen and tasted the elements of the dry lakes—sandstorms, whiskey, rocket engines, nitromethane, and maximum velocity penis-shaped land speed vehicles—as they coalesce on a lunar landscape in the Mojave Desert, will tell you this: The sands will come again. Just ask Jocko. Or Wally Parks.

(Author's note: I must acknowledge a serious debt as per literary sources that informed this article. These include: The Nearest Faraway Place *by Timothy White (Henry Holt and Co. Inc.);* High Performance *by Robert Post (John Hopkins University); and* The American Hot Rod *by Dean Batchelor (Motorbooks International).)*

*(Originally published in S*uper Stock & Drag Illustrated*)*

top fuel wormhole

BLAINE JOHNSON 1962-1996

I have come to terms with the passing of Blaine Johnson this weekend at the U.S. Nationals. His death seems to signify, for this writer at least, the end of my interest in NHRA drag racing. Indeed, there is no one left to root for... What Alan Johnson's tune-up was accomplishing on this circuit was nothing short of awe-inspiring. Indeed, in an age when voracious parts consumption is standard operating procedure, it was quite refreshing to witness the machinations of an operation that was as tight and clean—as far as performance and lack of parts failures—as the Bros. Johnson. The taking of the NHRA Points Title was a given for this team—on a budget that was chump change in comparison to most of the "hitters" in Top Fuel. Unfortunately, their will be no asterisk in the record books next to the name of this year's eventual Top Fuel Champion in the record books—y'know, "Such-and-such won their first Top Fuel title after the provisional Points Leader was killed in action at Indianapolis." Nor should there be—but in my heart Blaine Johnson is the last Top Fuel Champion. His accomplishments resonate because his team—mostly a down-home family operation—slayed the competition with intellect, perseverance, and ingenuity.

My recollections of Blaine Johnson include watching him climb out of his fueler at the top end at Pomona, moments after whuppin' up on Larry Dixon Jr. for Top Eliminator at the World Finals last year. This was Johnson's first Top Fuel victory, and the exultation in his face was a joy to behold. Later, in January of this year, I saw Blaine tucked into the cockpit of their fueler on the pad at Bakersfield during a test and tune session. It had been raining sporadically all day, the tech-daddies saw a small window of opportunity to run some fuel cars, Blaine pulled into the water box, only to be shut down by more rainfall. His disappointment was evident by the pained expression on his face. These images will always remain with me—and they shall be fond reminiscences. Thank you, Blaine and Alan Johnson.

(*Originally published in* Nitronic Research)

PART TWO: THE CENTER OF THE SHADOW

HESITATION KILLS

(Los Angeles, 1996)

"Hesitation kills," Cuz'n Roy said, and laughed.

It's a Friday afternoon in Los Angeles; we are weaving through stop-and-go traffic on the San Bernardino Freeway and at that moment I negotiate a '71 Grand Prix through carnage comprised of upscale Westsiders in Lexuses, various sport utility vehicles and mini-vans, all of which had been snagged in a collision with a freaked and crying gaggle of immigrants in a chipped, varicose blue 1982 Toyota Corolla.

I see the pileup continue to metastasize so I punch the throttle, aiming the massive 2-ton projectile of Detroit steel bang on into the center of the chaos, which now resembles the entrance to a dark star. The eyelids on all four barrels of the carburetor open like the mouth on a porn queen and begin guzzling gasoline faster than a desert dog. Sundry automobiles continue careening and fishtailing, orbiting away from the spinning Toyota and its initial point of commotion as if by centrifugal force, creating a hole the size of a small crater that is plenty big enough for us to pass through unscathed.

In our wake I see disturbed yuppies already on cell phones to their insurers, lawyers and Immigration, speed-dialing before their vehicles have fully reached a dead stop. Airbags distend like bulbous pimples and car alarms cycle in a discordant and paranoid arpeggio. Stalled automobiles point in five directions, the petals of a broken flower. Pieces of steel, plastic and colored glass litter the interstate and I keep the hammer down, with twin puffs of burnt blackie carbon punctuating our exit from the scene of this massive pileup.

"Man, this is like a bad day at a stock-car race. Shouldn't we stop?" Cuz'n Roy half-chortles.

We both know the question is rhetorical. "What?" I reply. "And get caught up in that bureaucratic nightmare? Is that what Junior Johnson would've done at Daytona?"

We are en route to speed trials in the Black Rock desert, northeast of Reno. With that freak show behind us, we can concentrate on the prodigious amount of ground we are to cover on this eve. Along the way, we will partially retrace the steps of one Craig Breedlove, a land-speed racer who had built the first *Spirit of America* jet car in his dad's backyard in Venice in 1961. In the 1960s, Breedlove became the first guy to officially go 400, then 500, and finally 600 mph. These speeds were verified by stiff suits from a French organization, whose job description is to sign off on such esoterica. Now Breedlove was out at Black Rock, trying to reclaim the Land Speed Record from some Brits, who had held the title for over a decade. It feels right and patriotic to travel the roads Craig had taken to Bonneville in 1963, when he first achieved international notoriety and fame, stunning the motorazzi and the world at large with the first official 400 mph clocking. His goal is now 700 mph and beyond, ultimately puncturing the sound barrier itself. Mach 1. The Speed of Sound. There is no time for dicking around with cops, lawyers and insurers.

"Punch through the turbulence," Cuz'n Roy acknowledges. "It is the right course of action at the first sign of trouble. Otherwise you'll spill your beer."

Punching through the turbulence. It is a time-honored approach to overcoming the pitch, roll and yaw of any journey with a potential for doom and immolation. Become at one with outrageous, incomprehensible velocity and use it as your guide. Once upon a time around 50 years ago, in pursuit of Mach 1, ace fighter pilot after ace fighter pilot lost control and stuffed sophisticated military airplanes into oblivion in the Mojave desert; conversely, Chuck Yeager commandeered a Bell *X-1* rocket airplane and kicked in the joystick towards the first successful supersonic flight (which is to say, he lived) by this approach: when things get weird and jittery, yank on the go-faster for more thrust. Damn the demons of chaos and instability. If you don't you are a footnote to history and mere allegory; if you do, you bask in glory...

the cole coonce drag strip reader, vol. 1

"Hesitation kills," I repeat to myself. In an age of the neurotic, the paranoid and the self-absorbed, now more than ever definitive action and decisiveness are the only methods towards glory. Cuz'n Roy and I are on our way to see a guy attempt to turn Mach 1. In a car.

(*Excerpted from* INFINITY OVER ZERO)

MISHAP AT BLACK ROCK!

Breedlove's Record Attempt Is Off!

Black Rock, NV. October 28, 1996 - While attempting to break Richard Noble's Land Speed Record of 633.468 mph, Craig Breedlove's *Spirit of America* jet car crashed and was severely damaged. The attempt took place two days before his Bureau of Land Management permit to use the Black Rock desert expired.

On the first leg of the required back-to-back runs, Craig was well on his way to breaking the record, which is based upon two timed one-mile averages, when at a speed of an estimated 675 mph a burst of wind lifted the back of the car and pushed it up onto one side. Major damage was inflicted on the rear axle and rear frame of the car. Craig was unhurt, but obviously disappointed to be so close to the LSR after many years of research and development with his GE J-79 powered vehicle.

The car will be brought back to the team's compound in Rio Vista, CA to assess the damage and make repairs, but it appears unlikely that another attempt at the Land Speed Record could be made until early next Spring, permits allowing.

Breedlove is in the throes of a duel with Richard Noble, OBE, who is campaigning an LSR vehicle piloted by Royal Air Force "Top Gun" Andy Green, to be the first to eclipse the Speed of Sound on land. Currently, Noble and Green and their *Thrust SSC* twin Rolls Royce Spey jet-powered machine are testing in the Jordan desert in preparation for their impending Mach 1 effort at Black Rock.

Breedlove's ill-fated record run was his first attempt at reclaiming the LSR from Richard Noble, the first goal en route to ultimately breaking the Sound Barrier. Breedlove uses a single J-79—capable of 45,000 horsepower—mounted on the fuselage, directly behind the driver, an engineering approach in stark contrast to Noble's system of using twin 202 Spey turbofans, each capable of 50,000 horsepower, mounted on either side of the cockpit in what, in essence, is a 10-ton, rear-wheel-steer Batmobile.

Breedlove's mishap occurred after a promising day of testing the day before. He was able to hit 563 mph, but did have some trouble with the parachutes…

(*Originally published in* Nitronic Research)

BISCIGLIA CRASHES '48 FIAT FUELER

Wisconsin Int'l Raceway, Kaukauna, WI, August 2, 1997—"Nitro Neil" Bisciglia, who has been barnstorming the Midwestern US in his stroppy Fiat Topolino-bodied fueler (and trying to sort out a clutch anomaly that has dropped his performance potential considerably from a peak of 6.29), suffered a top-end crash that left him with two pelvic fractures and a trashed race car.

The crash occurred during a night-time match race against *Dawson's Demon* AA/Altered at a dimly-lit WIR facility—and just as "Nitro Neil" got 'er back in the 6.80s and the performance pendulum seemed to be swinging his way. His steel 392 mill kicked the rods at 1000 feet and his mill went kablooey. When he reached for the fire bottles the trigger hung... yikes!... and because the shut-down area bends, he had to guess-timate—while on fire at 200 mph—where the track actually was! Bisciglia misjudged his x and y coordinates and got in the grass (the guardrail stopped at the finish line, natch). He then mowed over a couple of hundred feet of fencing with his *Firepower Flyer* and caromed into the woods... Still cruising, the coupe's left slick hit a tree that r-r-ripped the rear end out from between Bisciglia's legs...This caved in the rollcage but at least the car finally stopped moving.

He swears he'll rebuild, but for the rest of this year he will just concentrate on the West Coast scene (which is hairy enough even though the tracks don't bend and there are some lights in the shut-down area!).

Meanwhile, his California compatriots (aka the Free Mexican Air Force) are building a new Stirling-chassied *Foothill Flyer* in Ken Castagnino's shop in Jackson, Ca. They hope to complete the new digger in time to enter in the California Hot Rod Reunion in mid-November.

(*Originally published on* Nitronic Research)

drag racing turned its back on me a long time ago

TARGET SPEED TWENTYNINE PALMS: THE GUERRILLA RENAISSANCE IS NOW

Jocko Johnson's high-desert campaign to meld the arts and sciences in an age that shuns creativity.

Strange and abstract notions oscillate in the desert. Out there, notions emanate from the minds of exiled artists, philosophers, musicians, and engineers. Their visions and their bodies of work are perpetrated in everything from abandoned Airstream trailers to sandblasted Geodesic Domes to thatched adobe recording studios as well as the research laboratories and wind tunnels of the high-desert military-industrial complex. All of this is scattered across the Mojave like the seed of Creation itself, and these strange and abstract notions—this collective consciousness—permeates the entire Mojave ionosphere like some bastardized electro-magnetic field where errant oscillations bang into other free range oscillations, ultimately creating extrapolation upon extrapolation until one man designs a motor that debunks the conventional wisdom of automotive engineering. His design proves that the internal combustion motor as we know it is a mistake. A failure. The motor that will supersede the four-stroke dinosaur has 25 cubic inches, 18 cylinders, no crank, no push rods and weighs forty pounds—wet. And this inventor plans to prove the superiority of his design in a land-speed streamliner whose target speed is 555 miles per hour.

I recently drove out to the desert to find that man and his motor. His name is Robert "Jocko" Johnson. Actually, it's just "Jocko" or maybe "Jocko Johnson," but it ain't "Robert" and hasn't been for decades. The etymology of "Jocko" dates back to 1953; apparently our subject had an unfortunate bout with jock itch while working as a teenaged apprentice at the Barris Kustom Auto shop in North Hollywood. Because of his reflexive scratching, Robert was dubbed "Jocko" by the shop owner, kustom kar czar George Barris. And despite his nickname's, uhh, sensitive origins, Johnson has refused to answer to "Robert" ever since.

Yeah, if you are a young, aspiring hepcat hot rodder and you are blessed with a nickname bestowed by an artist/designer of George Barris' esteemed stature, you immediately commence to signing your entry forms and your purchase orders that way. But a cool moniker was not all that Jocko was graced with by these folks—he was privy to some pretty serious science as well. Jocko was on the ground floor of a far out, kustom kulture factory that was a crucial link to what some art historians consider the Last American Renaissance.

And what a Renaissance it was: It was a maniacal era. It was an era as wide open as a deserted desert highway. It was an era when the arts were flourishing on all cultural fronts vis-à-vis the endeavors of cats like Coltrane, Jackson Pollock, Allen Ginsberg, Thelonious Monk, Carl Perkins, and Link Wray. The intoxicating sensibilities of this "go-cat-wild!" "beat generation" infiltrated the So Kal Kustom Kar Kulture to its core: It contaminated artists like Von Dutch as he meticulously pinstriped his hallucinatory visions onto hot rods. Meanwhile, Ed "Big Daddy" Roth was taking a pressurized cake-decorating tool to paint on anything that was in his path. And young Jocko was honing his craft and expressing himself by bending sheet metal.

Barris Kustom Auto, Jocko's place of employ, was cranking out some seriously bizarre race cars; folding, bending and carving sheet metal and aluminum for the Bonneville cats, the dragster guys and the art directors at the local film studios. In 1952, when Barris had been hired by local hotshot cam grinder Chet Herbert to design a streamliner body for the Bonneville speed trials, an epiphany lit into Jocko's cranium like a flash of ball lightning.

This vision coalesced in 1954 when the Herbert machine ran roughshod on eleven FIA speed records at the salt flats. It was prime time for the man to sculpt a streamliner for the proving grounds of Southern California: the drag strip.

By that time Jocko was porting flathead Ford cylinder blocks under Scotty Fenn's tutelage at Experimental Automotive. To consummate his understanding of Zen as applied to race car science, the Barris years were the yin of aerodynamics and metallurgy and the Fenn apprenticeship was the yang of fuel flow and combustion.

In Jocko's precocious teenaged mind, streamliners epitomized the marriage of aesthetics and technology. As an artist and a craftsman, Jocko grooved on the principles of Bauhaus Architecture: "…. Form follows function…. Universal space…point, line, plane…." and applied them both to the internal combustion engine and body contour. Intuitively, he felt that the streamliner was the most direct approach to Top Eliminator. Herbert's salt flat endeavors, as well as the Land Speed Records claimed in streamlined vehicles by Euro speed demons such as John Cobb and Malcolm Campbell, seemed to confirm this notion empirically.

So after two years of toil, sweat, r&d, aluminum bending and smoking left-handed cigarettes, the first dragster with a full-envelope body hit the strip in 1958: The *Jocko's Porting Service* streamliner. Jocko teamed up with "Jazzy Jim" Nelson and they hit the strips with Jazzy shoeing the car. The results were hardly the slam-dunk that Chet Herbert enjoyed at the Bonneville in '54 and skepticism and derision greeted Jocko every time the car limped down the track. Finally, after a year of dragging the 'liner with decidedly mixed results, the duo of "Jazzy Jim" and Jocko struck the mother lode. Powered by a Jazzy's 450 Chrysler running on nitro, they recorded a 1/4-mile elapsed time of 8.35

seconds at 178 mph at Riverside CA, obliterating a previous e.t mark of 8.54 that belonged to Art Chrisman. The run may have had as much to do with slippin' the clutch—something else Jocko and Jazzy were experimenting with—as it did with avant-garde aerodynamics. Whatever the reason, the results stood for themselves. And Jocko drank from the teat of vindication, savoring the mother's milk of a misunderstood artist.

But vindication was fleeting: Subsequent runs revealed a chink in the armor—the aerodynamics of the 'liner were too effective. At terminal velocity, the desired downforce actually pushed the fiberglass shell into the wheels, the body cracked and ultimately disintegrated.

The destruction of Jocko's speed-addled sculpture— coupled with the parts attrition inherent in running a blown hemi on nitromethane—put a serious dent in Jocko's operating capital, a budget more in tune to the lifestyle of a be-bop saxophonist than a cutting-edge Top Fuel enterprise.

Jocko began meticulously reassembling his hot rod Humpty Dumpty, while also concentrating on generating cash porting cylinder heads in his shop in Lakewood. Indeed, Jocko's Porting Service blossomed as a business.

Ultimately, an aluminum version of the 'liner (shoed by Emery Cook and powered by an Allison V-12 aircraft engine on aviation gasoline) turned a time of 195 mph, but it was too little, too late. The consensus at the strip was that the 'liner's weight handicaps negated the advantages of the tremendous downforce and the streamlining craze went the way of the hula-hoop.

He continued chiseling steel cylinder heads, with a client base that read as a Yellow Pages of cool: dragster guys like Mickey Thompson, Ernie Hashim, "The Sour Sisters," "Big Daddy" Don Garlits and Connie Kalitta. Gasser gods like Stone, Woods & Cook and K.S. Pittman were bangin' on the door of Jocko's Porting Service in Lakewood.

"He lived across the street from his speed shop in Long Beach and some mornings we would have to wake him up to work on our heads," recalls Don Ratican of *The Sour Sisters* Top Fuel team. "But as an engineer he was head and shoulders above everybody. In those days, on a scale of measuring visionaries, Art Chrisman was a 10 and Jocko was off the scale."

But gradually all this precision tinkering morphed into another milieu, another form of craftsmanship altogether. In 1966, Jocko began sculpting as a fine artist. Seriously. As a career. And his sculptures were not unlike his streamliners: scrappy, yet smooth. Fluid. Sinuous with a deliberate sense of motion. He was a hit with the wine and goat liver crowd. This was liberating, this was freedom, while the automotive world was becoming increasingly uptight and monochromatic—"sheesh all these dragsters look and run the same," Jocko musta thought, "but what I can create with a chisel and my two hands is infinite and unlimited." Which would you choose?

In any typical sculpture, he would showcase his raw sense of aesthetics and his resourcefulness—something that drag racing taught him: You take the best of whatever's handy and transform it into something provocative and efficient. In one of his more famous works, he incorporated bondo and rebar into a plaster sculpture that he based on the shape of a cow's thighbone. He sold this to the Irvine Corporation for a cool 500 skins and the city managers had the artwork planted in the sandbox at the local playground.

And despite the sustained popularity of his work on an iron motor—including plenty of gigs subcontracting to Keith Black Racing Engines (whose radical 426 hemi motors were the bullet du jour), Jocko's disillusionment with the drag-strip scene and its generic L7 aerodynamics continued to swell. Jocko ultimately bailed on porting heads and fell in with the longhaired bohemians of Laguna Beach for a while. When that scene got redundant, he shed his skin once more by relocating to the high desert, where he gathered ironwood from the dusty tundra for raw material for his sculptures.

And everything was peace, love and yucca trees. But a paradigm shift occurred in the drag strip world—this time without Jocko. In the winter of '71, "Big Daddy" Don Garlits had rocked the world of the drag racing intelligentsia, snagging Top Fuel Eliminator at the Winternationals as well as the equally prestigious March Meet in Bakersfield—with a rear-motored digger, a heretofore-experimental design that until then had never caught the fancy of the trophy queen.

Had the alloys, materials and basic framework of Top Fuel dragsters caught up to Jocko's theories about the supremacy of streamlining? Piqued, Jocko knew he had to scratch that itch once again. So off he went to Florida, to sculpt the definitive Fueler, with Garlits providing the horsepower and the venture capital.

top fuel wormhole

From the giddy-up, the Jocko/Big Daddy collaboration seemed doomed to failure. As a barnstorming competitor who had to honor two professional circuits as well as a plethora of match racing obligations, Garlits had too many fires to put out to devote sufficient attention to the radical *Wynn's Liner* project. The futuristic machine came in over budget, overweight and behind schedule.

In late '73 the *Wynn's Liner* debuted at the American Hot Rod Association's Grand American meet at Orange County International Raceway—and, coincidentally, within earshot of the swing sets that teeter-tottered in the sandbox of the Irvine Corporation.

Disappointingly, the car laid an egg, qualifying last in the 32-car show—a position that neither Garlits' nor Jocko's egos could process or tolerate. The car wouldn't fire during eliminations. At speed, Garlits said the 'liner wanted to lift off, space age aerodynamics or not. Jocko adamantly refutes this, remarking that Garlits DID in fact lift off twice—in conventionally bodied dragsters in the '80s.

And unlike the resilience of the streamlining effort in '58, the clash of engineering philosophies and worldviews doomed the *Wynn's Liner* to a fate of rusting in some barren landfill, as a testament to failure and folly of human endeavor. A few years back, it was restored sans hemi and entered into Garlits' Museum of Drag Racing.

And as visionaries are wont to do, Jocko retreated to the desert. And dug in deep. And began fastening, forming, and fabricating a new streamliner known as the *Spirit of 29 Palms*. A vehicle designed to turn 555 mph at Bonneville. On alcohol. Cut to 1996. Your humble working journalist spots Jocko at a rod run at a dry lakebed. I eavesdrop as Jocko corners Alex Xydias (proprietor of the "So-Cal Speed Shop" in Burbank) and whips out a brand new pocket-sized centrifugal force-powered supercharger, a device Jocko had machined the day before the rod run. Jocko tells Xydias this ashtray-sized cylindrical supercharger will replace the archaic, bulky and inefficient GMC "roots" design that is *de rigueur* on today's dragsters and funny cars. Jocko insists that Xydias hold this pint-sized piece of kit. Alex looks kind of afraid of it.

I am not afraid of it and Jocko sense this. He invites me over to his camper for turkey tacos and Meisterbrau. I promise him I'll come see him and his inventions out at Twentynine Palms. Six months later, I do.

The road to Jocko's crib in the desert was an open road, the kind of highway that seems to confirm the existence of the mysteries and magnetism of the desert. Very few motorists, even fewer state troopers. The kind of road that clears the senses of any gratuitous phlegm. Invigorating.

I pass a couple of county highways that ultimately shadow the perimeter of the Twentynine Palms Marine Base. On the northern border of the Marine Base, a mere tossed coyote bone from Jocko's digs, a cat named George Van Tassel built—"thru the guidance of other worlders"—the "Integratron," a high energy electrostatic machine designed to recharge the DNA of a person (i.e. stop the aging process). The local Chamber of Commerce describes it as a "time machine for research on rejuvenation, anti-gravity and time travel." The structure is four stories high and 55 feet in diameter and is thought by some to be "a very powerful vortex for physical and spiritual healing". From the 1950s to the 70s, the Integratron was the site of an annual "Interplanetary Spacecraft Convention" and became famous as the location of Van Tassel's "Spaceport Earth."

As I kick up some dust on a dirt road on the perimeter of the military base, I think to myself that out on the perimeter of hell's half-acre, there is certainly ample room to stretch out and improvise. I was then buzzed by a below-the-radar F-4 Fighter. *WHHOOOSSSHHH!* I haven't even arrived at the mad alchemists and my senses are already overwhelmed by free-from improvisation in the desert.

As I pull onto Jocko's desert compound, salsa music is percolating in the distance, emanating from a monaural Spanish-language AM station that Jocko keeps switched on 24-7. "It's an uplifting sound and it has words I don't understand so I don't have to think about it," he said about the salsa. "It's precision musicianship—they just don't bang away at something in order to make a sound, they're all working together."

I found this comment ironic, considering Jocko's penchant for working alone, but I said nothing as he wound up and proceeded to explain the genesis of his new creation.

"I went out to Orange County for their last drag race. I hadn't been out there for 10 or 12 years—I didn't want to go, but a friend told me I had to go out there because they weren't gonna have anymore. I was in the pits for about three hours and I ran into a lot of my old friends—Keith Black being one of them. I said to Keith, 'Is everybody here doing what these guys are doing? I've been standing here for three hours and these guys here are taking their motor completely apart every single run.' I'm watching them throw the rods and pistons out and put new ones in and he says, 'Come here.' He took me into somebody's eighteen-wheel trailer and there was a bench along one wall that had these eight boxes that held eight rods and pistons, so there were sixty-four rods and pistons. The first three sets on that bench were used, they had a run on them. And I looked at him and I said, 'Do you mean this guy can only make nine runs today; he's got eight sets here and a set in the car now?' Keith said, 'That's right.' I said, 'What the hell is wrong with this picture?'"

"So on the way home that day," Jocko continued, "I told my friend that the combustion engine wasn't fully invented yet. He laughed at me and said, 'You're nuts, they went 276 mph that day' or whatever it was. And I said, 'Yeah, but what were they doing ten minutes later?' Basically throwing it away...," he laughed.

"I figured what I needed to do was figure out what in the hell was wrong with this. Back in the days when I was porting heads people would come up to me with their problems—I consider myself a problem-solver type. Not a refiner—go to the heart of the thing and search out the flaw.

"So I went and did this." He beckons and we climb up the steps of his portable speed shop. He unveils the PoweRRing 3 Cycle engine.

"We were still running old shit. So when I designed this engine I said, 'I'm going to look at the history.' So I started looking back farther and farther into time and I asked myself, 'Where did the crankshaft come from? Where did the rod come from? Where did the piston come from?' And it took me clear back to 1705 when they started building engines with steam. In the first steam engines they didn't use steam to push the pistons, they used steam to evacuate the cylinder. They put a little steam in there and when it condensed, it shrank—1700 times. From steam down to water. 1700 times. It evacuated that cylinder by putting a little puff of steam in there. Atmospheric pressure pushed the piston down. That's where you can do useful work."

Aww, "free downforce" as per a vacuum—a pet dynamic application of Jocko's and an application intrinsic to the PoweRRing's efficiency.

Jocko went on to tell me that he discovered that when the piston is on the compression stroke, the spark is ignited at about 30 degrees before top-dead center. So, when the explosion goes off, the piston is still on its way up. It's heading into high pressure and putting tremendous, often destructive, forces on the piston, rod, crank and bearings. The crankshaft has to turn an additional 25 degrees' before the rod can lean over and let the piston start its way back down. When the piston does start down, the leverage angle is only about an inch. "How tight could you get a nut or a bolt if your wrench was only one inch long?" he asked rhetorically. When the pressure is at its maximum, the rod is straight up the bore and restricts piston movement; so if detonation occurs, there's no place for anything to go, so the weakest link breaks, whether that's the piston, rod, crank or the engine block—something has to give.

His solution? Shitcan the crankshaft altogether. Use a very large camshaft instead. Because camshafts convert rotary motion to linear motion.

Jocko's PoweRRing 3 Cycle has 18 small cylinders arranged around a twelve-lobe cam wheel. Combustion occurs in one set of six cylinders after another, with the pistons exerting force on the cam-wheel, causing it to move. For every 360 degrees of rotation, there are 216 ignition firings, with six cylinders firing simultaneously every ten degrees of rotation.

He says he likes the idea of a radial engines because it would have the lightest weight per cubic inch and they are the easiest engines to cool. Capitalizing on the concept of circular ignition, Jocko's engine is a radial, but with a cam operating the pistons and minus any connecting rods or crankshaft.

"Current engine design, he says, "derives from a steam engine built in 1705; it was the first engine to use a crankshaft to convert reciprocal motion into rotary motion and pass it along through various gearboxes and transfer devices. This system is obsolete in light of new knowledge. Since high torque is inherent in my three-cycle engine design, the engine would be placed right next to the wheel, with no gear reduction except for a reverser. This engine is very compact, shaped like a wheel and no wider than a standard auto wheel. It leaves a lot of space inside a car for other things."

At this point Jocko and I saunter back onto his front yard where a full size mockup of his new streamliner sits. Jocko plans to unveil his 18-cylinder, 25 cubic inch radial motor—capable of 400 horsepower—in the arena of the Land Speed Record wars. The monocoque streamliner is officially known as the *Spirit of 29 Palms* but nicknamed "the triple-nickel" because of its target speed of 555 mph. After this combination conquers the combustion-driven land speed record, Jocko envisions installing the 'liner as a local tourist attraction, not unlike, say, the Integratron up the road.

"I'll rivet the skin onto the framework. It will be super rigid, it will be like an airplane but with the internal structure of a bridge," he says. "I will start with two engines, so it will be firing six cylinders every 5 degrees of rotation." If he needs more power for his LSR effort, he'll just insert another PoweRRing—they only weigh 40 pounds or so.

His wife (and sometimes collaborator) Joanie was working on a series of sculptures with recycled phone wire as Jocko and I talked. At this point the discussion swung from the PoweRRing—which he isn't going to bother to patent (he considers engineering ideas public domain)—towards the theory and application of streamlining itself.

"Every inch of those bodies is functional, " he says in reference to his spaceship on wheels. "Every curve, every line—the whole thing is about completely covering the car, getting the maximum use of the downforce, and doing it with a minimum of drag. The first one I built…the tail end of it was radically different from anything."

I ask him what made that vehicle—the *Jocko's Porting Special*—set the world on fire.

"The air came off the top of the body at the back and rotated down and tried to get underneath the tail," he answers. "It's low pressure down there. They created a set of vortices that would cancel one another out. That minimized the drag… because the bigger the wake you leave, the greater amount of power it takes to create it."

Yeah… Not unlike his sculptures and his streamliners, Jocko himself has a very low co-efficient of drag. He is free to create beatifically with a minimum of turbulence. And if his latest creations are above the ken and understanding of America, its master capitalists and its engineers, that is not the point. The point is this: He's on to something—not unlike turning 8.35 in the 1/4 mile in 1958.

But unlike 1958, the drag strips are no longer the proving grounds, the high desert is. And it has always fostered creativity.

Once the archetypal misunderstood genius acclimates him or herself to the godawful climate and gets in tune with the rattlesnakes, the scorpions and the coyotes and the sporadic blasts of supersonic reconnaissance aircraft on maneuvers, he can let it all hang out in his own private Skunk Works. There are no board meetings or focus groups in a place where the stars are absolutely infinite, and where the wind seems to whisper that anything is possible. When time and space got it on, and—BANG—the heavens climaxed, the seeds of creation must have spilled onto the Mojave. There are no rules and there are no limitations there... Whatever you want to bestow upon humanity is limited only by your perseverance and your imagination. Just like Van Tassel, Jocko knows the desert itself is a concentrated chunk of eternity. He knows that life is short and progress is crucial to the meaning of life. Recently some nostalgia dragster guys approached Jocko about porting some heads, just like the old days... "Why would I want to do that, that's a step backwards." Pause. "Drag racing turned its back on me a long time ago," he mused. "Now it's my turn to my back on it."

"People are afraid of progress," he says, perplexed. But not in the outback of Twentynine Palms, apparently, where folks intuitively understand the obvious: History only happens once. And history is being made right now in the California desert. Jocko's moment in history is NOW. It's our loss if we can't recognize a defining moment in history as it's going down.

(Originally published 1997)

THE UNIVERSE IS EXPANDING: MACH 1 AS THE BIG BANG

In the Northwest corner of Nevada, in the shadow of Granite Peak on the Black Rock Mountain Range, there dwells a valley whose innards are the desiccated bowels of a prehistoric lakebed that stretches nearly 80 miles longitudinally.

One gets the feeling that this here prehistoric lakebed has seen its share of paradigm shifts—and weathered them all. It is a very cynical landscape: A cracked, upturned seabed that is mostly gypsum and lithium and is surrounded by abandoned mining claims etched into gargantuan lava rock whose elements make up half of the periodic table. It is hard to fuck with.

And this charred chunk of alkali has a history that resonates both spiritually and in a secular fashion: 100,000 years ago when the Ice Age melted into the Stone Age, the condensation yielded the leviathan Lake Lahontan, a body of water with a mass greater than most sovereign states in the Northeast of the US of A. This wonder of nature eventually evaporated into playa dust, not too long before the local Pauite Injuns were pulverized by "Superior Caucasian Forces" from Virginia City, forces who understood that the Black Rock desert was a strategic fork in the road, both for Bible-totin' homesteaders who could bear right into the Oregon territories and for till-the-wheels-fall-off 49ers who could hang a louie, follow the Truckee River into Donner Pass and do some righteous prospectin' in Gold Country out California way. Parenthetically, this intersection's dusty tributary is known as Nobles' Trail, named after a golddiggin' trailblazer.

All of this went down on a lakebed that is so uninhabitable only scorpions would call it home. Yet in the presence of all that history in the American Outback, you get the feeling that time is completely still—a notion reinforced by the service in the local coffee shop—or that the universe is expanding at a velocity us mortals can't fathom. Either way, you realize this is the perfect tableau for humanity's attempt at emulating a supernova via traversing land faster than the speed of sound...

And although ol' Nobles has been picked-over coyote meat for over a century now, the terrain that bears his name is still a launch pad into unchartered territory, most recently for two teams of Land Speed Record crusaders, one from across the pond in the United Kingdom and the other hailing from the far side of the Donner Pass. The trail these folks set out to blaze had a mother lode somewhat more esoteric than Nobles' cache. For the teams of *Thrust SSC* (UK) and the *Spirit of America*, paydirt was thus: the honor of traveling at the Speed of Sound. Mach 1. On Land.

Ironically, the point man for the UK operation answers to the name of Noble, and is an honest-to-goodness Order of the British Knight, christened by God and the Queen as Richard Noble, OBE. Noble and his minions were here to make history and, in many ways, they were also here to observe tradition— the tradition of seizing one's destiny, a tradition perfected by other folks passing through these parts such as Nobles, Kit Carson and, more recently, Spencer Tracy.

top fuel wormhole

What all the aforementioned have in common besides the Black Rock desert is adversity: Nobles had the elements, Carson had the wily Pauite Indians, and Spencer Tracy had Lee Marvin (cf. *Bad Day at Black Rock*, probably rentable at your local video emporium). Likewise, for adversity, the *Thrust SSC* and the *Spirit of America* teams not only had each other, they also had to endure a plethora of seemingly insurmountable elements (floods, lack of venture capital, sandstorms, lack of venture capital, fod (foreign object damage), lack of venture capital, etc.).

This is the story of how Richard Noble and a band of compatriots not only overcame adversity but actually stared it down whilst engaged in a shootout the likes of which Washoe County, NV hadn't seen since wily ol' Chief Winnemucca and his scrappy Paiutes nearly staved off genocide.

*****

In 1983 Richard Noble turned 633 mph at Black Rock and reclaimed the LSR for Great Britain in his *Thrust 2* jet car, taking it away from the late Gary Gabelich, a California drag racer and Rockwell test pilot who clocked a 2-way speed average of 622 mph in a hydrogen-peroxide powered rocket in 1970. Noble's conquest struck a raw nerve in Craig Breedlove's craw—and in his sense of patriotism. Breedlove was the 5-time holder of the LSR in the 1960s, as well as the conqueror of many barriers -- 400, 500, and 600 mph—in his *Spirit of America* jet cars. As Noble had tea and crumpets with the Queen, Breedlove immediately began drawing eyelid diagrams of a third-generation *Spirit of America* that he felt was sleek enough not only to enable him to procure the LSR but also to slip through the last great barrier: Mach 1.

But to sell his dream to America and to his sponsors, Craig needed an adversary like Ike needed Khrushchev. So he approached the then-LSR record holder, Noble, and confided in him his aspirations towards conquering the Sound Barrier. Noble took the bait. Immediately both men jettisoned their relatively prosaic lives—Breedlove was now a realtor, Noble was now marketing recreational aircraft—and focused all of their energies toward their new goal.

A funny thing happened en route to the epochal "Duel In the Desert '97" in the Great American Southwest, however...

You see, both Breedlove and Noble had ambition but were lacking three other elements critical to his success: 1) Venture capital. 2) A crew. 3) A design for a vehicle that would somehow subvert the laws of physics and aerodynamics as applied to the turbulence inherent in supersonic travel—forces which would most likely launch and/or shred the vehicle and its driver. For in a motorcar traveling at that speed some of the pressure and shock waves which would envelop the vehicle would have no way to diffuse themselves as they hit the floor and then reverberated UNDER the vehicle, acting like a 750 mph catapult. As Noble himself described it, "At Mach 1, you're either on the ground or you're ten miles in the air at a force of 40 g's." Blimey.

So, yeah, Noble sets off to meet the esteemed Ken Norris, designer of both Sir Malcolm Campbell and his kid Donald Campbell's revolutionary LSR machines, to explain his plight, i.e. that he had the "want to's" real bad but no design team nor plan. And in a crucial and profound stroke of luck, Norris's earlier appointment, Ron Ayers (a retired guided missile designer from the Brit military-industrial complex who is as renowned in his field as Noble and Norris are in theirs), is caught in cross-town traffic and arrives at Norris's digs the same moment as Noble.

Before the chance encounter with Noble, Ayers had no desire to design a Mach 1 motorcar (and very little interest in motorsports in general). "My immediate reaction was to distance myself from the project," is how the elderly, erudite, avuncular aerodynamicist recalls the moment that Noble pitched him the project. "To drive at supersonic speeds would clearly be extremely dangerous, and indeed, it could well be impossible. I pointed out to Richard that even keeping the car on the ground would be extraordinarily difficult." But Noble knew fresh meat when he saw it, and commenced to dog-and-pony-showing his way into Ayers id and sense of purpose. Suffice it to say, Ayers became the "*Thrust SuperSonic Car*'s" first conscript—and its prime architect.

Indeed, the next day Ayers went into his garden, got out a pad and pencil and began free associating... "How can we keep a motorcar stable as it passes from the transonic to supersonic speeds..." Ayers continued to sketch and the *Thrust* began to take shape. "...It will need two jet engines, not for thrust but for weight, drag and downforce...they will have to live on either side of the cockpit..." His approach to cannonballing through the turbulence of Mach 1 was an aerodynamic application tantamount to the bigger hammer method. "...We will not finesse this per se, but punch through the sonic barrier...the center of gravity must be forward, but not so fore that it actually burrows into the desert floor and resurfaces in Eurasia..." "Everything that isn't lift is downforce..." The only logical shape this beast could assume was the bastard, mutant spawn of the *Batmobile* and Lockheed's SR-71 Blackbird spy plane—i.e., the gnarliest, baddest contraption to attack the jet stream since the Cold War ended. It was gorgeous.

And for all its designed inefficiency, it was practical. Richard Noble concurred emphatically with Ayers' take on attacking Mach 1. "The key thing in this is stability," he told me out on the playa. "Anybody can stick a jet engine on a chassis and light the fuse. Ron and I sketched out something and we thought, 'My God, this is really rather good. This could work very well. Right: twin-engines, aluminum wheels' and then Ken (Norris) says, 'There is no room for steering'—and it started to build from there."

(You can imagine the conversation amongst the *SSC* design team: "Yeah, Ron it's bitchin'—but where do we put the torsion bars?" In an epiphany, *SSC* Chief Mechanical Designer Glynne Bowsher—one of a succession of aerospace hitters hornswoggled by Noble and intrigued by the notion of breaking the sound barrier on land—concluded that in order to shoehorn a steering system between the framerails, the *SSC* must turn by the two in-line rear wheels. Talk about form follows function...)

The *Thrust SSC* was housed and fabricated in a spare hangar in Farnborough, UK, the locale of what, in essence, is the British Skunk Works (in other words, the hangars for her Royal Majesty's stealth and supersonic aerospace programs). Suffice it to say, the bulk of the *SSC* engineers who became intoxicated with Noble's dream already knew where Farnborough's commissary was well before Noble approached them for help...

As the design came to life at Farnborough Airfield, Noble canvassed the breadth of the Jolly 'Ol, banging on boardroom doors for financial support and hosting seminars at campuses and air shows in order to recruit a pit crew. Interestingly, his stirring pitches appealed to the hoi polloi more than the suits in the corridors of power. The hoi polloi formed the Mach 1 club—"give us a few quid, drop what you're doing and come with us to America to break the sound barrier"—and became another indispensable element to the *Thrust SSC*'s eventual success.

And finally, another crucial element was in place. That is, Nobles' choice for a shoe: A soft-spoken-yet-buff, dashing, Royal Air Force pilot named Andy Green whose physique, psyche, and demeanor were ideal for the project. Indeed, Andy Green could have been culled straight outta' Central Casting. The team was in place.

And after some CFD data and rocket-sled testing confirmed Ayers' theories on supersonic travel, the vehicle was completed. But before the conquering of Mach 1 in America was to commence, the team trudged off to an RAF air base in the Al Jafr desert in Jordan during November of '96 for some shakedown runs, with the blessing of ol' King Hussein. Testing the synergy of all systems on this technological marvel commenced: Computerized suspension, telemetry, satellite uplinks, communications, aluminum wheels, rear wheel steer, twin Spey 202 turbofan engine, support vehicles, etc.

All systems seemed to be speaking to each other, but a full dress rehearsal for the upcoming mission in the Black Rock desert would have to wait, for then came the prerequisite trial, error, and anguish that, if you study your motorsports history, seems to accompany all LSR efforts. In a Middle Eastern desert that is dryer than microwaved kitty litter, it rained. And rained. And flooded.

Indeed, as Ron Ayers related in retrospect: "According to the weather statistics, November should have the ideal combination of moderate temperature, low wind, low precipitation, and few dust storms." It was, in fact, quite the antithesis. The *Thrust SSC*er's arrival at this arid Middle Eastern desert was akin to fording a river: At the air base where Thrust was stationed the flooding was moving so fast that it appeared to be pushing stones ahead of it. Finally, Glynne Bowsher pointed out that the stones were actually floating camel droppings…

Meanwhile: Concurrent to the SSC frantically evacuating the flooded desert in Jordan, days before a provisional Bureau of Land Management permit at Black Rock expired, Breedlove caught a crosswind at 675 mph as his *Spirit of*

America streamliner "Wrong Way" Corrigan-ed and assumed the attitude of a traffic circle. It was the fastest U-turn in history.

"I didn't know that I had the side wind," said Breedlove. "I was confused. I wouldn't have run had I known what the wind was."

In fact, it was one of those moments when a bad case of "Go! Fever" short-circuited logic. With the permit dwindling and bad weather encroaching, Craig knew his window for making history was finite. As he was strapped into the car early that ill-fated morning for his record run, Craig had requested a wind profile. It came back, "Crosswind One-point-five mph." When the *SOA* crew fired the J-79, it developed a fluid leak and was shut down. As the crew tightened some fittings with their wrenches, a cloud cover blew in over the playa, obscuring Breedlove's vision. He continued to wait, and kept his game face on while still strapped into the cockpit. Finally, the clouds lifted and Craig could see the 13-mile black stripe that was his sole guidance system down the course. Finally, four hours after the original time of departure, all systems were go and Craig requested another wind profile. The response over the radio was "Crosswind at One-Five mph." Knowing that the *SOA* could only withstand a crosswind of 5 mph or less, in his zeal to go 700 mph Craig inserted a decimal point in the wind profile... He interpreted the transmission as "1.5" not "15" mph.

When the car tipped up on its side and went into a skid, "I had dirt in the windshield, and I really couldn't see what was happening," he said. "I thought I'd probably had it, that this was going to be it."

The next available permit for speed trials would be in September, 1997.

*****

On the eve of the press conferences in Reno that will hail the Mach 1 attempts, I arrive at the Reno Airport after spending the flight engaging in heavy and heated discourse with a geeky film buff about the aforementioned Spencer Tracy movie. I am heavily mythologizing not only the flick, but also the actual location of Black Rock itself. He's not buying it.

"Yeah," I said with authority, "there is a coffee shop called 'Bruno's' that is right across the street from the train station used in *Bad Day at Black Rock*. It has to be the same diner coffee shop where Spencer Tracy—with his only good arm—karate-chopped Ernest Borgnine in the throat."

"Well that can't be," the geek in the seat next to me sniffs, as he ramps his bifocals up the bridge of his nose. "I have the laserdisc in my library and on one of the Second Audio Programs the director, John Sturges, explains at length how they used these abandoned railroad tracks they found in Bishop, California for the train scenes. That fictitious coffee shop was actually a set on a back lot in Burbank."

"I'm telling you they shot this film in Gerlach, Nevada. I've been there AND I've seen the movie. Spencer Tracy gets off the friggin' train in Gerlach."

"That sir is empirically impossible," the geek bleats. "The production never set foot in Nevada. Rent the laserdisc."

"Laserdiscs are Satanic."

When the plane lands, en route to scoring a rent-a-car I go to the Information Booth in hopes of procuring a map of the Gerlach area—I've been there before, but this is the kind of terrain where you just don't want to get lost. There is a kindly, slightly senilitic Chamber of Commerce croater behind the counter who asks me where I am headed. I tell him, "Black Rock," so he says, "Lovelock, it's right here, " and he points to the town of Lovelock on the map.

"No," I say, "ummm, Black Rock, out by Gerlach."

"Ohhh; Tomahawk, it's right here, just take I-80 east past..."

"No, no, no," I interrupt and point to my destination on his map, crinkling it a little bit. "Black Rock, out by Gerlach."

"O-h-h-h, Black Rock. That's easy: Just take I-80 east to Fernley and take 447 north to Gerlach. It'll take you right to the station where Spencer Tracy got off the train."

"Actually," I pipe up, "that movie was shot in Bishop, California and on a back lot in Burbank."

"You have a nice drive, sir."

top fuel wormhole

"Ladies, gentlemen, and members of the press, we are here to go Mach 1. Getting the record back does not interest us. Going 700 mph does not interest us. We are here to go Mach 1."

Thus sayeth Richard Noble hisself from the podium at a press conference in a downtown Reno casino a couple of days after Labor Day, 1997. His audience was a motley mix of motorsports journalists, a couple of local betacam crews, some curious tourists (who strolled away from the keno girls after gazing through the tinted casino windows at what looked to be a phallic-shaped 10-ton spaceship that had landed by the valet parking), and some local street people who were intrigued by the commotion and had sniffed out the prospect of free Danishes and coffee.

Noble's "No Sleep 'till Supersonic" gauntlet was throw down just hours after his exhausted troops had arrived in Nevada on a blitzkrieg rock-and-roll-180 flight from the Farnborough hangar, jet lagged, sleep deprived and immaculately clad in matching green uniforms.

Cut to: the *SOA* press conference at a casino across town. Craig Breedlove was nonplussed by Noble's earlier speech and retaliated by saying, "I spoke to Richard early on in his design process and he'd said that he'd decided they needed a twin-engine design and that was where we differed.

"I said, 'Well, I really don't think you need two,' and he said, 'All land speed record cars have always underperformed.' I said, 'I really haven't found that to be true—I had a J-47 that I really think I could have reached 600 mph with. Maybe you experienced a lot higher drag numbers than I have.' In any case, that was their philosophy: Really screw the car down, just suck it down with a lot of ground effects. Just power it through—(and) it's a very stable way to do it." But not the *SOA* way.

"The problem I saw at Black Rock early on in this design concept with Richard was sinking in," Breedlove continued. "I went to Ken Norris and asked what their (*SSC*) ground loadings were and he told me they were at 13,000 lbs. (of downforce). I asked how they were distributed and he said, 'No, that's on the front wheels.' I said, 'Well, you're aware that you guys are going to have so much rolling drag that you guys are never going to get the record.' He said they'd been discussing that and the only thing is that Richard is very reluctant to point the car up any because of the flying problem."

Conversely, for his Mach 1 endeavors, Breedlove in essence eyeball-aeroed a projectile in the shape of an arrow. Using a hot-rodded J-79 General Electric jet engine from a Navy F-4 Phantom fighter aircraft for motivation, Craig visualized a sleek, narrow dart that would partake of the J-79's 22,650 pounds of thrust (45,000 horsepower) and finesse the shockwaves that emanate when a vehicle climbs through a transonic slipstream into—BOOM—a supersonic slipstream.

"When we ran *Sonic 1* at 600 mph (1965) we had no weight on the front end. I'm not saying that's a prudent way to do it, but that's just the fact of the matter. Somewhere between 13,000 lbs. and zero is the speed record."

****

After seven years of research and development as well as "dancing-as-fast-as-I-can" cajoling of corporations, the match was finally on: A quintessential California hot rodder arm wrestling a permutation of the British military industrial complex.

But although the match was on, there were still many obstacles in the path of both teams, not the least of which was negative cash flow. To facilitate the arrival of the Brits from Farnborough into Reno Int'l Airport—keep in mind it required 250,00 gallons of jet fuel to top off an Antonov AN-124 Russian cargo plane (the only vehicle in existence with enough trunk space to transport the Thrust's 80-ton portable skunk works)—Noble appealed for alms via the London Daily Telegraph and the Internet. The vox populi responded with a vengeance. *Thrust SSC* got its jet fuel.

Ultimately, 20 percent of the funding for the Thrust effort came from Noble shaking the virtual bushes of cyberspace. Amazing.

*****

"My best wishes to all involved in Thrust SSC's *attempt to be the first through the sound barrier on land. This project is a graphic illustration of British enterprise and engineering at its best. Good luck. The whole country is behind you."*—Tony Blair, British Prime Minister.

"It's all about beating the British system. If there were any British government involvement (in Thrust SSC*) we would end up with somebody on our board, okay? And this has to be a little organization that is very flexible and can dance and weave. The last thing we want is that sort of person on the board."*—Richard Noble.

*****

In May of '97 the Brits had made a return trip to Jordan for more shakedown runs—they managed to get the *SSC* up to 540 mph, which was apparently all that patchy surface could handle—and they were treated like royalty. Pomp and circumstance is not much in evidence in Gerlach, NV when the *Thrust SSC* mates first arrive. The Brits are homeless. Gerlach is a town of 300—counting the scorpions—and lodging is sketchy. There is one motel, "Bruno's," which is also the name of the bar and the coffee shop, all of which are named eponymously for the town czar, a lanky, bent elderly Italian with the kind of disposition only slightly surlier than that of Benito Mussolini's. Despite *Thrust SSC*'s scout team undertaking a reconnaissance trip in April to secure the permits and lodging crucial to their mission, it has all turned to shit: Bruno double-booked all the available lodging and ultimately rented his rooms to the highest bidder: the *SOA* contingent.

Right then, the Brits are boycotting that turncoat Bruno. They adjourn to the bar next door, The Miners Club, and discuss Plan B. After enjoining Bev, the barkeep, to "Give us a fag, wouldya' love?" (Loosely translated, "I'd like to purchase a package of cigarettes"), the affable Brits begin making friends with the locals, particularly Bev.

So picture this: Richard Noble and his lads (20 clamoring Brits clad in matching RAF-green) are hoisting Coors in a dusty, desert Dew-Do-Drop-Inn (this about as bizarre as it gets, in my book) when one of Noble's crew members shushes the entire bar. The local teevee news is reporting on that morning's press conference ("Going 700 mph does not interest us. We are here to go Mach 1...") at the casino in Reno. Suddenly the videotape cuts to the chipper studio humanoid broadcaster who closes the report with this coda, "Noble and his team are taking Saturday off in observance of Princess Di's funeral."

Simultaneously Richard Noble, OBE does a "say wot??" double-take while his overworked and underpaid entourage cheer and Bev pours more drinks.

They didn't get the day off. Nor did they care, really. All of which underscores this question: What is it about Noble that inspires his troops, his lads, to persevere in high-desert heat to erect a portable self-contained military-industrial complex that meets the criteria for the digital era's standard for data gathering, all on a dry lakebed that time forgot?

The answer is that is it is not explainable by the notion of "technological enthusiasm," a phrase that has recently come to explain everything from hot rodding to the Apollo moon shot. The answer is deeper, more atavistic and completely primeval. The answer has roots that extend into the quintessence of matter: The universe is expanding. By extrapolation, consciousness is expanding, constantly encroaching into realms of the unknown. The technological enthusiast must go THERE, the technological enthusiast will devour and outmaneuver whatever is his or her way: Pauites, the laws of aerodynamics, Newtonian physics, whatever.

Thus you have some of the finest minds of our lifetime sleeping on other people's couches, on their hands and knees picking up pebbles off the desert floor, all so they can have their moon shot.

Nobody exemplifies this "technological enthusiasm" more than Ron Ayers. Although retired and in the twilight of his stay here on Planet Earth, Ayers was as active as any of the fresh-faced Mach 1 Clubbers on holiday from the university.

top fuel wormhole

Nearly a month after the Thrusters had arrived and were continuing to creep into the transonic speed range, I eavesdropped on Ayers as he was explaining his theories on supersonic travel in a motorcar to a bewildered and besotted patron in the Miner's Club. Ayers was using a shot glass as a prop that represented the *Thrust SSC* and was gingerly gliding it along the surface of the bar to illustrate his theories about subsonic, trans-sonic, and supersonic pressure waves and how they would affect the handing of the *Thrust SSC*.

The guy at the bar was asking Ayers why don't you Brits just put the hammer down and go Mach 1 and be done with it?

Ayers explained the *SSC* design teams rationale for chipping away at ever-increasing speeds: "The aerodynamic forces would be simply enormous, enough to lift the car and throw it around like an autumn leaf in a gale," he said. "The crux of the problem is knowing how the flow would behave underneath the car at sonic speeds and what would happen to shockwaves in that region."

The guy on the bar stool next nodded as if he comprehended Ayers' riff.

"The most important thing," he concluded as Bev the bartender repossessed the shot glass and put it to less theoretical use, "is that we don't obliterate Andy."

*****

And so it went at Black Rock: It was a month replete with sandstorms, rain, and incessant fod. Early on, Breedlove had "fodded" his engine when he sucked a bolt into the combustion chamber. At times it was like *Waiting for Godot*. It was a month of hurry-up-and-wait, hey maybe tomorrow is the day. It was an exercise in endurance. Occasionally sandstorms would kick in and nullify the very thorough "de-fodding" (removing debris from the 13 mile courses) that took place during the day. In addition to the capricious, recalcitrant weather that made a mockery of the Mach 1 club's perpetual de-fodding efforts, the Brits were plagued with a malfunctioning on-board computer that would sense non-existing turbulence and kill both engines at 400 mph. The *SSC* software *phreaks* would chase after the jet car at 180 mph in a hot-rodded XJ12 Jaguar and blow some fresh code out off a laptop into the onboard computer's SCSI port.

Through all of this both Bruno's and the Miner's Club in Gerlach became like Algonquin Rooms for the LSR maniacs who gathered on the playa in search of the Big Bang. The conversation was always good. It was during these nights that I engaged Noble in a dialogue about overcoming obstacles. He insisted that the two forays into Jordan prepared the Thrust team for any possible catastrophic eventuality.

"The problem with Jordan," he said, "is that we built a car that was extremely unconventional and very complex. We took it out there with a very green crew, so we had the problems of sorting out the crew, sorting out the car and, even worse, sorting out the desert. It hammered the hell out of the car...(after) we cleared 170 miles of stone. And a lot of that was on our hands and knees."

Another night I got a similar recollection from Andy Green. "We had gone out there with a car with a lot of features that people said couldn't work: rear-wheel steering, twin engines, the computers," he said. "We went out there and we had a lot of problems with rear-wheel steer. And the engineering fixed it out there in the desert—we got the car to work right out there in Jordan. Everything that could have gone wrong with everything we had did—and we fixed all of it. The only thing we couldn't fix was the weather."

"The biggest obstacle wasn't the fod or the weather," said Simon Rogers, one of the *Thrust SSC* microlight pilots whose job description was to patrol the desert looking for fod. "Some days we would have to abandon a run because I would spot camels straggling across the track or Iranians rampaging across the desert smuggling massive amounts of petrol in a lorry (tanker truck)."

But perhaps the finest quote I was able to extricate from the Brits came from Green when I asked him what possessed him to be the first driver of an automobile to burst through the Sound Barrier. He said, "Nobody knows what's there because nobody has ever been there."

It was a haiku for the technological enthusiast.

*****

top fuel wormhole

I asked Andy Green to describe the differences in handling a Tornado fight plane and the Thrust SSC. "The car has a lot more acceleration than a jet fighter," he said. "It has two jet fighter engines with half the weight of a jet fighter—tremendous acceleration." He said he enjoyed his "holiday" from the RAF while he was moonlighting with the Thrust team. "You only run when the weather is nice, everything is good for you and the vehicle is perfectly sensible."

*****

Einstein proved that space and time both bend. Empirical confirmation of this phenomena existed at Black Rock on the day the Brits went supersonic. There is a parallax of cones that delineate the boundary of the race course, from the shut down area through the "measured mile" speed trap all the way to the launch pad. With the human eye, the cones gradually meld into the floor of the lakebed itself. Off on the horizon, a puff of dusty exhaust blossoms like Teutonic smoke signals as the crewmembers spin the *Thrust SSC*'s turbines and purge the afterburners of its Spey 202s. But this dervish of pyrotechnical activity transpires approximately 45 degrees off axis of the parallax view. Space bends. You are witnessing the curvature of the Earth.

"*Thrust SSC* is rolling," the radio hums. For the first mile of the record run, the machine is merely cruising at speeds that would not bat the eye of a highway patrolman in Montana. This is precautionary, to avoid creating a vacuum in the 202's intake which would suck pebbles and arrowheads off the lakebed and into the motor. At the Mile 1 marker Green stomps on the loud pedal. Instantaneously, copious amounts of thrust sock the RAF hero in the solar plexus and he's blazing across the lakebed with a rooster-tail of dust and exhaust in his wake as tall as Noble's phone bill. The trajectory of the vehicle appears to be bending on an exponential curve, even though it is straight as a Southern Baptist. Everything is strangely silent, despite the fact that the machine must be making prodigious thunder in its wake. (Isn't it?). Suddenly, the trajectory appears to change and is completely linear... it is absolutely boogeying... *Thrust SSC* enters the measured mile and... silence... a mushroom cloud begins to manifest itself in the wake of the vehicle and then WHHHOOOOSSSSHHH....

fuck that is loud! The sound of two fighter plane engines with turbines spinning at warp speed rattles the playa and the schoolhouse in Gerlach. Time bends.

*****

On October 13, 1997, one day before the 50th anniversary of Chuck Yeager's supersonic rocket ride in the Bell *X-1* airplane, Andy Green broke the sound barrier on land. He recorded speeds of 764.168 and 758.102 mph, at Mach numbers of 1.007 and 1.000. The timekeepers at the United States Auto Club could not confirm these numbers as an official FIA record as the prerequisite "back-up" run missed the one-hour window by 43 seconds. Two days later, Green again performed back-to-back supersonic runs—this time within the allotted hour—at speeds of 759.333 (Mach 1.015) and 766.609 mph (Mach 1.020), with an official two-way average of 763.035 mph.

As his crew packed up the *SSC* portable skunk works, Richard Noble made no mention of his impending afternoon tea with the Queen of England. However, he did say, "I'm going to Brazil to hide from the creditors." The *Thrust SSC* will be mothballed in a museum, never to run again.

Craig Breedlove is still on the playa, albeit with a new goal: to be the first man to travel at 800 mph on land. He clocked 636 mph as this story was filed.

*****

And there you have it: The theoretical work of Ayers, Bowsher, Noble and the entire entourage of the *Thrust SSC*—as articulated by Andy Green's cockpit acumen—has been established. And it confirms this notion: The universe is expanding. Just ask Mr. Ayers the next time you see him at the Miner's Club, having a drink with Spencer Tracy.

(Originally published in Drag Racing Monthly.*)*

THE SOUTHERN CALIFORNIA EXPLODING INEVITABLE

THE EPIC SAGA OF THE SURFERS

There is a philosophy of the world that states that there is a common realization about the interconnectivity of all things physical and spiritual—that there is a unity at a profound level—and that our actions have somewhat infinite repercussions. This discipline is known as Zen. In the mid-1960s, it was a philosophy that was integral to the machinations of an offbeat trio of Nitro Bums from the west side of Los Angeles: Bob Skinner, Tom Jobe and Mike Sorokin, aka "The Surfers." It defined their approach to the application of nitromethane vis-à-vis compression ratios and blower speeds. It defined who they were as individuals.

```
the cole coonce drag strip reader, vol. 1
```

This is the story of how these three men stood the World of Drag Racing on its ear via their theoretical approach to life as applied to a Top Fuel dragster. It is the parable of two abstract yet linear thinkers, Skinner and Jobe, and their driver, Sorokin, and how they discovered that the path to Drag City and the trophy queen was also the path to nirvana and enlightenment.

It all began just a few lunar cycles before Baba Ram Dass coined the phrase "Be Here Now," but this chestnut of wisdom could have been The Surfers' mantra. For these shrewd and mischievous nitromaniacs, the drag strips of Southern California were a blank slate to gingerly project their desires and sensibilities in much the same way a Zen Master approaches the mysteries of life: Head First. With No Rear View Mirrors. This was not just about merely kissing a trophy queen on Saturday night. This was an exercise in all things theoretical and philosophical. It was an exercise in consciousness expansion. It was a journey.

And it was the ideal time to catch a wave, so to speak. The opportunity to express one's self in the State of California then was as wide open and infinite as the blue waters of the Pacific Ocean. The only limits were one's resourcefulness and ingenuity... And for approximately three revolutions around the sun it was absolutely high tide for the collaboration between Bob Skinner, Tom Jobe and Mike Sorokin. The Surfers ruled.

Although The Surfers made the universe shudder with their unique approach to both Top Fuel racing and, uhh, life itself, the genesis of their racing endeavors was much more prosaic than you would imagine. Its germination was in the days of Ozzy & Harriet and Googie Hamburger Stand Americana and it specifically took root on the corner of Jefferson & Sepulveda in Culver City, California. There stood a burger joint known as the "Nineteen." Named eponymously after its nineteen-cent hamburgers, it was the epicenter for Cafe Society as interpreted by street-racin' Southern California hot rodders. And its atmosphere, vibrations and "extracurricular activities" resonated deep in the soul of Mike Sorokin, at the time a lead-footed Venice High School student.

"The thing about the Nineteen was, not only did they have cheap food," recalls local digger driver and one-time street racer Ron Hier, "they had a great big parking lot. We used to hang out there because we used to street race and 'Sork' was one of the guys who hung out there.

top fuel wormhole

"When we first started hanging out with Sorokin at the 19," Hier continues, "there really weren't any drag strips—except for one all the way out in Santa Ana, and there were no freeways in those days. It was Gene Adams, Craig Breedlove and his '34, Leonard Harris, Mickey Brown, John Peters. What got Sorokin into racing was hanging out at the 19 and street racing with the guys." After describing a crash "near the railroad tracks" involving a now-mega-famous race car driver (who shall remain nameless) Hier concludes that, "I can't believe none of us got put in jail."

Hier, who sold Sorokin a '34 Ford that was used to drag down Sepulveda Boulevard, mentions that Sork's desire to race led to an ego battle with his old man, a conflict stereotypical of the era's teenage rebellion. "His dad did NOT like drag racing... he didn't like street racing, he didn't like drag racing, he did not want Mike driving. He would come over and try and talk all of us out of racing." Suffice it to say, the elder Sorokin's pleas were the proverbial fallen tree and the "fast crowd" at the Nineteen was its empty forest. Ben Sorokin's admonishments fell on deaf ears, mostly because he couldn't be heard over the roar of un-muffled internal combustion engines and squealing tires as they roared down Lincoln Boulevard.

Simultaneous to "Sork" sharpening his reflexes on the malt shop circuit as well as in gas coupes and a D/Fuel dragster on the strip, Santa Monica City College students Bob Skinner and Tom Jobe began tinkering mischievously in academia with what, in essence, was the pursuit of a double major of chemical prankster-ism and the theory and application of nitromethane. And as the drag strips and the freeways experienced their concurrent boom, these two whiz-kid brainiacs pooled their brainpower with a local construction worker and schemed together on running a Top Fuel car out of a motel garage. It was the perfect opportunity to apply their studies to the real world...

"Skinner and Jobe, when they put the car together," Hier recalls with bemusement, "...it was just a hare-brained idea." Bob Skinner doesn't dispute Hier's assessment. "I had dabbled in street racing. I briefly ran a B or C/Gas car," he recalls. "I had just got back from a three-month vacation and Tom Jobe and Jim Crosser said to me, 'Okay, we want to build a fuel car.' And I just said, 'Okay.' Most things that I have done along the way have been sort of spontaneous impulse without a lot of thinking about it. So when I came back and they said, 'We want to build this car,' I just said 'Great' and we just kind of got into it."

Hier remembers how the team raised its venture capital: "Skinner and Jobe got together with Bob Skinner's mother—who owned the Red Apple Motel there on Wilshire Boulevard in Santa Monica—and got her to sign for a 'furniture loan' for something like $5000." Skinner and Jobe immediately cashed the check for the non-existent "furniture" and began gathering parts and pieces for their AA/Fuel Dragster, which was kept in a spare garage at the Red Apple.

Jobe sums up their rationale for running a Top Fuel dragster out of his Mom's motel's garage thusly: "It was a time when anybody could participate. When we started all we had was enthusiasm. We didn't know nuthin'. We were just a bunch of street racers from Santa Monica," he says. "My brother raced in a stock class with a Chevy and I was his motor man. He street raced six days a week and would go to the drags on Saturday night, but we just got tired of the 'class' deal. He won the Winternationals in '60 and runner-upped at the US Nationals, but he was always getting torn down and all that crap. We all kinda' dabbled with C/Gas Willys and Mike drove a (C/Altered) roadster coupe with George Bacilek," he remembers. "Anyway, all of us had messed with different classes and we finally said: 'Classes? That sucks! Let's build a dragster,' but we didn't know how to build one, you know."

In other words, the only "competitor class" where Skinner and Jobe could dwell as free-thinkers was a class whose framework had no real... framework. Top Fuel.

So Skinner and Jobe began tugging on the shop apron strings of the local chassis builders and fabricators like a pair of hyperactive nephews that forgot to take their Ritalin. "There were a lot of (dragster) guys around here," Jobe notes. "Every day after work we'd hit all the garages—there was a bunch of them in Mar Vista—we'd go to every one of them and ask some questions 'til they'd throw us out and then we'd go down to the next one. We (finally) found out enough stuff because we had to build the whole thing ourselves; we didn't have any money to buy anything."

top fuel wormhole

They might have been strapped for cash, but Skinner and Jobe were loaded with an intellectual camaraderie that couldn't be bought. "Tom and I had a great ability to work together," Skinner acknowledges in references to the sculpting of their short, scruffy, minimalist dragster. But their other colleague had a somewhat less theoretical take on drag racing and according to Jobe, "Our other partner just dropped out soon after we got the thing running."

But just getting their homemade dragster running, nay just getting the digger to fire was an excruciatingly painful learning curve, according to SoCal drag-racing fixture Tom Hunnicutt, who was crewing for his friend Jim Boyd's *Red Turkey* AA/Fuel Dragster the day The Surfers unveiled their creation at Lions Drag Strip in early 1964.

Hunnicutt says of that afternoon, "They kept pushing up and down trying to get the car to fire and it wouldn't fire," he laughs. "I don't know if they had the magneto in wrong or what, but they kept pushing it on the return road for a long time—it wasn't just once. It was a bunch of laps." About this initial impression, Hunnicutt recalls thinking derisively, "'These guys aren't drag racers, who are they?' They were kinda' geeky."

This is the phase where Skinner and Jobe were fine-tuning the chemistry of all things material and physical—and enduring the scorn of their opponents because their homemade, homely digger was a real back-marker. Even if they could get the motor to fire, part of the boys' dilemma was that they had yet to settle on a driver who could viscerally and intuitively interpret their cerebral approach to Top Fuel racing and run it through the lights with the butterflies horizontal. Before Skinner and Jobe ultimately settled on Sorokin to shoe, there were a litany of drivers who attempted to hang ten in the cockpit, including "Lotus John" Morton, a journeyman sports-car racer who was sweeping the floor at Carrol Shelby's place of employ (where Skinner also punched a clock). Morton, who had a reputation as being absolutely fearless and could handle any piece of machinery that had a throttle, describes his one-day tenure as shoe of The Surfers AA/Fuel dragster this way:

"The dragster ride happened when I was at Shelby's," Morton states in a passage from his biography, *The Stainless Steel Carrot*. "I got in the car at the strip. Really got packed in. I was sitting there in that thing thinking, I have really got myself into something. Here I was a sports car racer and had never driven anything down a drag strip before, not even my dad's car, and I was about to drive the fastest thing they made. I was scared shitless. The thing was so powerful the centrifugal force of the clutch was trying to push itself out. I revved the engine and the sound ripped out like an explosion. My whole leg was trembling on the clutch.

"I let it out. Everything was a blur, the whole world went fuzzy. I let off for a second, just a tiny bit, and got pissed off at myself and floored it again. On my other runs I never let off but it didn't matter; the thing was so fast I did a hundred and eighty my first run and that was it, never any faster. I put the clutch in at the end of the run and waited for the thing to stop. By the time it did, I could feel my leg was still shaking, like a dog shitting razor blades. But I did it. Something made me do it."

Morton's eloquent and punchy account reveals something about the state of The Surfers' racing effort: For a couple of geeks, all of a sudden Skinner and Jobe were making beaucoup horsepower. But they lacked the final piece to their puzzle: A driver who could harness all that horsepower and ride the bulbous, minimalist machine bareback. And then Sorokin passed Skinner's reflex test of catching a series of falling coins, hopped in the saddle and history was about to be capsized.

According to Skinner, "It's hard to say how it all evolved because we had (Bob) Muravez driving and we had Roy Tuller driving, then 'Lotus John' drove, then we had Mike driving for us and we got rid of him and had other drivers driving for us. Somehow we came back to him (Sorokin) and things started to work better for us. Maybe we got the car running better, maybe he got better but I feel like we all kind of evolved together."

For Sorokin, this was nirvana indeed. His ambition was to be a professional dragster driver and here was an opportunity to hammer the throttle, kick out the jams—and get paid. Notoriously hyperactive and quick as an outhouse mouse on the Xmas tree, Sorokin was a fearless capsule monkey who thrived on going into orbit no matter how sketchy the conditions on the launch pad. Sorokin had *Go! Fever* as bad as any Southern California boy, and he was willing to get himself strapped into a nitro-burning rattletrap rocket no matter what the circumstances.

"He was so damn good at what he did. And all he wanted to do was win," remembers Jobe. "He wasn't interested in arguing about the nuts and bolts, 'that's your problem;' he didn't even care."

With the triumvirate simpatico, and Sorokin dependent upon win lights for his rent and lunch money, The Surfers arched more than a few eyebrows amongst their contemporaries and competitors with their fashion sensibilities, their engineering prowess and uncanny knack for racking up Top Eliminator trophies. This unnerved the competition—a couple of Surf City hodads were killing 'em at Drag City—but it thrilled the railbirds and it gave the media a human-interest "hook" to ratchet up their race reports. The whole "surf" thing, however, was a ruse...

"None of those guys surfed," remembers Hier. "None of 'em had a board."

Sorokin tried to keep the image of beach bums in perspective. "Surfing kind of scares me," he confessed rather dryly to Drag World. But his droll backpedaling was too late. The die had been cast.

Jobe, musing on The Surfers' sartorial ensemble of Pendeltons, deck shoes and skateboards, says, "They didn't know what to think of us, we were thought of as just... this was before hippies... but we were thought of as just some long-haired freaks from the beach."

"They were definitely different," recollects Roland Leong, nowadays the pit boss on Don Prudhomme's Funny Car but then proprietor of the infamous *Hawaiian* AA/Fuel Dragster that claimed Top Fuel Eliminator at the '65 and '66 Winternationals. "I remember seeing these guys at Fontana and Bakersfield and they pulled in there with an open trailer with a '55 Chevrolet and uhh, like uhh, 'Who are these guys?' They called themselves 'The Surfers,' right? And me, coming from Hawaii, that wasn't my idea of a surfer, you know what I mean? I guess in California terms they looked 'beach' kinda' guys, but in my eyes..."

"When you think about it, at the time we were all young and the word 'nerds' wasn't in our vocabulary," Leong adds. "But looking back, they looked like the intellectual-type as opposed to some greasy drag racers, which is what we were all known for at the time."

Regarding the perception of The Surfers as beach-bum misfits and geeky oddballs, Skinner—who now answers to the name "Roberto"—was oblivious. He says, "Some people live their lives and other people live their lives but at the same time it's like they're standing off at a distance and watching themselves. I've never been that observer."

Skinner maintains there was no contrived image, but others theorize that the persona of beach buffoons with sand-in-their-snorkels was a calculated, theatrical red herring. But archrival Leong saw through the skullduggery of the Surf City minstrel show. "All of 'em were pretty smart guys," he says. "With the budget they had to run on, they did an excellent job. They didn't have the funds, so a lot of their stuff they had to make or spend their money very wisely. They didn't have a lot of what we call perks, you know what I mean?"

"It wasn't very long before they were pretty dialed in," Hunnicutt corroborates.

Indeed, soon the drag-strip world was talking about the beatniks from the bay, not out of bemusement but out of respect. It was obvious The Surfers were onto something... Just ask the denizens and the vanquished dragster drivers of San Fernando, Long Beach, Fontana Drag City, Riverside, Bakersfield, Irwindale, Pomona, Fremont, Amarillo, Salt Lake City, Pocatello, Union Grove, Rockford, Maple Grove, Atco, and Denver. At every one of these venues, The Surfers either bagged Top Eliminator, recorded Low Elapsed Time or turned Top Speed of the Meet—and sometimes all three. (In Amarillo, they won two match races on the same day. Roland Leong's *Hawaiian* AA/FD was bongoed in a towing accident so the track manager enjoined The Surfers to go best-two-out-of-three against local hitters Eddie Hill and Vance Hunt... the Californians swept both matches.) They were no longer geeky gremmies. They were Heroes.

****

To: Joe Buysee, Lansing Michigan From: Mike Sorokin, Mar Vista, CA
Hi Joe,
Thanks for the nice letter. I'm glad we didn't disappoint you at Bakersfield. It's fans like you that make our efforts worthwhile.
I'm sending you a t-shirt. It's used, but clean. I'm sorry I have to send

you a used one, but there are no new ones around. I don't think we will be in the Michigan area this year, but maybe next season.

Sincerely,

Mike Sorokin & The Surfers

****

The wave continued its crest. Skinner asserts that, "At that point in life I would say that we were totally focused on our deal." In a separate conversation, Tom Jobe agreed and then elaborated on their approach to conquering Top Fuel. "We went at it in a very conventional fashion," he said. "All the guys that had the goofy combinations were never gonna do it… (and) if you had a mainstream deal you couldn't get banned. We had a very clear view of that. 'We've got to attack this from a mainstream angle.' That way your advantage is invisible."

Ron Hier explains one example of their focus and aversion to "goofy combinations" was to remove parts they considered superfluous. "They never had run an idler belt on their blower," he mused, "because Tom Jobe felt that it was just another accessory that they might have a problem with, something else that could break. So when they put the motor together and they wanted to change belts, they would unbolt the blower and tilt it forward until the pulley was underneath the belt and then push it down onto the manifold and bolt it down. All during the time they were running that car, they never lost a blower belt."

On the absence of the idler pulley, Skinner is nonplussed. "We figured we could just get along without it, so why have it if you don't need it?"

****

Hi Joe,

What's happening? Not too much going on around here. We're building a covered trailer for our tour and we don't have much time for racing at the present time. Our race with the Goose will be our last local race.

Our car isn't exactly beautiful, but it IS functional. Beauty doesn't always get the job done. We are building a new car which should be pretty nice looking.

Full body and all that trick stuff.
 Well, maybe I'll see you pretty soon.
 Mike

****

In 1966, Roland Leong's engine czar Keith Black went on record in *Hot Rod Magazine* as defining a 75% nitromethane mixture as "heavy." Ergo, 100% was not just volatile—it was certifiably insane. Of course, this was the percentage that Skinner and Jobe considered ideal for their tune-up. To the mighty Surfers, cutting the nitromethane with alcohol was even more absurd and non-linear than using a blower pulley. More is good, too much is better, right? But were these yin and yang yahoo alchemists pushing the envelope of internal combustion beyond its tension threshold? Were The Surfers off their trolley? Had they gone too far? On the contrary: At this moment The Surfers were the manifestation of a phenomenon that happens in physics all the time: When envelopes are pushed, the parallel lines of, say, method and madness, bend and distort, and at some point they are no longer parallel, at some point they actually intersect. Method and madness become the same thing... Madness becomes rational. The Surfers had reached that lucid intersection.

Ron Hier depicts "the lunacy" of Skinner and Jobe's fuel mixture: "They originally started at about 50% nitro but Jobe didn't like the (lack of) accuracy of the hydrometers. He thought they were a bunch of crap because they couldn't get the right mixture on them; you were never sure what it really was, so he said, 'If you just pour it out of the can we could eliminate that (uncertainty).' That was Jobe: Eliminate all the mistakes. So instead of mixing it and getting a bad mix he said, 'We'll run a 100%.'"

Another theory was that the beakers were too expensive for The Surfers' budget. Ironically, this is a rumor that Skinner and Jobe started themselves. It was really quite unnerving to see Sorokin gleefully pouring pure, undiluted nitromethane into the tank—all because his team couldn't afford any more beakers. Skinner expounds on the "no hydrometers" rule this way, "What we used to say was that we didn't want to break the hydrometer, but basically what we were trying to do was get as much energy out of the fuel as possible. Our game plan was about efficiency... to try and maximize the potential power that was available in the fuel. It took a long time to do that."

So what was the percentage? "100%," he answered. "Well not 100% but close... we had some stuff we put in there, y'know? We had some additives that took some percentage, something anybody could buy to stabilize things a little bit... in the neighborhood of 1 or 2%."

Jobe concurs about the percentage, but adds that the decision to run this outrageous percentage was strategic on a variety of levels; most importantly, it shrewdly negated The Surfers from falling prey to their own pranksterish tactics. "Since most of those guys could add nitro and kill their motors—we couldn't add any more because we already had the whole thing, right? We had it planned that you couldn't destroy the thing almost no matter what you did. The other guys would typically run 70 to 80% nitro and if you could get them panicked they would add another 5 or 10% and blow the thing up."

Yep... Despite their public image as oddballs who ran 100% nitromethane because all their hydrometers were broken, an image they helped cultivate themselves, in reality this cagey alchemy was another trump card for these wiseacre college kids from Santa Monica. It was a pearl of wisdom they had gleaned from their academic studies...

"I was going to college—mechanical engineering—and I just set about studying nitromethane," explained Jobe about what led to a witch's brew of pure nitromethane. "I would get the head of the chemistry department or whoever and get them all involved in what we were doing—and they'd cop a plea right away and say, 'Hey, I don't know how to do anything really, I'm just a teacher'—then they'd find out what we were talking about was going to get drug out to the starting line on Saturday night...So I'd say, 'Hey, you've got to keep me straight on the theory, I want to make sure I don't start deciding that gravity pulls from the side and get screwed up out there,'" he rhapsodized.

"So I set about studying how nitromethane worked," he continued. "The reactions, both when you burn it and when you detonate it and how they differ; what causes it to detonate versus burn; what attitudes increase or decrease the tendency to detonate. At that time there was a lot of literature out because there had been some train-car explosions and other unexplained explosions that happened with nitro so a lot of research had been done where they dropped

55-gallons drums of the stuff from towers and shot it with 50-caliber machine guns trying to figure out how these tank cars went up in, I think, Illinois.

"That was the basis of what made our deal run good," Jobe determined, "figuring out the nitro angle of it. And then figuring out how many BTUs were in 60%, 70%, 80%... Also," he proffered, "I was old enough to where I had watched the transition from gasoline to alcohol at the drag strip; when I was, say, ten years old I was watching 'em put together alcohol and gasoline—which don't mix, right?—so at the starting line one of the crew would come up and grab the frame of the dragster and start shaking it to mix the stuff up, and I'm watching this as a little kid and going, 'Man that's stupid. If alcohol is good, why not just throw the gasoline away and go with the alcohol?'"

Remove all obstacles in the path, eh?

"When we did our deal we were going, 'Why use alcohol? Let's just throw that shit away. That stuff doesn't make it go... It's just pollution.'"

Jobe's old man was a jeweler and his workshop became The Surfers' impromptu research and development laboratory. "We continued our experiments at my dad's factory in Santa Monica," he says. "He had some jeweler's lathes that we used to make all kinds of goofy nozzles. Do you remember in Science Class, Bernoulli's equation? That defines all the stuff you need to know to make a nozzle... Anyway, we made 'em look just like the pictures in the science book."

The "Kinetic-Molecular Theory of Gasses According to Jobe" is indeed the crucial element to The Surfers' success. Beyond that, it is also a blueprint on the mechanics of running a Top Fuel dragster—thirty years later. Outrageous nitro percentages, thin nozzles subjected to ludicrous amounts of pressure, and low compression are *de rigueur* for a contemporary fueler. But in '64, it was considered radical and suicidal. The Surfers debunked this as myth... by using a water faucet as a flow bench. Yes, a water faucet...

"We made us a flow bench out of a water faucet that had 60 lbs. (of pressure) which, at the time, was what most fuel injectors had. Ultimately, we made a whole fuel injector but then we found out that was stupid because then you don't get any contingency money from Hilborn or whoever. Why throw away contingency money? So we just used Hilborn, but we made all the nozzles—we were into 200 lb. fuel pressure but we never told anybody. We had little tiny nozzles, but lots of 'em, in order to atomize the stuff. You can't burn liquid," Jobe clarified.

"We found out that we could up the ignition's amps, we could take fuel out of it." Why less fuel volume? "All it's doing is flattening your wallet. The more you atomize it, the less you have to put in to get the same amount of burnable, combustible stuff."

The r&d at the jewelry workshop yielded a tangible, palpable difference between Skinner and Jobe's digger and virtually every other machine at the race track: That is, the way it sounded. Tom Hunnicutt explains, "Their car sounded like no other car. You could tell when it was their car. If there were 100 Top Fuel cars and they all sounded the same, their car was completely off by itself. Their car was louder than anybody else's and it had more fuel lines on it than anybody had ever seen." Hunnicutt says about their swift conquest of the fueler wars: "They were kicking ass and not breaking anything. It was the perfect team."

Skinner describes The Surfers' mechanical ethos this way, "Efficiency, reliability was important to us," he said. "Occasionally we had to take the head off or something. Occasionally we would break a roller tappet, occasionally we would lose a head gasket. When we ran the 64 cars at Bakersfield we didn't have any problems."

Because The Surfers were such a well-oiled machine and maintenance man-hours were minimal, this created ample opportunity for these free-thinkers to, uhhh, skateboard while the rest of the fueler guys were thrashing between rounds of competition.

"Skinner always had some skateboards to play with because we didn't work on the car a lot like everybody else did," Jobe says. To compensate for a lack of fiscal horsepower, the ingenuity of The Surfers manifested itself on the plane of psychological warfare; the boys occasionally deployed the skateboards as a weapon to combat their opponents' deeper pockets and cubic dollars.

As Jobe tells it, "On the way to the drag strip we would talk about 'What can we do to them today?'" he says. "'What weird thing can we lay on 'em?' in ways they wouldn't even figure out. We needed all the advantages we could get. A lot of the guys we had to compete against were well funded... The Lou Baneys and the Keith Blacks. All of those guys had really nice stuff. They had, like, new parts."

Jobe remembers, "... a Sunday afternoon race at Fontana. All the bad guys from back East were gonna show up," he says. "They were all puttin' the mouth on us in the press saying what they were going to do to us West Coast guys. It was about an hour's drive to Fontana from Santa Monica and we were talking and riding along and thinking, 'What should we do today? Let's not work on the car. We'll come down and pick up the car at the other end and while Mike and his girlfriend pack the parachutes we'll service the thing.' We could service the whole thing in about five minutes. We said, 'We'll push right past the pits and we'll put it right back in line and we'll get out the skateboards and we'll go torture 'em in their pit area.' So we did that—fortunately we didn't break any lifters or anything," Jobe remembers. "So we'd get the skateboards out. We'd go over and watch these guys (tear down) and we'd say, 'Man, you guys sure are smart; you guys know how to work on these things and everything. Man, you guys are good!' They didn't know what to think of all that. By about the third round one of these East Coast hitters said, 'Damn, don't you guys ever work on that thing?' We said, 'N-o-o, we don't work on it because we really don't know that much about it. We'd just screw it up, it's better just to leave it alone.' And this guy is like, '(*slowly*) What-the-fuck-is-this-all-about?' In the last round we got the mouthiest of the bunch, Bobby Vodnik, and we beat him and left 'em all shaking their heads.

"Nobody ever found about the mind games, because we never talked about it," he concludes.

****

To: Joe Buysee, Lansing Michigan
From: Mike Sorokin, Mar Vista, CA

Hi Joe,
We will NOT be at Union Grove until June 25th. You can bet we will be trying to beat the Goose, we haven't run the car for a month and I'm forgetting how to drive the darn thing. I hope your pal loses his buck. I think he will. We still have a few tricks to try.

I have been married for about a month. I like it.

```
top fuel wormhole
```

We are not worried about the strip conditions. The car handles good and it has two chutes. We actually made No. 1 on the Drag Racing Magazine poll for the West. We were very happy about that. We are planning on running the US Nationals.

We didn't get any color pictures in the article because our car isn't pretty enough.

You don't have to thank us. It's a pleasure to meet fans like you. I just hope our future performance doesn't let you down.

Well, I'll see you later.

Mike

******

"Sorokin was a real high-strung kind of guy, very nervous," says Tom Jobe. "He kept to himself and he loved to race." On a typical Sunday morning, after rendezvousing at the Red Apple, The Surfers would stop for breakfast whilst en route to San Fernando Raceway. Once seated, Jobe describes Sork's hyperactivity thusly: "Mike would be sitting there and he could not keep from bouncing his feet, jumping up and down and vibrating at the table.

"The guy was so high-strung that nobody could beat him at the starting line. And if you wanted him to be just a little bit quicker, you could just wind him up: You know, 'Mike, so-and-so was saying that their driver could whip you' and that would really make him vibrate. And if somebody actually pissed him off they could forget trying to beat him. I don't know if he went into higher revolutions per minute or what, but he would really be quick," Jobe remembers.

"He would just drive anything, but fortunately by the time we got rolling he was getting tired of all the coupes and roadsters and he wanted to drive something fast—and make some money too."

The biggest test of Sorokin's mettle transpired during the '65 UDRA meet at Fontana. During a semi-final heat the boys had blown the side out of the block. It was their only bullet in the entire inventory and until that moment, "it lived like Methuselah," according to Sorokin. But rather than pack it in, our heroes improvised. They turned the car on its side, jammed the piston all the way to the top of the bore, removed the dead hole's connecting rod, taped the crank journal and wrapped it with a hose clamp, taped cardboard (!) over the gouge on the inside of the block to keep from hemorrhaging oil and threw the pan back on. For the half-dead 392's swan song, they dosed the remaining 7 cylinders on 99%, fired it up, and Sork staged the discordant, vibrating wounded machine like nothing was out of the ordinary. Despite the frenzied thrash, Sorokin expertly cut a gate-job that was sharp as a switchblade, and was scarfing up asphalt in a discombobulatory pell-mell fashion until the entire backfiring mill detonated and went kablooey at the top end. They lost the match, but won the respect of the entire drag-racing community with that gonzo, anarchic attempt to win a $1000 purse. Sorokin got more ink than the event winner...

"When we got done with one of those deals, Mike would just look at you like, 'Is it time to go?' and he'd hop right in knowing full well that the whole side of the motor is made out of cardboard and silver tape. There was a hose clamp around the crank where a rod used to be," he concludes. "He didn't give a shit. 'Oh yeah, let's go.' He loved it."

As The Surfers' star continued to rise, Sorokin met Robyn Rains, a part-time trophy girl at the digs. "She is the best parachute packer I have," said Mike, "and it's nice to have a pretty girl to look at instead of all the racers."

Robin packed the chute at all the races, including the '66 March Meet at Bakersfield, an event that has been described as "the purest drag race ever." It was an absolute orgy, there were 102 AA/Fuel Dragsters entered in Top Fuel Eliminator that weekend. The Surfers outlasted 'em all—and for punctuation they set a National E.T. record of 7.34 seconds.

Skinner reflects on Sorokin's contributions to The Surfers' triumph at Bakersfield like a calculus problem: "You can't really pinpoint who does what," he reckons, "but in order to win some drag races the car has to be running, the driver has to be able to not only get the thing down the track but leave at the right time. Plus, after a while he got to where he could control the throttle, where initially what he used to go was start the thing up and put the throttle down.

"I remember one thing that he said at Bakersfield. We ran the first round and ran a 7.40 and he said, 'The track is really good, I think I can put the throttle down all the way on the next pass.' And he wasn't used to being able to do that. He definitely developed some finesse."

But it was a culmination of elements, including all that r&d on the jeweler's lathe. According to Skinner. "We worked a lot with our fuel injector—we evolved the fuel injector. Up until we won Bakersfield we never had a new blower. At Bakersfield we had a new/used blower. We were never on the cutting edge with expensive gadgetry."

But The Surfers' ken and karma transcended the limitations of their gear. It was their awareness that was "bleeding edge." Intuitively, if not intellectually, The Surfers knew that matter and energy was interchangeable and both are keys given to humanity to open any door we seek. The Surfers chose the door to the Kingdom of Nitromethane, whose sacramental temple was in Bakersfield.

In the Winners Circle at Bakersfield, the paparazzi went bananas, with flashbulbs bursting like asteroids during the Big Bang itself. It was glorious, with the bespectacled Skinner mugging for the camera in the reflective light bouncing off the Miss Hurst Shifter Trophy Girl's cleavage. Fame. Wealth. Top Eliminator. The Madcap Savants from Surf City put 'em all on the trailer. And as stars shone on Kern County that night, as oil derricks teeter-tottered off in distance, the grunions were running at a motel in Bakersfield: Mike and Robyn Sorokin celebrated their triumphs in a cosmic sense and their son Adam was conceived. All across Creation, The Surfers were shooting the curl. Finally, they had achieved a spiritual duty greater than themselves.

But at their zenith, The Surfers encountered a fork in the road. Skinner and Jobe were burnt on drag racing and sought new challenges. "Skinner and I could see that the only guys who were ever going to make a living in this deal were the owner/driver/operator: the Prudhommes, the Garlits's, the whatever," said Jobe. "You could see that it was already headed in the direction. We worked a lot of hours," he continued. "I went to school and had a part-time job and worked on the dragster. We were always just scraping by—and just barely. A lot of times we would show up to the drag strip with a crank that wasn't even balanced...Mike wouldn't be able to even see once he got halfway down the track the thing was vibrating so badly...He didn't care, 'Whatever...Let's go.'

"We told Mike, 'Hey, if you don't think that you have to do this for the rest of your life, why don't you look at it from the standpoint that we went out and did a bunch of wild shit, had a great time, kicked a lot of ass, took a lot of names and we're all in one piece and we don't have a nick on us. Let's just forget about it.' He said, 'No, I think I want to keep going. I like doing this.'"

Skinner says, "We were really able to walk away." Sorokin, however, was a different story. Sork was totally wired on driving a digger. Quitting the business wasn't an option.

Sorokin reflected in the Santa Monica Evening Outlook on his perpetual yen to kick out the jams on the drag strip. "I spent two years at City College studying electronics because I thought it was the thing to do," he said. "I found out this is what I wanted to do most. I think everybody has some kind of dream. This was mine and I'm living it. You can't ask for much more."

****

Hi Joe,

How are things in the armed forces? Drag racing is getting rougher & rougher. We ran at Irwindale yesterday. It took a 7.57 sec. to qualify in a 16-car field. We broke in the third round after beating Gotelli-Safford and Tommy Allen. My writing is bad because I am holding my month old son, Adam. Very good-looking kid.

Anyway, in about a month, I think I will be driving the Hawaiian. The new car we were building when we quit racing is almost finished and it is without a doubt THE best looking car in drag racing. Richie Bandel, from Brooklyn, bought the car. We all hate to see it go. The old car is still for sale.

Well, G.I. Joe, take care of yourself and good luck.

Mike

****

Sorokin's next gig was driving for another titan of engineering, Ed Pink, which lasted for a couple of months. He then drove for Blake Hill for a month. Next, he got the call when Roland Leong decided to campaign two fuelers, one powered by a Chrysler 392 and the other sporting a newfangled 426-hemi powerplant.

"Sorokin drove the 426 car," recalls Leong, "and we won the Stardust meet in '67 at Vegas." Keith Black was wrenching, Roland was cutting checks, and Sork was swapping pedals—a formidable collaboration on paper, but one that failed to set the world on fire in reality... It's not like they stunk up the joint, they didn't; it's just that this combination just did not crush like Black, Leong and Sorokin were all used to. When Roland downsized to one fueler, he went with Mike Snively as the driver.

****

Hi Joe,
How's things in the Army? Good I hope. I was very happy to have won in Las Vegas. The win was badly needed.
It doesn't take people very long to forget past accomplishments. I hope this won't be the only big win. The cars around here are unbelievable. We ran 7.26 last week and didn't qualify!
Keith Black is a pretty good guy to race with. He is plenty sharp. (My writing and spelling is terrible)
Well, goodbye for now, say hello to your mom.
Mike

****

Reflecting on the trajectory of The Surfers' endeavors, Skinner said, "It was kind of a curiosity, kind of an adventure to go on." His reward was the process and not the goal... "I've taken a different path in my life than most people have," Skinner said. "I'm interested in life-long learning and I'm trying to continually grow as a human being. My interests are much more spiritual and philosophical than trying to be famous or achieve something on a material level."

For Skinner, his drag-strip endeavors were informative on an almost existential level. "I'm sure that having the success (we had) did something for my level of confidence," he said. "It helped me realize that I could be independent and I could solve problems and solve them in a different way than the average person. I see myself struggling with.... structure."

Ironically, drag racing hipped Skinner to the structure inherent in the symbiotic relationship that exists between humanity, technology and a given environment. "Tom is the person who masterminded our combination for the engine," Skinner continues. "A lot of it really was kind of like a science experiment. It was nice recently that we were honored at the banquet for the Drag Racing Hall of Fame. I thought to myself, 'What if someone asks me, 'how did we do that?' I'm not really sure, but I know on some level we made friends with all the parts and we had very intimate relationships with each of the parts. In order to do that, you have to be able to look at the part and on an abstract level. You have a conversation with the part. You look at the bearings and the bearing kind of talks to you and tells you what it needs so it won't get hurt."

****

Hi Joe,

I was really saddened to hear about (name is illegible). He was a VERY nice guy.

I was layed off at work. They didn't appreciate my taking two weeks off to go to Bristol.

We didn't even qualify. A 7.35 in the first round was good enough, but a 7.40 in the second wasn't. Plus the engine melted a couple of pistons. That engine is extremely temperamental. Only 6 days to the meet at Lions. I hope Black does the right thing and performs some of his miracles. He was talking about using an Enderle injector. That's the only thing that hasn't been changed in the engine.

Well, I'll talk to you after the 15th.

Mike

****

In the waning months of '67, Sorokin was back at the strip, shoeing a somewhat generic slingshot under the employ of Bakersfield racer, Tony Waters. In their three races together, they went out in the first round of competition each time. Sorokin and Paul Gommi, a fellow SoCal fueler freak, had ordered a new digger and they picked up the chassis on December 29th. The two of them looked forward to the holidays to blow over so they could get the car ready for the new season. "I talked to Mike the morning before we went to race in Orange County, see?" recalls Leong. "And what he did was he just picked up a brand new chassis from a guy in Colorado I guess, at the airport."

This was the last race for Sorokin as a hired gun. With Gommi, he would now be owner/operator.

"He didn't like the car he was driving, but that was a ride, right?" Roland says. "He was going to start putting together this brand new chassis, he bought the chassis with his own money and he wanted to know if I had some parts that he might need to finish the car up. I said, 'Yeah, we'll talk about it. Then he asked me if I would be home Sunday…" Leong pauses when he remembers the weekend of December 30th, 1967 when the flaws in the clutch technology were showcased in a most grisly manner.

As Morton alluded to in *The Stainless Steel Carrot*, clutches had a tendency to pull the bolts out. After a few laps under maximum torque, the asbestos disks would periodically shred apart and would create a domino effect throughout the bellhousing. Ultimately, the flywheels cut through the aluminum bellhousing and the chrome-moly chassis like a buzzsaw through Brylcreem. This was one of those nights.

Tom Hunnicutt was sitting in the bleachers with Jim Boyd during the first round of eliminations. "Sorokin left the line and got about halfway down and I remember this horrendous metal sound. I remember looking straight down (from the bleachers) and as he went by, I remember seeing the light off of the top part of his helmet," recalls Hunnicutt. "The rear wheels had stopped—this was at 220 (mph) or whatever—and the front part of the car was gone." At this point the bolts sheared and the flywheel cut the chassis completely in two. Worse yet, the rear end seized and was freewheeling inside the rollcage at 218 mph. This forced Mike out of the cockpit. "He was half out of the rollbar. I thought to myself, 'Maybe he's trying to get away from it… why is he standing up?' About that time the tubes dug in and he started tumbling. And every time it went over, it was like a rag sticking out of a ball all the way down the drag strip, all the way to the end… It was the worst thing I have ever seen."

After the horror and the screaming and the god-awful grinding subsided, there was silence. Everyone on the premises was stunned. Some folks were literally in shock.

"We walked back to the pits," Hunnicutt continues, "and I remember Frank Pedregon was putting his car back on the trailer—and he was in, he was qualified. Jimmy was in denial and kept asking him, 'What hospital are they going to take him to? Maybe we can go see him.' Frank finally had to tell him, 'Jimmy, he doesn't need a hospital.' It was one of those things you don't forget for your whole life."

"Anyway, even in the staging lanes I talked to him a little bit about it (getting together on Sunday)." Roland recollected. "I guess as long as I've been doing this, I've kinda seen it all so to speak…But it's kind of an eerie feeling to just talk to a guy before he gets pushed down and the next time you turn around he's dead."

Once again, the universe shuddered because of Mike Sorokin. But this time it was from his passing. Sorokin's son was a year old. He vaguely recalls the phone ringing and hearing his mom screaming when she was given the news. It was perhaps drag racing's darkest moment, and at the very least, an ugly punctuation to the legacy of The Surfers.

****

April 11, 1968.
From: Roxanne Gibson (Note: Mike Sorokin's sister-in-law)
To: Pvt. Joe Buysee
Dear Joe:
I just finished reading your letter, it's so sweet and thoughtful of you to find time to write me, I know how hard it is to keep up with your letter writing. I don't know how you do it.

Joe, I just feel sick inside about all that goes on over there. I wish like crazy you American guys didn't have to be over there. I also received today a letter from our gal Robyn. She's fine and Adam too. They left for Spain April 7th.

That's too much about your license plate, my birthday is April 18th, so I'll be thinking about, "Roadrunner" except I'll be 28…wow, 27 years older than your car.

So long for now, Joe.
Roxanne

(Pvt. Joe Buysee died of a rare brain disease in December, 1970. Depending on whether you ask his family or the government, it may or may not have been related to exposure to exotic, strategic chemicals during his tour of duty in Southeast Asia.)

****

And The Surfers were this: They took the promise of America, tipped it over, and ran it out the back door. They chose their moment, took the trappings of our American Dream and manipulated it to their own ends, baby. And then they moved on because everything is ephemeral in the universal scheme of things, a theorem proved by Sork's shocking and profound passing. The memory of The Surfers and their exploits, however, continues to influence and affect everybody who was touched by their presence and anybody who saw them run.

In March of 1997, The Surfers were inducted into the Drag Racing Hall of Fame. Skinner didn't even know it existed. He showed up at a black-tie affair in striped two-tone red pants, a flannel shirt and a Panama hat. Jobe was equally perplexed. Ron Hier relates the following anecdote from the ceremony: "Like Jobe said, 'We did it and that was that—and now I'm in the Hall of Fame, I can't fathom it, how did this happen?' So I told him, 'You gotta look into it a little more and understand what happened to drag racing after you left.'"

But Jobe is nothing if not a crisp, clairvoyant thinker and he knows the perfect wave is rare, indeed. He saw that the parameters and the scope of drag racing would be narrowed into a diameter thinner than his own fuel nozzles, that the scope of something defined as unlimited would narrow into something quite finite. "Rules create a funnel," Jobe explained in very matter-of-fact tones, "and at the end this just creates red dragsters and green ones and blue ones." He continues to describe the inevitability of homogenization. "Rules end up defining the vehicle: The wheel base, the height, the width. The only thing left is the color," he said, "and that is taken care of by the sponsor. That's evolution." One hundred percent.

(*Originally published 1998*)

DRAG RACING IS MUCH MORE PUNK ROCK THAN ANY SLACKER GEN X SHITHEAD WITH AN OUT-OF-TUNE GUITAR

Yeah, Yeah, Yeah. I know, I know: You are young, beautiful, and you live in Babylon Hills, California, 90210. You are trying to get a handle on this Grand Guignol play aka "life." You are frustrated, misunderstood, beat up by the pain of being alive, and at the same time you are seeking out the proper mode of expression, the milieu that trims your foliage. You are seeking your muse, but at this point will settle for a job. Even that pursuit, however, is frustrating and futile. It seems that the kooky global economy means that the chirren' of upper-middle-class honky imperialism are lucky to get a gig at the local Brazier Burger (although one can immediately begin careering in the dynamic, engrossing, gravy-train fields of distressed property repossession, telemarketing, West L.A. parking enforcement, stuffing envelopes at the regional IRS depot, ad blahseum).

You are boxed into a corner. Blocking the only exit out of this dead-end lifestyle and cash flow cul-de-sac is a riot squad of non-inhaling, bleeding-heart liberal do-gooder politicians who are in cahoots with constipated "fiscal conservative" billionaire robber barons. Together, they are asphyxiating the job market, kowtowing to the whims of Alan Greenspan and the Federal Reserve, leaving the young adults of the U.S. of A choking on the exhaust fumes from opportunities headed down yonder way. Between NAFTA, GATT, and the Third World Population Bombs in the neighborhoods, not to mention the greed of ravenous senior citizens cherry-picking Social Security entitlements (with the yunguns providing the credit base!) until it's barren as the salt flats and I'm gonna grab my gee-tar and tell my troubles to the world! Ooh, you poor suffering, sniveling, shiftless, ingrate, trust-fund fuck…

I think I hear my bullshit detector ringing louder than a smoke alarm at an AA meeting. The truth is thus: the denizens of White Flight, California comprise of complainers, bellyachers, cable teevee fuckoffs, and pampered bourgeoisie bongheads, indifferent and/or oblivious to the fact that there is fuckall to give their dreary lives meaning. If there is something that can breathe some fire and moxie into the simpering spirit of this slice of failed humanity (and I maintain there is—read on if you dare), this society chooses to ignore it.

Perhaps because of the ubiquitous presence of teevee (both "interactive" and merely passive), kids today are bored, jaded, and unlike, say, our youth-gone-mad predecessors of the 1960's, not terribly motivated. They demand that their entertainment is served to them—they don't seek it out, and certainly do not create it. I know, I know: "Tell me what can a poor boy do, 'cept to play in a rock 'n' roll band." Oh god, not that shit, again—smash a fire extinguisher against my skull before I have to listen to another Silver Lake indie rock band regurgitate Paleolithic minor-mode rock riffs whilst some "riotgrrrl" vocalist atonally spews out whatever passes for vitriol these days (probably some half-baked rant against the vaguely monolithic White Male Power Structure, while we know that on L.A.'s Day of Reckoning—April 29, 1992—she had hauled ass out of the city on the I-10 East in her pre-owned Honda Accord, to be nestled safely in the confines of Mom and Dad's cushy condo at Big Bear. While her City of Angels burned like Dante's Inferno, she was channel surfing, a remote control device in one hand and a Diet Coke in the other, scrolling through the televised coverage on cable, hoping the darkies did not torch her band's rehearsal studio in Echo Park)...

Bullshit rock bands aside, these kids don't get a whole lot accomplished—at least nothing tangible or relevant to the human condition. (This is just my opinion, of course; I do not consider the creation nor the consumption of, say, the Paisley Dorktones' new interactive 10" Dolby CD-ROM (encoded in Bi-monophonic SurroundSound!) particularly interesting, exciting, fulfilling, or invigorating. I would rather watch a nitromethane-guzzling dragster explode and disintegrate at 300 miles-per-hour; now that's entertainment!).

(The whole notion of a "slacker" society, I'm sorry—I just don't get it. Not only to choose to blame our insufferable indolence on a lack of cash flow, resources, and opportunities, but to wear the insignificance of life in the 90's like a badge of honor... What? Tell it to the Serbs (now there is a resourceful bunch!) and the Croats, rivethead. We are privileged peoples, livin' large in the Land of the Eternal Sun.)

Yep, the kids of the 60's were some busy buckaroos. That's right: hippies were more ambitious than you! What with campus demonstrations, love-ins, extended holidays in Southeast Asia, multi-media slide shows projected on the likes of Nico and Edie Sedgewick, riots on Sunset Strip, and a whole lot of consciousness expansion—who had time to complain about the futility of existence?

If all that was not enough, there was another cultural renaissance occurring simultaneous to the Electric Kool-Aid Acid Tests and the Summer of Love. For, back in the day, the kids were also shakin' some action at the local drag strip. This was where the young gearheads displayed their gumption, bravado, and intellect. They showcased these attributes in machinery they crafted themselves (generally speaking)—contraptions that resembled a spaceship as much as anything else. These were formally known as "rails" or "dragsters."

"Drag strips," "rails," "dragsters." What the hell is drag racing, you may wonder? It is a socio-technological phenomenon that is louder, faster, and more primal than either grindcore or the Big Bang itself, that's what.

top fuel wormhole

Drag racing was born at the dry lakebeds and the abandoned military airstrips of post World War II Southern California, and these locations remain a staple of hot rodding. The mood and vibrations at these exhibitions of unbridled horsepower are very primal, chaotic, and apocalyptic. Despite the clouds of smoke and fire that might obscure the action, a message cuts through the haze and fumes–a message the gearheads and hepcats and kittens intuitively understand: speed is a metaphor for freedom.

The premise of drag racing is simple: two cars race in a straight line for a distance of 1/4 mile (1320 feet). The first car to the finish line is the winner. And although the premise is linear, by as early as the 1960's the approach to these contests became increasingly surreal, bizarre, and abstract. Drag racing became an art movement.

Aesthetics aside, miles-per-hour is the real objective here. And in order to satiate their voracious thirst for speed, speed, and more speed, out-of-control mechanical savants sculpt strange looking combustion-driven time bombs—y'know, "dragsters". To complement the car's unorthodox yet minimalist appearance, the motors and the fuel are equally exotic–your basic Chrysler engine is now supercharged or injected, and the fuel (the engine's blood) is either maximum octane airplane fuel, methanol, or the highly volatile nitromethane (a fuel classified as a Class A Explosive by the Department of Defense).

So how does this relate to the problems of the Age we live in? In an era of fiber-optic saturation, of sensory overload, of electronic bombardment, if you are not going to build and race a dragster, then what is a valid mode of self-expression? Going to USC Film School for six years so you can end up directing infomercials or rock videos (which are basically the same thing, now that I think about it) after deluding yourself into thinking you would create your generations' *On The Waterfront*, or *8 1/2*, or *Five Easy Pieces*, but hey man, if your career catches a break you can still direct a "Feature Film" (ooohhh!), like the sequel to *Reality Bites*—the working title is *Reality Swallows*—and in this film Winona Barrymore plays an affluent Melrose chickee reduced to a South Central crack whore after her hip lifestyle collapses due to her incompetence at the West Hollywood post-modernist coffee klatch/tattoo parlor/performance art gallery (where she worked as a curator's assistant until she was fired after summoning the rent-a-cops—played by Corey Feldman and Eric Estrada in *hil-ar-i-ous* cameo appearances—to oust Cher's conceptual artist/nouveau beatnik boyfriend from the premises when he shat on a lava lamp statue of Socrates—turns out this was just Act 1 of a "performance piece" that Mr. Cher had entitled "Judge Ito" (tragically, our young heroine mistook the "artist" for a common homeless guy defecating in the foyer); but to complicate the plot of *Reality Swallows* Congressman Sonny Bono—that's right, the previous Mr. Cher (as himself)—finagles a deft political power play with fellow Republicans Jesse Helms (Charlton Heston), Phil Gramm (Clint Eastwood) and Bob Packwood (Don Knotts) that destroys National Endowment of the Arts head honcho Jane Alexander (as herself) (this after this GOP Gang of Four uncovers evidence that Ms. Alexander green-lit the controversial "Ito" piece, forcing her to resign in disgrace); which then capsizes her lifestyle into a downward spiral that finds Alexander estranged from High Society and ultimately a street person, walking the streets of Compton, where she reunites with her estranged daughter—you guessed it, Winona—and the two of them pool their only marketable talents in Post-Reagan America, re-uniting as tag team of mother and daughter strawberries), or, a more realistic career opportunity (after depleting your parents nest-egg because you insisted they pay for your education)—yes, even more degradingly, you wind up schlepping as "production assistant" on a dubious gangsta' rap video, pampering that insipid no-talent "director" fuckwad in the "DreamWorks" baseball cap while on location at Florence and Normandy as AK47 recording artist MC Cinque lip-synchs his "catchy" militant anthem "Colonel Sanders is the Joseph Stalin of My 'Hood"? Do you really want to base your life on a career and a subculture as dehumanizing as all of that?

Another option, perhaps, is to start a post-punk rock'n'roll combo, but man is that tired.

And boring.

On the California cultural horizon, not only are there entirely too many indie rock bands and student filmmakers, there is an intolerable glut of twelve-stepper tattoo emporiums, performance art fanzines, and waitresses auditioning for a bit part on "Baywatch"...

```
top fuel wormhole
```

So what is a poor SoCal riot boy or grrrl to do? You want sensory overload? You want to rage against the machine, mall-breath? You want to blow shit up?

Well check this out: Drag racers blow more shit up on any given weekend than Timothy McVeigh's Michigan Militia, the SLA, and the Hezbollah combined. And they do it righteously. If you want to get radical then smash your television, get a job laying bricks (assuming you're not getting fat off your parents' morally dubious mutual funds) and sink all of your cash and free time into running a race car at the local drag strip. The hep thing about this endeavor, race fans, is that it's completely Karl Marx approved—Anyone can do it! It's totally DIY! You can borrow your granny's grocery-getter and run 'er down the ol' 1320–they have a class for you at the local drag strip (it's called "Stock Eliminator"). Or you can build your very own dragster from the ground up (or, if you aren't much of a backyard tinkerer, commission one from a professional chassis builder). An even doper scenario is to purchase an old front-engine dragster (most of these "rails" were built in the '60s), shoehorn betwixt the frame rails an early Chrysler hemi engine (recently liberated from an '58 Imperial rotting at the local Pick-Your-Part), and GO! man, GO! Whatever your decision, be it the more labor intensive and paycheck-siphoning dragster route, or the decidedly more financially-benign street-legal "stocker" or "doorslammer" reality, the drag strip has a place for you. But before you make your decision, remember the rule of "cubic dollars" which is stated as thus: "Speed costs money—How fast do you want to go?" If you want to go 200 mph in the 1/4 mile driving a dragster, it is gonna cost some dead presidents—but nobody at the drag strip is gonna tell you you can't run a race car. Only you can tell yourself that. To put this another way, in drag racing all limitations are self-imposed. Drag racing is of, by, and for the people (kinda like punk rock used to be, remember?).

Sure, you could get killed in a race car... but to hear you Gen X'ers tell it, you got nuthin' to live for anyway because life is banal and pointless, right? So dumpster that hopelessly out of tune guitar, quit your feeble "low-fi" indie-rock band, (or drop out of art school, ripcord on your nowhere "modeling," "acting," or "documentary filmmaker" career), shitcan your trendoid threads, and get some grease under your skin. Live the American dream, goddammit. For about the same amount of money and gumption necessary to "self-produce" and press a 45 Rpm 7" record, you can create beaucoup smoke, noize, fire, and thunder by running a race car at your local drag strip. This is a much more noble and glorious mode of expression than being in a band. (Indeed, one would be hard-pressed to find a more boring and pointless outlet for the psychosis and angst of life than banging out more tired barre chords on a shitty guitar. Punk rock, actually music altogether, died with Sid Vicious. Show some respect for the dead, will ya? Quit.)

So if you are mad at the world, or just plain bored—quit yer yappin'. You and your buddies can pool your resources and run a dragster. Just get it together, or shut up and fuck off. The local drag strip is the only logical cafe society for today's real dissidents; it is our Tiananmen Square. It is a place where the stakes and envelopes are pushed (things explode and people do get hurt), and that always makes for interesting art. And until that Silver Lake "riotgrrrl" climbs into a maximum-horsepower dragster, I will consider her pose as a tortured artist completely innocuous, irrelevant, and rather pathetic.

(Originally published in Bikini Magazine)

MURPHY MAKES HISTORY AND MARCHES TO GLORY *(excerpt)*

Goodguys 39th March Meet, Famoso Raceway, March 13-15, 1998—Wam! Bam! Wallakazaam! What a rootin' tootin' drag race! And it all boiled down to two dragsters—the venerable awe-inspiring, Jim Murphy-shoed *W.W. Two* machine against the immaculate fresh-outta'-the-oven *Foothill Flyer* slingshot (shoed by "Nitro Neil" Bisciglia)—squaring off for all the prestige and glory that is part and parcel of winning Top Fuel Eliminator at the March Meet.

The box score will reveal that Murphy did a masterful job of negotiating *W.W. Two* past the traction-deficient bottom end and posted a quarter-mile elapsed time of 6.26 seconds to defeat the *Foothill Flyer*, which began spinning the tires about 300 feet into the run whereupon Bisciglia prudently shut off the engine while savoring runner-up status. But this doesn't do the March Meet justice, and once the smoke cleared after this final pair of fuelers BA-WHAPPED their way down the quarter mile, it was hard not to reflect on a March Meet that was absolutely loaded with awe-inspiring moments...

Indeed, there were so many highlights, this writer is at a loss as to where to starting litanizing them; The beginning would be the logical place to start, I guess, but that was Friday night's qualifying session, which was rained out—no epic moments there. But come Saturday, it was hellzapoppin' right off the bat, courtesy of Denver Schutz. Schutz catapulted his way to the #1 qualifying position of the 8-car show (where he stayed) with an early shut off (!) 6.01 @ 209 mph, a run that was as smooth as a baby's keister to the $1/8^{th}$ mile—in fact, the Eirich, Schiller & Schutz *Ground Zero* fueler clocked an unprecedented 203 mph at half-track—before tire shake forced Schutz to abort the run. "Everybody's accusing me of shutting it off early all the time, falling on my ass in order to save (the engine)—well, I'm tired of doing that! But it was vibrating so bad down there, the tires were so far out of balance, I couldn't see," said an exhilarated Schutz, champing at the prospect of driving it out the back door come race day. No matter how stunning, however, this wasn't the run that sent the railbirds into orbit. Nor was the #2 shot by Mike McClennan, who wowed 'em with a rod-tossin', crank-charrin' 6.09 @ 218...

The biggest damage to the spectator's and participant's sense of reality transpired during the final session of Top Fuel qualifying late Saturday afternoon, when the wheat began to separate from the chaff. Amongst the 21 cars entered, the list of non-qualifiers as of Saturday afternoon would make for a pretty decent hot-rod harvest unto itself: *Champion Speed Shop, Fuller & Dunlap, Pure Hell, The Birky Bunch,* the *Foothill Flyer, W.W. Two, Steiner & Berger* and others were all in line to get tickets to Sunday's dance.

Dunlap punched his ticket early, clocking a 6.15 at 216 mph, which enabled the *Mike Fuller Motorsports* machine to enter the show—and also kept him out in front of Butch Blair's barrel-rolling *Fugowie* fueler which was doin' the monkey at 180 mph through the lights and playing pong with the guardrails while upside down. (Butch was okay... the once-gorgeous race car was actually fairly intact except for a missing rear wheel and slick, an obliterated set of front tires, a bongoed blower set-up and an inch or so of chrome-moly missing off of the top of the roll cage... yikes! Suffice it to say, Butch, who is an excavator and contractor when he ain't running a Top Fuel dragster, operated very little heavy machinery the rest of the weekend; in fact, nothing more strenuous than a blender. Doctor's orders!)

More high drama manifested when "Nitro Neil" attempted to qualify the brand new Stirling-chassied *Foothill Flyer*, which arrived at engine czar Ken Castagnino's shop at 6 am the previous Monday morning—sans motor. It had been a tumultuous, topsy-turvy week for Neil, car owner Pete Jensen, engine donor Ron "Pro" Welty and the rest of the *Foothill Flyer*'s "Free Mexican Air Force," as they thrashed on the dragster for five days, ultimately towing to Bakersfield without having even fired the engine.

More than one member of the nitro cognoscenti raised an eyebrow in disbelief as the FMAF worked like an Alabama chain gang to finish prepping the new car, only to smoke the tires during their first two qualifying attempts. All that overtime paid off, however, as Neil silenced the non-believers with an in-the-pocket 6.37 at 224 mph, a clocking which prevailed for 8th and final position on the eliminator ladder.

Once the euphoria of Bisciglia's accomplishment was digested, the place went absolutely ballistic after the *W.W. Two*'s subsequent benchmark performance, the obliteration of the 250 speed barrier, as Jim Murphy turned a time of 6.25 seconds @ 250.00 mph. What makes this feat even more startling is the notion that is was all a mistake... "It was a little unexpected," said *W.W. Two* czar, Jim Herbert. "We tried to soften everything just to get down the track—we weren't in the program—the new combination (Mastodon aluminum heads) seems to be making a little different power curve."

Herbert's driver describes this momentous run as kind of a turkey—at last initially. "I held the brake, it was a screwed up run. it was real doggy off the start." After Murphy let go of the brake handle, the tires started spinning again and the car veers toward the guardrail, so Murphy grabbed the brake again! "It was really screwed up," Murphy reiterates. But all this tugging on the brakes loaded the motor *REAL GOOD*... when Murphy finally let go of the brake at about 700 feet into the run (while heroically hugging the guardrail) the motor was makin' bacon like Farmer John on disco biscuits... "It was pullin' and pullin' and pullin'," said Murphy later. "I was gonna run it right to the light—I wanted to make sure we got in. We didn't want to be sitting out."

"I don't like a lot of speed; speed hurts things, luckily it didn't this time," Herbert revealed. (Actually, further evaluation proved they had hurt a main bearing.) "He got a little disorientated down there," Herbert continued. "The car was still moving at half track on him, he kind of lost where he was at and when it did hook up it started to haul ass." Herbert tersely doled out praise for his driver: "He drove the wheels off of it; we're here to be in the show. I'm not a very good loser."

(*Originally published in* Drag Racing USA)

JIM HERBERT R.I.P.

MARCH 3, 1999—It is with great sorrow that I report that Jim Herbert, majordomo of the *W.W. Two* AA/Fuel Dragster, passed on this morning.

Details are still forthcoming, but apparently it was heart related. The timing of his passing is somewhat ironic because his health had been sketchy for years, but he really seemed to be getting healthier lately.

I was discussing benchmarks recently with some Internet bleacher bums and some folks mentioned the 6.000 that Ted "the Bad Lieutenant" Taylor recorded in the *W.W. Two* car as a definitive moment in drag-strip history. We would be remiss to mention that Herbert's hot rod was the second slingshot in the 5's. He also tuned his latest driver, Jim Murphy, to that 250 mph moon shot at Famoso.

I had the honor of "getting next" to Herbert during the course of my drag strip journalism endeavors—which is to say he would return my phone calls. Straight up, nobody commanded my respect more than this man—and I have had the pleasure of meeting a plethora of both abstract and forward thinkers in a variety of mediums. Herbert, however, had really been in a groove for the last decade or so. It was a real privilege to meet the man as he truly hit his stride.

One of the most epic sights in drag racing was watching Herbert snap the ground wire off the mag and *WHAPP! WHAPP! WHAPP!* the mighty, beastly *W.W. Two* fueler would awaken with a roar. Herbert would point the driver (Taylor, Gary Ritter, Murphy) into the beams and with these few graceful and economic hand gestures he would let everyone gathered around the starting line know exactly whom they were reckoning with.

"Epic." "Graceful." Hey! We should all hit our marks with such dignity and panache. Jim, the drag strip community will be poorer without your presence. You were truly a hero, whose penchant for setting racers and race fans on their ear was matched only by your humility and modesty.

I can't tell you how happy I am for you. You had the opportunity to shine like a diamond, but you were never ostentatious. You will be missed.

(*Originally published in* Nitronic Research)

"W.W. TWO" IN BAKERSFIELD TEAR-JERKER

Goodguys 40th March Meet, Famoso Raceway, March 13-15—It was perhaps the most poignant final round in the history of the sport...

Facing off against "Wild Bill" Alexander for the honor of Top Fuel Eliminator at the Goodguys March Meet was the *W.W. Two* AA/Fuel Dragster, the defending champs, who were sans their esteemed point man, Jim "the Lizard" Herbert, who had passed on to the Great Flow Bench in the Sky a mere ten days prior, a victim of a heart aneurysm.

Herbert died with the secrets of his tune-up still locked in his noggin. Defense of the March Meet title was left to his surviving teammates (who were ambivalent about campaigning the dragster in Herbert's absence but were persuaded to go racing by Herbert's widow, Cheri) and their ability to unlock and decipher the secrets of a complicated matrix of nozzles, weights and measures that comprised the blown-Chrysler-on-nitro tune-up that had been taken to the grave. Befitting of a man of his stature, the winner of Top Fuel Eliminator at the March Meet was also the recipient of the Jim Herbert Memorial Trophy.

During qualifying, the chances of driver Jim "Holy Smokes" Murphy and the rest of the *W.W. Two* team transforming their appearance here into a proper wake seemed remote. After three qualifying attempts, they anchored the bump spot with an elapsed time of 6.23, far off the pace set by "Swingin' Sammy" Hale in the *Champion Speed Shop/Juxtapoz* Chevy-powered fueler, who had rocketed to an unprecedented 5.87 at 232 mph to snare the pole position.

(As a parenthetical to Hale's benchmark—"We're going to bypass the .90s," is how "Swingin' Sammy" prophesied the run—bodacious manifold pressure kicked out both the ingress and egress lines of the oil system, creating a geyser of Torco that lubricated the left slick like a banana peel on a back-lot sidewalk. As an oil-blind Hale fought for control of his 230 mph Valdez, jettisoned oil actually doused the driver in the next lane, *Circuit Breaker* hot shoe Howard Haight, who was busy swapping lanes—not once but twice—with the caroming *Champion* machine. To reiterate, in addition to Sammy, Howard Haight also received an oil bath… from the digger in the other lane! Howard, who has cut his teeth on a variety of mean machines including the infamous *Pure Heaven* AA/Fuel Altered, said it was the scariest ride he had ever taken.)

Despite the performance of the *W.W. Two* machine being well behind the curve of Sammy Hale's moon shot, during eliminations kismet, providence and perspiration intervened on behalf of Herbert's survivors… Murphy began the afternoon by zipping past Gerry Steiner, 6.11 @ 215 mph to Steiner's charging 6.13, 242 mph. (As a consolation, Steiner's boisterous assault on the lights stood for Top Speed of the Meet.) In the semi-finals, Murphy upped the ante with a 6.09 clocking that dropped Denver Schutz's trailing 6.29. (Note: *FTN* would be remiss in not mentioning Schutz's first-round opponent, Jack Harris in the Dale "the Snail" Emory-tuned *Nitro Thunder* dragster; these guys qualified 2nd at a rollicking 6.04 but had traction problems against Schutz. . .)

On the other side of the ladder, however, Alexander, shoe for Frank "Root Beer" Hedge's *Mastercam* AA/Fuel Dragster, was living like Little Lord Fauntleroy… During qualifying, Alexander posted a career best elapsed time at 6.08 (accompanied by a speed of 222 mph). Surprisingly, for all the accolades of a lifetime performance, this netted the *Mastercam* team the unenviable #5 position on the elimination ladder and pitted Alexander against "Swingin' Sammy" Hale. But in eliminations the *Champion* team made a strategic mistake as the Chevy put out a cylinder or two, lost and regained traction and sashayed to a losing 6.54 against Bill's superior 6.17 at an impressive 234 mph. Despite an aggressive clutch set-up, fate continued to bless Alexander in the semi-final round of eliminations. His competition, Rick McGee in the *Tedford, Hester & McGee* entry, appeared en route to an easy victory as the Mastercam machine struck the tires on the launch and limped down the racetrack. At 1000 feet, however, as McGee was all alone ten yards from the end zone, he fumbled, striking the centerline cones and was disqualified. McGee's transgression left Hedge & Alexander with the uneasy task of playing Snidely Whiplash to the *W.W. Two* team's Dudley Dooright...

Indeed, as Hedge emerged from the undulating clouds of tire smoke en route to his tow vehicle and was informed that he actually had won that heat, he was noticeably shaken and appeared rather distraught. "This is Herbert's race," he said, moments before regaining his senses and cranking up both the nitro percentage and the lead on the magneto.

Despite any perceived trepidation concerning spoiling a Cinderella story, the *Mastercam* machine was loaded like an elephant gun in the final round. The motor was as loud, over-the-top and boisterous as it has ever sounded. The burnout was particularly deafening. As "Wild Bill" pulled 'er into the beams, the blower straps caught on fire due to a leak out of the left header bank. Starter Larry Sutton (of Lions Drag Strip fame and an absolute Timelord of the Xmas tree) doused the flames with a fire extinguisher and motioned Bill into the beams (!); the blower straps caught on fire again and Sutton hit the extinguisher once more before giving Alexander the kill sign. Sutton then wheeled around and held up one finger to Murphy, signifying a solo shot to victory. It was a touching coda to one of the most emotional weekends in drag racing as crew members gathered around Murphy and the *W.W. Two* machine in a semi-circle, most of whom raised the right hand and the air and extended their index fingers in salute to their fallen leader. As Murphy popped the parachutes at the culmination of a 6.23, 208 victory lap, railbirds, racers and bleacher bums were openly weeping.

In general, the event was a slam-dunk success. The staging lanes, bleachers and porta-potties were all filled to capacity. Moreover, the impromptu tribute to Jim Herbert was as inspired as it was implausible. But the success of *W.W. Two*—in spite of the absence of their fallen leader—begs this question: When was the last time you cried at a drag race?

(*Originally published in* Full Throttle News)

THE CHAMPION SPEED SHOP'S TOP FUEL WORMHOLE

A Concentric History of the World's Quickest and Fastest Chevy on Nitro...

"Man from outer space or man trying to get there? No, he's not an astronaut, but he drives a dragster just fast enough to go into orbit. The man is Sammy Hale, driver from South San Francisco who here displays his new fireproof driver's suit which he donned Thursday after arriving at Quad-City Drag Strip for the World Series of Drag Racing. The suit features an airtight aluminum coating, is washable and costs about $150. 'It's worth it,' Hale said. 'Have you ever seen a man burned in a dragster?' Hale boasts the world's fastest and quickest Chevrolet, having turned better than 180 miles an hour"
-- East Moline Dispatch.

As experts in the fields of quantum physics and cosmology ponder the notion of whether or not Time Travel is possible, they would do well to study the South San Francisco-based phenomenon of the *Champion Speed Shop* AA/Fuel Dragster, a race team and machine that has torn a hole in the fabric of what we know as the third and fourth dimensions of space and time. They have claimed the honor of being the world's quickest and fastest accelerating Chevy on nitro*... it claimed this honor first almost forty years ago and has reclaimed the honor now.

Beyond these claims, its one constant is the occupant of the dragster's cockpit, one Sammy Hale. That's right, race fans: The same guy who, quick as an outhouse mouse, steered the *Champion* car to 180 mph in 1962 whilst putting the Chrysler-powered machine of Top Fuel potentate "Big Daddy" Don Garlits on the trailer at Half Moon Bay, was the same guy who rocketed to 239 mph last year in another Champion-sponsored front-motored fueler. (To ratchet up the *Champion* team's claim to utter domination, "Swingin' Sammy" Hale threw down a real moon shot at this year's March Meet in Bakersfield, turning an unprecedented 5.87 at 232 mph to claim Low E.T. of the Universe.)

But before we get into what launches Sammy into orbit, first we must set the way-back machine to intersecting co-ordinates of a) 1957, and b) Colma, California in the general vicinity of what the locals call South City. A sleepy, perhaps moribund town sandwiched between the Pacific Ocean and the San Francisco Bay, Colma is known for its abundance of cemeteries (most specifically the Holy Cross, Cypress Lawn and Olivetti graveyards on Old Mission Road), and is a town where the population of deceased surpasses the number of actual living, breathing taxpayers. It is where South San Francisco brings their dead. And in a charming paradoxical spin on the carbon cycle, some theorize that the preponderance of mulch and compost that seeped into the topsoil is why the "South City Hot Rod Experience" came alive here...

Although the creation of this scene was the local hot rodder's Big Bang, its origins were certainly humble enough. "One day on the school bus I noticed this little shack on El Camino Real in South City," Sammy Hale remembered. "There was this nice little '34 Ford pickup out there all painted red and striped and everything. A couple of more times we went by and noticed a sign and the next thing you know it's like, 'Hey, there's a speed shop there.' It was a big interest to see what they had so you'd go in and buy three feet of red plastic plug wire."

Indeed, in the beginning Champion Speed Shop was nothing more than a shack, operated by a stocky, entrepreneurial President of the Pacers Car Club, Jim McLennan (aka "the Smiling Irishman", aka "Papa Bear"). McLennan had married into the Padilla family, who ran one of the oldest plumbing companies in San Francisco. Patriarch Joe Padilla had been credited with rebuilding the town after various earthquakes and natural disasters. Although not necessarily blue bloods, they were pillars of respectability—and then their daughter up and married the scourge of society, a street racer. To appease the in-laws, McLennan began an apprenticeship as a plumber during the day. But at night and into the dawn, as Jim was burnin' black rubber through the billowing fog that would shroud the slick, lacquered asphalt at either the Great Highway or Brotherhood Way, his true ambition became as clear and as obvious as the clanging bell of a cable car: Set up with the proper piece of real estate, McLennan had a hunch he could parlay his passion for hot rodding into a living. And yes, his was a post-WWII success story worthy of a Horatio Alger book. But the real windfall of the Champion Speed Shop was more than just the fruits of commerce. It engendered not only a cottage industry but some would maintain a friggin' art movement. A renaissance. But not without some support from the in-laws...

"My grandfather went down there and said, 'If you're going to do this, you need to do it right,' and they built this 10,000 foot tilt-up," is how Bobby McLennan explains the Padilla family's role as patron of the arts. The new building was on Mission, around the corner from the wooden shack the Padillas considered an eyesore. The new shop was a magnet indeed, attracting scores of young and not-so-young motorheads. And when not wrenching, polishing, fabricating or hanging out, the more mature gearheads would adjourn to Malloy's, the watering hole where all the grave diggers and speed demons bellied up to slake their thirst and buy each other rounds. McLennan said emphatically that, "Every drag racer in the country has had a drink at Malloy's. Kalitta, Garlits, Prudhomme, they were all there." Beyond the touring professionals, guys with names like Bruno Gianoli, Don Cordo, Andy Brizio and others helped make Malloy's a sort of satellite office of Champion. In '58, between discourse at Malloy's and the Speed Shop, McLennan set up a partnership with "Terrible Ted" Gotelli (aka "the Goat") to run a couple of rails, with Jim doing the driving. In addition to driving Gotelli's Chrysler-powered *Organ Grinder* digger, McLennan also campaigned his own dragster. Jim's dragster was a wicked Scotty Fenn Chassis Research job, powered by a bored and stroke 364 c.i. mouse motor ("We started out with a 327 and put a 1/4" stroker in it," Jim recollected) that Weber Cams dubbed the "World's Fastest Chevy" in their trade ads.

Eventually Jim extended the forks and campaigned the Chassis Research car as a gasoline-powered twin-engined deal, a combination that lasted about six months. Regardless of the setup, the machine was the pride and joy of the neighborhood, attracting kids on bicycles every time they heard the motor turn over. Likewise, impromptu test-and-tune warm-up runs down Old Mission would wake the dead and bask the patrons at Malloy's with a comforting mist of nitromethane that would secrete down the esophagus and seemed to complement whatever poison the bar patrons were imbibing at the time. In a commercial sense, the dragster acted as an attraction for the Speed Shop, where the scene continued to flourish and explode. McLennan partnered with Don Smith, a horse trader very adept at working the phones (and nowadays the proprietor of High Performance Distributors). Paint shops, body shops and other speed shops began to punctuate the landscape of this once-somniferous town, and McLennan branched out as a race promoter and speedway owner/operator. Out of the germination of his ideas, money and resources a renaissance flourished. Half Moon Bay, Cotati Drag Strip, Champion Speedway, and Fremont/Baylands Raceway were all under the Jim McLennan umbrella. The ripple effect was pretty profound: Andy "the Rodfather" Brizio, who mounted all the wheels at Champion's shop, was the starter at Half Moon Bay. He then set up shop as "Andy's Roadsters" out of one of the side doors at Champion and then, ultimately, splintered off into his kit-roadster empire.

But beyond providing an opportunity for the regional craftsman, the new speed shop gave the local kids who were 21-or-skidoo'd out of Malloy's a sense of place as well—it was the center of their universe. "Every street racer, every guy who would go to the drags was there," is how Hale describes the energy at Champion in the 50s. "It was just a whole spectrum of personalities and man, there were a lot of crazy mothers who used to race on Wednesday and Friday nights out on Brotherhood Way. The nickname for the place was 'The Zoo' because there were so many people that came and went, it really was like a zoo. It was a social club."

Ahh, but it was more than a club; it was a friggin' hot-rodders' skunk works, a proving ground for innovation, both in performance and in safety. Although in 1956 Jim Deist began mounting braking parachutes on dragsters down in L.A. and shortly thereafter began experimenting with aluminized firesuits, these innovations had yet to catch on elsewhere and were not readily available. But due to higher and higher-velocity dragsters running out of real estate while attempting to brake to a stop in the truncated shutdown area at Half Moon Bay, necessity became the mother of invention for McLennan. He envisioned stopping the dragsters with a parachute. The r & d for this device was utter slapstick, and transpired in the back of Ted's pickup truck: "I had gotten over to Robert's Surplus over in Oakland and gotten a great big 18' foot ribbon-type chute for $12," said Jim. Ted stomped on the gas and hauled ass own past Malloy's and Jim, who had been hanging on for dear life, tossed a parachute anchored to the tailgate like a kite. "Well, it deployed," chuckled Jim, "but it tore the tailgate right off of Ted's truck." The bar patrons roared with laughter and the undertaker pondered future supply-and-demand, but the safety device caught on locally after McLennan scratched his noodle and settled upon a triangular ribbon chute. Security Parachutes from Hayward had a new customer. "It worked great—we sold a lot of them," McLennan asserted.

Furthermore, two horrific digger fires on subsequent weekends at Half Moon Bay forced McLennan to consult with the safety crews at SFO Airport and brainstorm on fire protection. McLennan appropriated use of what the airport workers called a "proximity suit," a silver aluminum suit that would retard fire for about half a minute—a lifetime to a drag racer. Insisting on field-testing these devices at Gotelli's shop led to a literal trial by fire and more slapstick: Gotelli doused the shop floor with gasoline and set it ablaze, McLennan endeavored to sprint through the flames. Once in the inferno, he became somewhat disoriented, stumbled and fell before crawling out of the conflagration. "I didn't get burned," Jim related, "but we knew then that it worked. We did some goofy things..."

But even with distribution networks being what they were in those days, the concept of the proximity suit caught on amongst the dragster drivers. It could be argued that Deist came up with these safety features first, but the efforts of McLennan ratcheted up their profile in Northern California at the very least. And anybody who wore a proximity suit definitely remembered it. "You'd put that thing on and you'd itch for a week," Sammy Hale said.

Unfortunately, the proximity suit wasn't the only irritant chapping hides. Both the Goat and the Smiling Irishman were strong-willed and hard-headed Type-A personalities—maybe a collision of egos was inevitable. But when Gotelli replaced Jim with another driver one weekend, "It really pissed me off," McLennan remembered, not realizing until years later that Gotelli had Jim's best interests in mind—the Goat could not bear to see Jim hurt, what with a wife and mouths to feed. Jim recollected, "I thought he was pissed off at me for some reason and I hadn't done anything wrong." Their communication chasm bloated; in 1960 Gotelli and McLennan split as race partners, and Gotelli started his own speed shop down at the south end of Colma, a shop that still thrives in the original location.

After the split with the Goat, the onus of raising a family and the tremendous responsibility of spinning plates with his growing business interests convinced McLennan to hang up his proximity suit. The job fell to the cool-as-a-cucumber Sammy Hale, who was old enough to vote but not old enough to patronize Malloy's. Hale reminisces about being tipped about the vacancy in the Champion cockpit this way: "I used to hang out there all the time and buy stuff and just hang around. Don Cordo said, 'Hey smart-aleck, how'd you like to drive the hot job?' I said, 'What hot job?' He said, 'The dragster—the one in the back.' I said, 'Yeah man, haul that mother out here, I'll make a pass right down Mission Road,' right? He said, 'I know McLennan's thinking about getting a driver because he got a bunch of oil dumped on him in the Goat's car and his wife don't want him to drive no more.' It was between myself and another guy who got ruled out because they figured he was dropping bennies and smokin' grass or something. I figured I got chosen because I got hip to the fact that they were looking for a driver and I started hanging around more and offering my services working on the car."

In November of '61, Sammy was called up to bat. "I kept my nose clean and didn't insult anybody," he reckoned. "The twin-engine gasoline setup went by the wayside and Jim decided to go back to running a single engine on fuel. Finally, I got a chance to take a ride in it. He told me drive it just as hard as I can, as far as I can. That's what I did. After 3 or 4 passes I finally got it through the lights under power on a real slippery track up at Cotati." After losing his cherry, "Swingin' Sammy" was thrust into the limelight. "The car was already installed on the *Drag News* Mr. Eliminator list," he recalled, "and we challenged Romeo Palamides for the #5 spot. That was my introduction to driving in competition, a Mr. Eliminator deal. Fortunately, I won.

"Things moved along pretty fast," Sammy calculated. The Scotty Fenn rail was supplanted by a new 114" Kent Fuller chassis with a body by Wayne Ewing, gorgeously scalloped like a space aged aluminum crustacean. At 1130 lbs. the digger was light as a half-ton of grated Parmesan. "The first time we ran it we went 180 with it," Hale said of the new car's debut in January of '62, "which was a milestone. Nobody had ever gone 180 with a Chevy before." Before the final round of eliminations, Jim and Sammy had a pow-wow about harnessing the horsepower and creating more traction, a conversation that underscored McLennan's savvy.

"We were having a real hard time making the car handle correctly because it was wheelstanding," Sammy recalled. "Jim just said, 'Hey, instead of just going up there and standing on it, frying the tires and popping the front end just do the best you can to get the revs up real high like on a normal run. Just drive it out but don't give it all the clutch.' In other words, slip the clutch. I drove that sucker out there smokeless and ran a 8.36 at 180 mph."

Their partnership quickly blossomed into a mutual-admiration society. "Sammy was always so quick on the line and the car was so light," McLennan reminisced with pride. "We always gave them a holeshot..."

But there was more to the combination than an exquisitely-tuned mouse motor in a light-weight frame with a lickety-split speed demon pushin' the pedals: There was also the South City attitude, a philosophy of battle spawned by the pique between the Smiling Irishman and the Goat. "After Gotelli opened his speed shop, that's when the war really started," confirms Bobby McLennan. Both in business and in competition, Gotelli and McLennan, former partners, were now hotheaded enemies and cross-town rivals. This created a certain strategy that infiltrated the drag strip, a South City-style code of conduct. When a driver from South City pulled up to the starting line, the boxing rules of the Marquess of Queensbury were ignored and the values of Patton and Rommel were substituted. It was sand-in-your-eye and chivalry be damned. It was the art of the burndown and these starting-line mind games were as crucial a component as any cam grind. Hale diplomatically explains the ethos this way: "I think in a particular circumstance, the hotter that car gets, the better it is. 'Hey, the thing is just now warm enough to run.'" Or melt.

In July the McLennan/Hale collaboration was on a real jag, accentuated by dropping Connie Swingle in Garlits's digger at Half Moon Bay. Hale turned a speed of 180.36 miles per hour with an elapsed time of 8.40 seconds, while the Garlits machine recorded 187 miles per hour but still lost with an elapsed time of 8.50. The spry, lightweight Chevy dragster that was enabled by the shrewd and inspired mind of "Irish" McLennan as well as the graceful-yet-insidious moves and reflexes of "Swingin' Sammy" continued to outmaneuver the competition...

"By October of '62 we had won quite a few meets and had worked our way up to #2 (on the *Drag News* List)," Sammy remembered. They raced Vance Hunt for the #1 spot but dropped a two-out-of-three in Houston, TX. "It was trying to wheelstand and there was no guardrail. I didn't want to drive the car off the side of the drag strip. I lost the first round, won the second, lost the third because the car was wheelstanding. Kent Fuller was there and was very adamant about not putting any weight on the front end. I was virtually begging him, 'Just throw another 15 lbs. or 20 lbs. on the front of this thing, I can beat this guy out of the hole so bad he'll never catch me,' but he wouldn't do it. So we lost." It was a pivotal, crushing defeat that precipitated the parting of Hale and McLennan.

Their eventual separation was hastened by McLennan taking on more business ventures, and by the time he opened Champion Speedway in 1963, a roundy-round track out by some projects near Candlestick Park, he was overwhelmed. "He couldn't do both, so he decided to stop running the fuel car," Bobby said. After McLennan brokered a deal with Masters & Richter to assume operation of the dragster, they put a Chrysler between the framerails—and "Big Bob" Haines in the cockpit. "I was flat-ass broke, living at home with my parents. I got a job as a crank-grinder, which was my trade," Hale recalls.

But withdrawal from running a digger was more than either "Swingin' Sammy" or the otherwise bodacious Papa Bear could handle. McLennan adopted a pre-owned Fuller car and hastily prepared it for the Winternationals in '63. Once again, Hale was the shoe, but Sammy felt the car lacked the smooth-yet-tight composition of the original model and said it handled like a monkey on delirium tremens and the disc brakes were equally dicey. Citing that the car pulled through the beams because the brakes wouldn't grab firmly enough, Sammy red-lighted against "TV Tommy" Ivo in the first round.

"Jim was one of those guys that if he lost or got beat he wanted to throw $1000 on the top of the barrel and race again." After the ignominious loss to Ivo at the Winternationals, they towed up to Fremont to race the next day. The trip led to a big argument. "I finally told him, 'Hey, if you think it's cool to run it like that, you drive it.' He got in the car and tried to drive it and got beat by some guy in an unblown Chevy," Sammy said wistfully. "That torpedoed our relationship. Actually, that was the end of the small-block Chevy thing until, well, forever—until it was resurrected in 1985."

"Sammy is like a third son to me," Papa Bear said recently, giving credence to the notion that sentiments once expressed in the heat of battle are no reflection of his true familial feelings. (Moreover, before the end of the decade Jim and Ted also resolved their differences.) And beyond his family and friends, McLennan had a reputation in the business world as being proud yet humble, and authoritative yet giving. Ultimately, his temperament helped create a successful professional environment and an outrageously quick Top Fuel car. But slinging rocks at the Chrysler-powered Goliaths of Top Fuel began to lose its appeal and became increasingly frustrating. In '64, Champion quit racing the digger. The McLennan family concentrated on race promotions, real estate ventures and food concessions. As he matured, Bobby went after a business degree. His younger brother Mike eventually went into plumbing.

Hale, meanwhile, continued to terrorize the drag strip. He drove Vic Hubbard's unblown Chevy; then the Chrysler-powered cars of *Masters & Richter, Gotelli Speed Shop* ("I damn near made the down payment on my house from what I made on that car"); and finally, Jesse Perkins' *Cow Palace Shell* AA/FD.

But as drag racing entered its post-Altamont era, Sammy recalled, "I was really burned out on it." The time was right to split the scene; historians reckon this was when drag racing entered its dark age; when it began to implode, succumbing to the forces of its own gravity, collapsing upon itself like a black hole... Cotati and Half Moon Bay went away; Champion Speedway was torched twice (and is now a vacant lot out by the projects of Hunters Point). The Goat ran a rear-engined fueler well into the disco decade, but for all practical purposes the South City nitro scene vaporized. The *fin de siecle* was complete when Jim closed the Speed Shop in the late 70s. Poof. The drag strips were now a ghost town and the speed merchants of San Francisco were Lost Planet Airmen, indeed... As the implosion of energy continued, it seemed like the drag racers would never get spit out of the ass end of this dark star...

But according to the mathematician Gödel, time is like a river, which meanders around stars and galaxies whose gravitational pull creates whirlpools. In other words, time can wrap itself into a circle. Anyone walking along the direction of rotation would find oneself back at the starting point—which is where the *Champion Speed Shop* AA/Fuel Dragster found itself, apparently, when its saga resumed gingerly in 1985. Bobby McLennan describes the Rebirth thusly: "Roy Brizio contacted me and said, 'You know this nostalgia thing is going crazy, we ought to put one of the old cars back together.' I said, 'You're nuts.' We were going to do a restoration which I didn't work on at all, and present it to Dad." Brizio enlisted the help of his high school pal, Tony Bernardini, who was running Four Star Automotive and the whole she-bang became less an episode of the Twilight Zone and more like an Andy Hardy movie. "It didn't have an engine," Bobby explained, "Bruno Gianoli had an engine, a blown street-rod engine with fan belts—it didn't even have a blower belt." At a birthday bash at Malloy's, the restored dragster was push started on Old Mission Road. Once again, glasses were held high and across the street the dead rolled over in bewilderment. The Champion boys were going racing again—it's just that nobody told the driver. "I hadn't talked to Sammy in fifteen years. I was nine years old when he was driving" said Bobby McLennan. "He didn't seem really excited about it..."

"I guess Bobby thought he didn't know me well enough, right?" Sammy said. "I remember distinctly when Roy called up and said, 'Hey, we built this car and we asked Frankie Silva to drive but he's got problems with his girlfriend or something, he doesn't want to do it and we'd really like you to drive it.'" Sammy was ambivalent indeed. During the 70s and 80s, in order to both get his ya-ya's out as well as make ends meet, he had turned to bicycling Tour de France-style, as well as grinding cranks for the sports-car crowd. The last thing on his mind was drag racing and his initial response was tepid. "I said, 'Okay as long as it's not going to be a throw down competitive thing.' He said, 'All you got to do is smoke the tires, you don't have to drive too hard. We're just doing it for a show and to get everybody back together.' I borrowed a firesuit, I had no inkling I would ever drive a race car again." Nor was he the only member of the team caught off guard—they didn't even have a toolbox. "I had a briefcase with our tools and spark plugs in it," Bobby remembers sheepishly.

Soon thereafter, they not only got a toolbox—they got serious. The Brizio recreation of the Scotty Fenn model was campaigned for show as a twin-engined tire smoker by Mike McLennan (now driving the *Smith & Maher* AA/FD, as well as the infamous *Mob* AA/Fuel Altered), while Sammy shoed a remake of the Fuller slingshot fueler. By 1990, after experiencing a modulating wave of success and failure, the Champion team and its small block Chevy-powered digger was dominant again against a battery of iron Chrysler 392s. But their success just agitated the competition, who at this point included salty speed merchants like Jim "Lizard" Herbert, Don Argee, George Wulf, Jesse Perkins and Mike Fuller, all of whom had stepped a little too close to space-time bending whirlpools that sucked first and second wave nitromaniacs into running a Top Fuel car one more time. Indeed, these guys found themselves with an opportunity to showcase their intellectual prowess (again!) and settle some vendettas that had been festering for decades... None of these folks considered this a stroll down memory lane; this was an opportunity to correct history's glitches. So they stepped up the hardware: And just like the first go-round, aluminum hemis began to infiltrate the framerails of the front-engined fuelers. The Chevy faced utter obsolescence. The hemi crowd continued to run quicker. The Chevy digger's performance stagnated. It got ugly for the South City bunch. "We had to catch up," Bobby said, who was tuning the car with Bernardini and Sammy. "We were grenading parts left and right." More ominously, he reveals that, "we were as close to putting a Chrysler in the car as it's ever come."

Due to its shape, running a Chevy on nitro is a real mother of a thermodynamic conundrum. A true Chevrolet engine is defined by the geometry of the ports, particularly the exhaust. In this traditional design, there are two ports that are siamesed together and their proximity to one another invariably creates entirely too much heat. With nitromethane used as a fuel, the heat factor rises exponentially, thus creating a tuning nightmare, as the fuel-flow parameters must operate within a razor-thin margin of error... too lean and not only do parts melt but the potential for a harrowing hydraulic situation (ka-boom!) looms large; conversely, if the fuel flow is too rich and the head gaskets are jettisoned, more boom-boom. The atomization of the fuel is crucial as well; "you can't burn liquid," as the man said but with the Chevy you need a specific volume of raw, unburnt fuel to cool, soothe, salve, and bathe the exhaust ports of the heads. Ergo, the cam grind is a delicate factor—nay, every friggin' factor is delicate and precarious. And if it ain't perfect this baby ain't nuthin' but a not-so-smart bomb.

Which is to say, the challenge is making the sucker flow properly after subjecting 'er to a whole lotta fuel volume it wasn't designed for... "Our biggest drawback is the heads. I don't care what you do to it, the very best small-block Chevrolet head, with the siamese exhaust ports, comes to about 65 percent of the Chrysler head (in volumetric efficiency)," Bobby said. Then he confessed that, "I was getting pressure from my family (to run a hemi) who were saying, 'You know, you are working too hard,' But there were pieces of the puzzle that just didn't make any sense—a little bit in the fuel pump, a little bit in the clutch, a little bit in the mag. And then all of a sudden..."

```
top fuel wormhole
```

"The Chevy is not as heavy as a Chrysler," is how Hale described Champion's advantageous method to its madness, a metallurgical marriage of a steel block with Brodix aluminum heads. "Instead of having a car that weighs 1800 or 1900 lbs. with a 450" motor, we use a 400" motor (and we) weigh 1675 or '85. We wound up with a fairly low compression combination and that was because the people that supplied us with certain pistons, they came as low-compression and we wanted to run. We thought, 'Let's just work around that.'"

The low-compression gag required more mag and more can, a mathematic equation that really appeals to Sammy's sensibilities. "I always figured the best way to build a bomb is to combine a ton of spark and a ton of fuel," he said after posting a mind-boggling speed of 239 mph last April. Hale may or may not have ever read the *Anarchist's Cookbook*, but it's no secret that the McLennan-Hale-Bernardini tune-up on the *Champion Speed Shop* fueler is gloriously apocalyptic, a notion punctuated by the occasional kicking out of head gaskets on the big end (WHOOOF!), which oils Hale in a blowtorch of fire making the whole endeavor that much more dramatic. Despite the flare-ups, the little Chevy continues to go rounds which means that after every win light, it's crunch time in the Champion pit area.

"You've got to wring that little Chevrolet out, so there's going to be more maintenance," Bobby confirmed. "And they're tougher to work on." Which means that the between-round exploits of the *Champion Speed Shop* crew is as completely over-the-top as the performance of Sammy and the race car itself. Invariably, between rounds some mighty gonzo and maniacal thrashing on the mill commences by Champion's motley consortium of Irishmen, Eye-talians and beatniks—it is a veritable rainbow coalition of asses and elbows orchestrated and choreographed by both Tony Bernardini and Bobby. "We need a couple of Latinos and a couple of gays and one lesbian to be acceptable in the Bay Area," Sammy mused about the chaos. "Then we would have a CALTRANS crew."

Perhaps the diversity is another intangible that has turned this Chevy into an absolute rocket ship as well as a sentimental hit with the railbirds, not to mention an angle that recently helped procure the patronage of *JUXTAPOZ*, an art-damaged Kustom Kulture 'zine that has coughed up some cash to ensure the car continues to make laps. "It takes a lot of different personalities to make a successful business run and it's the same thing with being a successful racer," said Bobby. Of his driver, Bobby relates that, "Of all those personalities you have to deal with, his is certainly unique." Which is why he was hired (again)... you would have to be somewhat different to want to go though this life sitting aft of a nitro-burning Chevy mouse as it winds through the traps at maximum velocity. And just as importantly, you have to dig the challenge...

"There is a limit to what this motor will take because of the port size and the valve size," Hale explained. "You can only pour so much liquid and air through that hole." Gödel said something similar about the volumetric efficiency of the wormholes in space-time—an equation that Hale isn't entirely comfortable with. "I don't bullshit anybody," Hale said after setting Low E.T. at the California Hot Rod Reunion in November. "I'm an old man, I shouldn't even be doing this." Perhaps. But Einstein would ask "Swingin' Sammy" rhetorically that in a Top Fuel wormhole, uhh, a dragster driver's age is relative, isn't it?

(Originally published 1999)

THE CRASH, BURN AND RESURRECTION OF A WORKING CLASS HERO

The "Wild Bill" Alexander Interview

This story is one of growth, transformation and alchemy as metaphor. Defined as "a medieval chemical philosophy having as its asserted aims the transmutation of base metals into gold," the process of alchemy involves the charring of metal, a procedure that the man who came to be known as "Wild Bill" Alexander witnessed repeatedly from the cauldron of a cockpit. Indeed, nobody has encountered—and dodged—more molten metal than the bold and angry prince who answered to the name "Alexander." Every trip down the drag strip was a potentially explosive exercise in metallurgical sorcery, which saw the alchemist himself grow and mutate from Hot Rod

Hooligan into hell-bent Speed King and Conqueror to, finally, Elder Statesman of the Nitro Wars.

Alexander began his ascent into adulthood with a bad mojo. As a dyslexic schoolboy from a broken home, Bill sought comfort and camaraderie in the Bel Airs, one of the many ubiquitous car clubs that sprouted up in SoCal during the 1950s. Concurrent with leaving home at 16, he finally found a field he excelled in—and a potential outlet for his prodigious anger: Speed.

His buddies talk about Alexander's precocious aptitude for wrestling with a hot job. "He was racing my '34 Vicky and it had a 3-speed on the steering column," one Bel Air member remembers. "The gearshift lever broke off in mid-shift and he never even blinked. I was riding in the passenger seat and I couldn't believe it. He just tossed it aside and continued shifting with a nub on the column."

In one of the great symmetries of the era, the unsavory street racing favored by the Bel Airs thrived in an impromptu arena that was nothing if not a civic embarrassment: the concrete banks of the Los Angeles River. Traditionally, rivers are florid metaphorical tableaus upon which life and culture flourish. Think of the Nile and its fertile lands which gave rise to the Pharaohs of Egypt, among them Alexander the Great. Then think of a narrow piece of muck and concrete that serves no larger purpose than that of a glorified drainage ditch. Yes, although it is known as the breeding ground of nothing except perhaps a case of dysentery, the L.A. River gave rise to the career of "Wild Bill" in the same way that the Nile enabled a rampaging young Pharaoh also known as Alexander to conquer entire empires.

At the concrete delta, Alexander's reputation grew while outrunning not only car clubbers but also the fuzz. One night, Law Dogs surprised the river-bed drag racers and attempted to broom the juvenile ne'er-do-wells into paddy wagons. The hot rodders peeled rubber and commenced to scattering like excited particles in a science experiment. Forced to improvise, Alexander resorted to scampering in his coupe like a coyote up the dusty bridle trails of Griffith Park and up into the Hollywood Hills. . .

The chaotic, dirty gear-jamming of the L.A. River ultimately yielded to properly sanctioned speed contests at El Mirage, Bonneville and San

Fernando Raceway. While operating a drill press during the week, the drag strip was where Alexander's star shone brighter still. Part working-class hero, part ultimate cockpit chimp, "Wild Bill" was subjected to and rode out the effects of imperfections in tire technology, as well as structural, metallurgical and thermodynamic failures. But he survived the frequent bouts with carnage in style: Shoeing Ernie Alvarado's *Shudder Bug*, Bill stood down the notorious and fabled *Greer Black & Prudhomme* AA/Fuel Dragster for Top Eliminator at Lions December 8, 1962, a dragster eliminated by only 7 other drivers. After crashing at Fernando in '63, he returns to the strip and, under the aegis of horsepower monger Jim Brissette, is newly christened "Wild Bill" Alexander as he sets Top Speed of his career in his first lap back. Later he sets Top Speed of the Universe, arguably at 202 mph, and then indisputably at 205.

Occasionally back in the 60s the drag racing press referred to Bill as Alexander the Great. This was apropos, as the precocious terror who became king of Macedonia at the prime age of 20 had an insatiable appetite for destruction and decimation. "Wild Bill" similarly had a scorched-earth policy. For reasons he wouldn't understand until much later in life, he was anti-social, misunderstood and kinda' mad at the world. Nobody escaped his agitation: competitors, officials or even teammates.

But, heck, after leaving a wake of wanton bloodshed and genocide, even Alexander the Great eventually mellowed and could be found dancing nude at the tomb of Greek poets. And after retiring as a journeyman in 1971, as the sport of drag racing took a turn Bill wasn't comfortable with, Alexander returned to the drag strips at the turn of the '90s with the genesis of California's front-motored "Prostalgia" Top Fuel wars. But his comeback is distinguished by the same jones for speed that characterized his first tenure in the hot seat; moreover, it is enhanced by a kinder, gentler demeanor and a new lust for life. Indeed, as runner-up at this year's March Meet at Bakersfield, while driving for "Root Beer Frank" Hedge's *Mastercam* AA/Fuel Dragster, Bill posted his career best elapsed time of 6.08 seconds.

*****

So some of the guys in the Bel Airs tell me you used to race on the L.A. river bed.

Alexander: Oh yeah (*nonplussed*). Generally on Friday night. At the time I didn't haven't a car. My buddy, Gary, had his '34 Victoria. Stan had a '57 Chevy—brand new—and we'd go down there and race with Tony Nancy, Floyd Lippencott, Jr. and Tommy Ivo, and all these guys and just street race in the river bed. It had this green slime down there so we had to find a spot with the least amount of green slime in order to race. Whoever's side had the least amount of green slime won, usually.

Then we went to the River Road—which is Forest Lawn Drive now. We'd get 4 or 500 spectators down there, pit areas, the whole thing.

But it was more than just the L.A. River. It was Glenoaks Blvd...

Alexander: When we were street racing there was a Frostee (Foster's) Freeze where everyone hung out. That's when I had my '34. You'd park yourself and if some guy came by with a hot car, there was a signal right there. He'd have to stop and you'd just pull out next to him. You'd race down Glenoaks as far as Brand Blvd, turn around and pull back into the Frostee Freeze.

How did you make the leap from street racing and running from the law into climbing into a digger?

Alexander: My brother had built a '41 Willys to run the lakebed (El Mirage). He got drafted and left the car at home. Of course, I wasn't supposed to touch it but instead I—whoop—took it out to the lakebed. It was kind of a dog; it ran 127 mph. A friend of mine said, "Let's get the rulebook and check it." We looked at the rulebook and we could take a 265 Chevy and de-stroke it $1/8^{th}$ of an inch and get it down to 259 inches, put a blower and an injector on it and we could run it in the same class, C/Altered. We did. The record at the time, if I'm not mistaken, was 129 and we took it out and ran 155. Just shattered it. Then we went to Bonneville and ran 172 and then it took back to El Mirage and ran 181—in a '41 Willys coupe that went everywhere but where you pointed it. It was the most ill-handling thing—of course, I didn't know any better because I had never driven anything out there.

After El Mirage one day, on the way back we went to San Fernando to run it and Ernie (Alvarado) was there. The next weekend they came and said, "Hey, you want to go to Long Beach?" Ivo runs 8.99—it was the first 8 second time (on gas)—in a dual engined, unblown Buick. Ernie, who was a roundy-round guy, went, "Oohh, I like this." The next weekend they came by and said, "Hey, you want to go to Long Beach again? And how would like to drive a dragster?"

When I was 14 my brother-in-law, Marty Elvehoff, had a slingshot altered that he was doing body work on at his house. I sat in it and I told myself, "Someday I'm going to drive one of these." So when Ernie asked, I finally had the chance. So we go to Kent Fullers' and we start building an aluminum body for it. We go down to the river road, fire it up and we had put the main jets in backwards. It was trying to hydraulic the motor. I'm down there trying to turn the fuel shut-off valve on and off, trying to make it run and it goes Ka-Blooey! and kicks the rods out of it—steel rods! We oiled down the river road... never even got it to the race track.

That had to be a portent of things to come.

Alexander: Oh yeah. So we build a new motor for it, we're getting ready to go to the races at San Fernando, loading the car up and the phone rings. Ernie's dad had just died. Obviously, we didn't run. That lasted almost a year. Ernie and his dad had just gotten close—it just devastated him.

Oh no.

Alexander: Finally, we got around to running it. We take it to San Fernando, I leave the starting line and you talk about a shock. It probably went out about 400 feet and I'm off the throttle, out of it, dead player. Get down to end and the guys come down and ask, "How was it? How was it?" I said, "Aw, bitchin'." Lying through my teeth... *ly-ing* through my teeth. "You want to make another one?" "Yeah!" Lying again. We go back and cool the motor down (we were running on gas), make the next run, go about 700 feet and the comfort zone is gone—I'm petrified—CLICK! It ran 145 or 147 and I'm making the turnoff and I'm thinking there is n-o way I will EVER get this thing to the end of the track.

A blown Pontiac on gas?

Alexander: A blown Pontiac on gas. Probably at that time, the most state of the art car built—Kent Fuller built it. So after the second run, they come down and ask, "How was it?" "Bitchin'! I loved it!" Still lying through my teeth. "You want to make another one? "Yeah, okay… *(under his breath)* Oh, God. . ."

We go back and r'n'r the thing, cool it down. We go up to make the last pass. The gas record at that time was 168 mph and it turned 165 mph—and I got it down to the end. I shocked myself. Doing that convinced me that I could do it.

Were there any other pivotal moments?

Alexander: Well, shortly thereafter I met my first wife. The only reason she went out with me was because I drove one of those cars with a parachute on 'em. We got married soon thereafter. So now I'd ask Ernie, "Are we going to run the car this weekend?" and he'd say no. This went on four or five weeks in a row.

What had happened was Ernie didn't want a married guy driving for him. He didn't want the responsibility. So he pulled the plug on me and put Tommy Ivo in. Tommy drove it that winter until the March Meet.

Was it still a hobby at that point or were you able to actually get some grocery money out of it?

Alexander: It was strictly a hobby. But after the March Meet, the car sat in Ernie's garage for four months and I got the brilliant idea to tell him, "Give me your garage, give me your push car, give me your trailer, give me the race car and I will turn it into a Top Fuel car—with my money, it won't cost you a penny." Duh. Dumb idea, right? I didn't have a pot to piss in, I'm married with one, soon to be two kids. He said, "Okay." So every penny I could beg, borrow and steal went towards converting the injector over: new nozzle, new barrel valve, all that stuff so we could run it on fuel. Edgar Hugglebuss and I went out to Long Beach every Saturday night and that thing would go 200' and it would turn right. So I'd get out of it. Edgar said if he had insurance he'd drive it. Right. That really pissed me off. So I told him, "I'm getting this (expletive) down there. It's either going to the end or it is going to crash—one or the other, I don't care anymore." So I legged it on down there and about the 300' mark, it turned right and I turned left and it went right through it. It did the same thing on every pass I ever made with that car. It was just one of those idiosyncrasies. From then on we went down for a long time and set Top Time or Low E.T. and then we'd get beat. Until a 32-car showdown there where we went and beat *Greer, Black & Prudhomme.* That was our first win and it seemed like we almost couldn't get beat after that. Until it crashed.

So from late '62 and into '63, you were among the elite fueler guys.

Alexander: None of us felt that way. At that time we were a bunch of kids having fun—a bunch of kids who knew we weren't going to live past 35. With Ernie's car, I never took a penny, although it made a ton of money.

So you didn't quit your day job at this point?

Alexander: It never dawned on me it could be possible. All the money went into the racing account which Ernie ended up keeping after I crashed. But after that I always took 33%. I did not drive for anything less.

Tell me about the crash.

Alexander: Mickey Thompson saved my life. The very first time we tried to run at Long Beach the inspectors looked at what was one of the first over-the-head hoop rollbars and they didn't like it. So they called Mickey on the radio and he said, "If you put two bars halfway up the rollbars down to the rear-end mounts, I'll let you run it." So we put two "sissy rails" on it. That's what prompted the body to be designed the way it was. Ernie hated those sissy rails so much.

Lujie Lesovsky (Indy car builder) built the body up on the sides and into the parachute pack to hide the sissy bars. He said, "I can't just stop here," like most of the guys did.

So you're saying this actually precipitated the design of, say, Stellings & Hampshire.

Alexander: Ernie's car was something that everybody went off of and made better. Ernie's car was kind of boxy. The *Greer, Black & Prudhomme* car was a little slicker—it looked a little smoother and nicer. Everybody smoothed 'em out, but Ernie's was the first of its kind.

Until that Sunday at the Pond in April of '63.

Alexander: Right. In those day we ran 15 or 16 pounds of air in the rear tires. We made the first run and broke the track record—mile an hour and E.T. Came back for the first round and instead of 15 or 16 we ran a pound less. "If that was good, this ought to be better." Same thing, Low E.T., Top Speed, track record. Come back the next round, it's a pound lower. So screw it: "If that was good, this ought to be really good." Went out and did the same thing. Come to the final round and one of the last things I remember is that we were another pound lower. My theory is that the tires finally got so low that it spun the wheel in the tire and at half track started spitting tire out and kicked the right hand tire off, blew it up, it drove it into the dirt, nosed in about 1000 feet and ended up clearing the flags over the finish line and then all hell broke loose. It just dug in and catapulted. Flat out, it blew a right tire.

After it catapulted, it came apart like a cheap watch. The front end broke off, the engine took off. People told me that the chutes came out when it was 20 feet in the air. When I got stopped, my hand was still on my shoulder like I had pulled the chutes. They did a magnificent job of getting me out of the car. Dave Wallace and Harry Hibler (track personnel) saved my life. Harry looked at me and said, "Goddammit, don't you die." I rolled my eyes back in my head and he said, "You son of a bitch." He thought I had died. They hauled me off to the hospital—we called it the butcher shop. Meanwhile, a friend of my wife's called her and said, "You and Renee can come live with us." My wife said, "What are you talking about?" "I just saw on teevee that Bill got killed out at San Fernando."

(silence)

Alexander: Yeah, heavy stuff. Ernie's damn near dead—he's in shock and was in the next room.

Besides that dark day at the Pond, how was it getting the "Shudder Bug" down the strip?

Alexander: That car taught me everything I know today. It was an evil car—I didn't know that at the time. At that time, it was state of the art. But it was an evil little bastard. It taught me how to feel the car, rather than let the car act and then I react. It taught me to turn the wheel before the back of the car ever reacted. It taught me to be ahead of it—to feel the car. Ernie's car taught me so very much—but it also taught me that life is very precious.

Maybe that's the car they should use in the drag racing schools. So when you came back, that was the advent of "Wild Bill"?

Alexander: When I first drove again I went faster and quicker than I ever went in my life.

Out of the box?

Alexander: Out of the box. I was worried that I would have this big flashback where I was upside down and on fire. It didn't happen, I just legged it on through there like it was no big deal. I don't remember the guy's name who was in the tower, but he said, "Oh, that's old 'Wild Bill' for ya'." I got stuck with the name.

This was with Hippo (Everett Brammer) and Jim Brissette, right? How did this partnership come together?

Alexander: Hippo went to Jim Brissette and said, "Would you put your motor in my car if I get Bill Alexander to drive for me?" He said, "Sure." Then he asked me, "Would you drive my car if I get Jim Brissette to put his motor in the car?"

We started out with a 354 and would smoke the tires, went to a 331 and would smoke the tires, and finally ended up with a 300-incher and the thing ran good. We could finally control the horsepower. But through all of that Jimmy decided, "Screw this." He ordered a brand new Woody Gilmore car, 144-inch-long come-catch-me-throw-me-down-top-of-the-line, with the engine about 3 inches off the rear end. It didn't have immediate success. Fastest car in the world for maybe two years, quickest car in the world for maybe four months.

The reputation was that the car would stay together for maybe three rounds.

Alexander: It would haul ass in qualifying. The first round nobody wanted us; second round everybody wanted us because they knew the rods were coming out at half-track. It was because Jimmy was making so much more horsepower and the car worked so good that it worked the motor that much harder. It would have main bearing problems, which became rod bearing problems. Jimmy tried everything—we drilled the main caps and had extra lines going into the main caps—and then the fingers started pointing. "Bill is driving it too hard." For the last eight months it was finger pointing, not by Jimmy so much, but by his friends and people at the races. Yeah—we're running 206 and a tenth of a second ahead of the field sometimes and "he's driving the car too hard."

What was your deal with Brissette?

Alexander: 33 percent, bottom line. I packed the parachute and drove.

The consensus was that Brissette wouldn't settle for anything but big numbers.
Alexander: Exactly. Blowing the engine up and catching it on fire—that didn't bother me. Blowing the rods out, getting oiled in, I'm okay with that. Ernie's car, every run we ever made, I got oiled in. But then we started blowing blowers off—this became rather serious. Actually, it became very serious.

We went to Fremont one night and whistled the sucker down through there, get about 900' and *ka-blooey*. We split the blower right down the middle. Come back, put the spare on it, go out there and whistle it through… *ka-blooey*. We split the blower right down the middle. Some guy who had already qualified goes over and pulls the blower off his car and goes "*plink!*" "I want to see you guys run over 200 mph." Jimmy throws that sucker on the motor, run it down there till' about 1100 feet, it sneezes and splits that blower. Somebody else walks over with another blower. Etc., etc. By the final, we leave the starting line, I've got the other guy covered and the thing is really hauling ass. I'm thinking, "All right!" And I'm whistling down there… Ka-blooey! It goes off. The blower lifts and comes back and hits me right between the eyes. The entire blower and the injector. It falls in my lap, it pulls my hands off the wheel and into my lap. This all takes place in a millisecond. I lift the thing out of the car, throw it out on the cowl, grab a hold of the steering wheel and I'm still trying to drive. There is oil on my goggles—they are all cracked by now. I take one hand off, wipe off my goggles. "Okay, I'm still fine." The blower goes, "clink, clink, clink" hits the tires, goes back in the air and hits me right back in the eyes again. This all sounds like bullshit, but it went "boink, boink." I went, "Aww, s-s-h-h-it." It hit the tire again, came back and hit me in the face and that is the last thing I remember until the ambulance guys were taking me out of the car.

When I became conscious the first thing out of my mouth was, "Did I win?" "No, you lost." "Aww, s-s-h-h-it." It ripped my finger from the knuckle down and split my nose from my forehead down. It was going, "*phffflltt. . . phffflltt. . . phffflltt.*"

And it was more of a mercenary deal at this point?

Alexander: If it hadn't have been for drag racing, I wouldn't have been able to have a wife and raise two kids. I worked during the day and I made more on the weekends than I did during a whole week. I was able to take care of my family and provide for them much better than I ever knew.

Who did you drive after Brissette?

Alexander: I didn't drive for a couple of years. Then Bob Sbarbaro called me from San Francisco. I would commute—all expenses paid. Plus 33 percent. I started driving for him but we didn't get along. Bob was very outgoing and loved everybody. I was very withdrawn and really a homebody. (At this point) I did racing for a living—not because I enjoyed it.

So it would it be safe to say that you enjoyed being in the cockpit, but not socializing.

Alexander: The only thing I liked about racing was driving the car. As far as socializing, I didn't do it. Maybe people got the wrong impression of me. But that was me and has been me—until not long ago.

I couldn't tell you why I was the way I was. I didn't know any different; I didn't know any better.

Why were you so mad at the world?

Alexander: I had a shitty childhood—a gawd-awful childhood. Walking the streets when I was 7 or 8 years old. *(Details deleted at Alexander's request)*. I hated the world and I was an angry, very upset young man who took my anger out on anything or everything.

But driving a fuel car had to be the ultimate release.

Alexander: It was the ultimate release, but as soon as I got out of the car the anger came back. It was a lousy way to live. It ruined my first marriage.

With a co-efficient of drag racing.

Alexander: Not really—that's what I thought. But in hindsight, I ruined that marriage. I was a pissed off young man who didn't know why he was angry. I didn't realize this until six or seven years ago. I have been trying to turn my life around for six or seven years.

top fuel wormhole

Isn't it interesting that the front-motored fueler thing has come back and you have a chance, perhaps, to undo some things?

Alexander: This is where you are exactly right. This is where I have a chance to make up for a lot of the bad things I said and the bad things I did. As far as moaning and bad-mouthing of sanctioning bodies—I made a lot of mistakes.

So there you were in the late '60s and the sport is getting more professional. How come you didn't ride that wave? Did your outspoken manner make it difficult?

Alexander: I had a wife and two kids I had to be responsible for. I had an opportunity to go on tour but I was afraid I couldn't make enough money to support them. My marriage was shaky, so I thought I should stay home and try to salvage it—which wasn't salvageable.

Do you regret that choice?

Alexander: No. I'm glad I did it. I would have liked to have taken the chance but I wasn't about to gamble with my wife and kids.

Is what you're doing now providing a venue for some of you guys who felt that you didn't get a chance to ride out that last wave as you saw fit?

Alexander: This has let a lot of us do what we wanted to do when we were younger—and maybe a little more talented. But it is allowing us to fulfill maybe a dream, or maybe the reality of something we stopped doing then because of families, business or whatever.

It takes a certain kind of mind to run a nitro car, particularly to tune one…

Alexander: Now you're out of my league. I know how to drive and pack the parachute—and mix nitro. And I try to stay away from mixing nitro because I just assume pour straight nitro in it.

(Originally published in Drag Racing USA*)*

NOTES FROM THE HEART (LAND HOT ROD REUNION) (1999)

Heartland Hot Rod Reunion III, Thunder Valley, Oklahoma, August 21-22, 1999—After catching wind of the notice that Jon "Thunderlungs" Lundberg is coming out of retirement for the weekend in order to announce this race over the public-address system and drum up support for his Drag Racing Archive project (www.drhra.org), I decided to drive to Oklahoma so's to archive this race on a digital audio tape machine.

Beyond "Thunderlungs," further ratcheting up the cachet of this event was the notion of a Top Fuel Shootout after qualifying on Saturday night, with front-engined fuelers from all corners of the continental US migrating towards Noble, Oklahoma in order to mix it up for a shot at glory.

Awright, so after spending the better part of Wednesday night scamming on hi-fi audio gear and loading up on chocolate espresso beans, by 9:30 it's time to hit the highway and eat some white line... just east of Pomona, I-10 to I-15 is completely bollixed with construction bottlenecks—after taking surface streets through the Inland Empire, ride at 90 mph till Flagstaff... cop a catnap at a rest stop, trip around downtown looking for coffee that hurts, hit the road again while keeping an eye peeled for peripatetic Top Fuel racers Ty Norton and the *Champion Speed Shop* bunch, both of whom should be heading east on I-40.

Once through Navajo country, meditate at the Cadillac Ranch on the outskirts of Amarillo—you know, the place where some eccentric Texan decided that stuffing a bunch of DeVilles vertically into a cow pasture is high art. I can't say I disagree with the man, but after avoiding the rest stops on I-40 for longer than my bladder could tolerate, I also left an artistic statement at this gallery of Cadillacs... once in Amarillo proper, pull through the parking lot of the Big Texan and look for drag racers... By pure happenstance, I ran into Sante Fe drag racer Mike Civelli and his bunch there once—great experience... No luck this time so I make for the interstate...

Drive 'til Elk City... get a $20 motel room amongst the itinerant rough necks and oil workers...

Sleep late. Drive into Norman, Oklahoma, a few miles from the drag strip. Check in at the Thunderbird Lodge, dump my bags in the room and amble toward the Ramada which is a couple of blocks away. Halfway out the door, I hear, "Hey"... It's Sammy Hale and Tom Homer, *Champion*'s truck-driving tag team. En route, Sammy guides the three of us toward a taxidermist operating out of a Quonset hut and goes into a Zen and the Art of Deer Hunting riff as we examine the stuffed critters...

Next: Hot lap it to the drag strip. The pits are filled: the grandstands are not too shabby, neither.

Picture this: Lundberg's on the mic be-bopping about "Chanel No. 5, nitro and tire smoke" as a pair of fuelers fire just as the sun goes down: "Wild Bill" and Sammy Hale roll through the water and then strike the tires simultaneously. *WWWHHHAAAHHHH!* The fabled match race between Hedge's cacophonous Chizler and *Champion*'s mighty mouse is upon us. *This is what Top Fuel is all about: 80 years of poise, sweat, attitude, chutzpah and experience are in parallel lanes.*

In a word, goosebump-inducing. Alexander lights both bulbs, then *Champion*'s tuners finish manipulating their fuel faucets and Sammy stages. Hale has half a car length out of the hole, but no more as they hammer down the 1/4 mile. Bill is riding Sammy for the duration, but can't quite catch him. Sammy gets off the throttle just before the eyes and a curtain of smoke from two lean cylinders envelops both lanes. It gets worse. Boom. A major detonation ensues, windowing the left side of the block, sourdough pretzeling the left head, ripping off the canard, puncturing the left slick and burning off the left parachute. Alexander *STANDS* on the throttle—he is probably the only guy who can see what is actually happening, when the smoke is so thick—and propels himself out of harm's way and Sammy crosses behind him and bank-shots off the guardrail, setting the grass on fire.

There was so much smoke that nobody except Bill and Sammy knew what was going on in the shut-down area. The reason they couldn't find Alexander is that he waited until the very last moment to hit the parachutes and then spun the car into the last patch of grass before the track ended in some woods and a perpendicular railroad track.

Alexander doesn't brake until a few feet before the last turnoff whereupon he pulls the chutes and does a Steve Kinser into the grass.

Much damage to Champion's framerails; they'll have to front-half the car... they are done until SPIR...

*****

After attrition sidelines both *Suhr & Lechtenberg* and *Champion Speed Shop*, The Winner-Take-All Top Fuel Shootout is a joust between Alexander and the injected Chrysler-on-nitro entry of *Beedy & Lutz* out of Illinois. Alexander's throttle linkage malfunctions costs him half a second off of the pad; "Rapid Robert" Beedy zips to the big end as Alexander gives chase, but to no avail. With a 7.03 at 180 mph to Alexander's 6.96 at 215 mph, an exhilarated *Beedy & Lutz* claimed the $3000 bounty, 500 of which they magnanimously bequeathed to the Make A Wish Foundation before the ink was even dry on the check.

This victory was a costly one for Hedge & Alexander in more ways than one. Beyond the loss of what was considered free money, the *Mastercam* car screwed the pooch. This ignominious defeat was the final insult in what has been a season filled with frustration for Hedge and Alexander, two of the most storied individuals in the history of the sport. Their team's cache of operating capital suffered because of the defeat, but beyond that, the tender feelings and finger-pointing cost these two legends their partnership. Alexander caught a plane home Sunday morning before eliminations began. It is this writer's opinion that the sport is poorer because of this unfortunate parting of ways.

*****

After motoring back to Los Angeles that evening and blowing by both Civelli and Norton during an electrical storm in the middle of the night, I caught up with Homer and Hale just east of Flagstaff on Monday afternoon as it drizzled. We stopped for coffee and a piece of pie at a local truck stop and discussed how tempestuous and bizarre the weekend had been for the California teams. After posing for some pictures with a wheelbarrow, we parted, amped on sugar, caffeine and carbs. It seemed to be the perfect diet for driving cross-country in the rain.

POSTSCRIPT: Re: The *Mastercam* vs. *Champion Speed Shop* drag race: That was a very fucking scary accident—and it really underscores a problem I have which is that I've gotten to know these guys personally and they have become my friends... I was *very* concerned about the safety of both these guys ("Swingin' Sammy" Hale and "Wild Bill" Alexander), two old gunslingers who have been participating in the sport since 1961 (!).

In essence, Sammy Hale's digger exploded and the detonation ripped and shredded all manner of hardware on the left side of the race car. The engine was shrapnel, it ripped off a canard wing (sort of a stabilizer) and shredded the left rear tire.

On fire and blinded by oil, Sammy drifted into the next lane where Alexander was... Bill had looked over and saw the magnitude of the inferno that was engulfing Sammy Hale... keep in mind that this is all going down right at the finish line at around 230 mph, where they are supposed to stop the dragsters. Instead of trying to stop, Bill ignored the brakes and the parachutes and motored past Sammy Hale who was out of control at this point.

True to Alexander's premonition, Sammy Hale came into his land and smacked the guardrail, ultimately setting the grass on fire.

It was the most brazen example of bravado cum mental kung fu I have ever witnessed...

(*Originally published on* Nitronic Research)

"SWINGIN' SAMMY" HALE EXITS FROM CHAMPION SPEED SHOP COCKPIT

11-4-99, Novato, CA—The driver whom many drag strip pundits consider the Nureyev of the form, "Swingin' Sammy" Hale has relinquished his position as driver of the *Champion Speed Shop/Juxtapoz* front-motored AA/Fuel Dragster and is taking a hiatus of unspecified duration from dragster driving. At 58 years of age, Hale has driven nitro-fueled dragsters for the Bay Area-based Champion team sporadically since 1961, a partnership whose longevity was a major factor in its fan appeal.

In addition to the rather unprecedented continuance of their partnership, other details contributed to the team's tremendous Q factor, not the least of which is their choice of propulsion: a small-block Chevy, an engine whose delicate geometry has turned off virtually all other nitro warriors because of the volatile challenge the engine presented. Although Hale expressed frustration with idiosyncratic performances of the Chevy-powered machine during the 1999 season, he acknowledged that other-worldly performances such as a barrier-breaking 5.87 elapsed time last March and an event win at the Goodguys

Hot Rod Nationals at Indy tempered a few rather fiery incidents during the course of the year. Hale cited other reasons for the primary motivation for his departure from the *Champion* hot seat, most specifically familial commitments, as well finding a new location for his business, Sammy Hale Crankshafts.

Despite his departure from the cockpit, Hale was emphatic, however, in pronouncing *Champion*'s choice the de facto approach to rotating the Earth. "Every time you pull up to the line," he said, "you should be trying to put up your best numbers." Because of its diminutive weight, Hale has been a proponent of the Chevy mouse. Later in the conversation he conceded the tremendous strides made by big-block Chevrolets in the front-motored fueler wars, but he also expressed bewilderment at why anybody would not run a combination similar to *Champion*'s. His sentiments in this regard emphasize the mental battle between those who favor the more conventional and sturdy Chrysler hemi and unorthodox approaches such as his former team's.

Hale was non-committal about the length of his leave of absence from the sport. Underscoring how amicable the departure was, Champion team owner Bob McLennan expressed hope that Hale would grace the team with continued intellectual input, an element both McLennan and co-tuner Tony Bernardini have mentioned as a contribution to the recent success of what assuredly is the most avant-garde entry in front-motored fueler racing. But even McLennan admitted that posting numbers like the 5.87 karate chop this year, Hale had "done what he needed to do."

"It was a great year (for us), but by his standards it was not a successful year," Bob said. "He is by far the most competitive person I know."

Indeed, it is that ravenous approach to competition that is upsetting the balance he is trying to maintain in his life.

"The first thing on my agenda is to relocate the shop… I'm in the middle of a traumatic business relocation," Hale emphasized. "This (his crankshaft business) is a one-man deal—I don't wear the *Juxtapoz* suit seven days a week."

Once that is sorted out, Hale says he "wouldn't be deaf to some ideas about (running a fuel car). I still have some different ideas about cylinder heads which got sidestepped with the *Champion* car."

(Originally published in Nitronic Research)

MIGRANT APES IN THE GASOLINE CRACK OF HISTORY

Rocket cars. Rocket dragsters. It was only a matter of time before the technology designed to put a man on the moon and vaporize entire cities was appropriated by the speed demons on wheels...

It's simple: the common method for propulsion of the rocket dragsters utilized the following method: pressurized nitrogen forces the hydrogen peroxide onto a silver plate and the ensuing, instantaneous chemical reaction creates a tremendous cloud of hot stream that is force fed out of a nozzle, creating thrust.

Rockets summon, tickle and reanimate many primal notions dormant within the collective human consciousness: they tap into the memories of fire and they evoke the spirit of the transcendental, the exaltation and elevation of the human body and of the human spirit... *"They wanted to escape from their misery and the stars were too far for them"*—thus spoke Zarathustra and Friedrich Nietzsche about the very banality of existence... Rockets are the stuff of Jules Verne books (*From the Earth to the Moon*) and Fritz Lang movies (*Frau Im Mond*), of Arthur C. Clark and Stanley Kubrick and *2001: A Space Odyssey* whose symphonic score (Richard Strauss' "Thus Spoke Zarathustra") observed a human destiny far beyond the confines of Planet Earth; of the Ancient Chinese and tossed bamboo tubes filled with saltpeter, sulfur and charcoal as part of ceremonial fires and noisy explosions scaring away evil spirits. A full millennia subsequent, this is the stuff of the Sung Dynasty attaching canisters of powder to spears and using the projectiles to repel the invading Mongol hordes... *"Thunder that shakes the heavens"* was the Chinese description of the dual elements of physical devastation and psychological terror... The Mongols appropriated the technology for use in their conquests of Baghdad and from there rocketry spread into Europe... As the Dark Ages gave way to the Renaissance, Sir Isaac

Newton solved the theorem of equal and opposite reactions, which became his Third Law of Motion and a pithy explanation of how a rocket generates altitude and velocity... This is the stuff of unmanned rockets built from the blood of indentured Hebrews, subjugated into aiding the Third Reich as it bombed the shit out of London in its quest to establish a Master Race; of the Space Race and the rocket to the moon with spacemen in aluminum suits establishing beachheads on extra terra firma... This is the stuff of our id and a Jungian subconsciousness—of "migrant apes in the gasoline crack of history" as William Burroughs said—of apocryphal legend and honky imperialism and of dusty teenagers ratchet-strapping forgotten solid-fuel rockets onto the hoods of their rusted Chevy Impalas and smashing man and machine into the eternal oblivion of desert stone...

(*Originally published in* INFINITY OVER ZERO)

~~It was only good for a flower pot~~

THE MAD! ROCKET SCIENTIST

As a totem, or a weapon, or a propulsion system—whither from Biblical times through the days of Mongol Invasions, beyond the Dark Ages into the bomb factories of Germany, from the launch pads of NASA and finally touching down onto the drag strips of 1970s' America—the bark of a rocket has always been as fierce as its bite. It is the stuff of the physiological. It is the stuff of Ernst Mach—sensory and tactile and now hard-wired into our metaphysical fabric. It is the stuff of visionaries, daredevils and crackpots. It is also the stuff of dairy farmers moonlighting as rocket scientists...

*****

"You couldn't see the person next to you," says Brent Fanning, aka "the Mad! Rocket Scientist." Fanning is reminiscing about when he and his wife Vicky ran the *Outer Limits* rocket funny car at drag strips across America to supplement their incomes as dairy farmers.

Outer Limits was supposedly a Corvette with a rocket engine, but by the time the Fannings were done deconstructing and reconstructing the fiberglass body by installing a series of colored bulbs they had bought at the hardware store and then wired in a hokey chase circuit, it was basically unrecognizable as anything off of a Detroit assembly line, much less of anything on this planet. If the no-budget sci-fi film *Plan 9 From Outer Space* needed a car as a prop, this was their interstellar baby...

Yes, at a Texas dairy farm whose barn is transformed into a garage for a rocket, the hydrogen-peroxide-powered monolith known as *Outer Limits* would dwell silently and become quite the conversation starter for an agrarian culture not exactly known for its verbosity. The Fanning's neighbors, most of whom were also farmers, would gather around the monolith and kick the tires, like goats looking at a watch. Brent would tell them the principles of running the rocket car, which he had researched over at Texas A&M, using the university's networked computers as a font of knowledge and rocket science. He told them how the NHRA muckety-mucks had reluctantly attended a test of the rocket car way out in California and the men in suits were less than enthusiastic about even watching it run, much less signing off on a license for somebody who calls himself the "Mad! Rocket Scientist" racing something called "the *Outer Limits.*" Fanning told his buddies how they even had flown in a bona fide NASA engineer to supervise the test, who was actually kind of baffled about how Brent had put this particular system together.

*****

While discussing rockets over a couple of beers one night, I tell Fanning that Craig Breedlove once said to me, "Everybody knows that anything under seventy-percent hydrogen peroxide makes for nearly useless rocket fuel." Fanning couldn't disagree more about watered-down hydrogen peroxide as a monopropellant.

"We used to dilute it with water so we could make more steam. I'd put Vicky in the stands while we made a run. After the car ran, if she said she couldn't see the person next to her, we considered the run a success, regardless of the speed."

The speed. In those days, the rockets were running so much faster than the Top Fuel dragsters, track operators would lie about the elapsed time and terminal speeds so as not to upset the National Hot Rod Association and its insurers. This was an ironic about-face to the rather common practice of hyping "popcorn" times over the public address system and in the trades as a way of generating more interest in a given race track and its events.

Indeed, the same muckety-mucks who reluctantly oversaw the Fanning's rocket test out in California, sent out threatening letters about revoking the licenses of drivers who went too quick and too fast. Philosophically and intellectually, the rockets were beyond what the Druids could process.

Fanning's *Outer Limits* was the last vestige of the rocket-car subculture, a once-burgeoning scene whistling across the drag strips: The names of the cars underscored a weird synthesis of nationalism, post-psychedelic individualism and futurism: *the X-1, Vanishing Point, Miss STP, Stratosfear, Moon Shot, Screaming Yellow Zonkers, the Free Spirit, Spirit Of 76, Age of Aquarius, Captain America, the Pollution Packer, the American Dream, USA-1, the Conklin Comet, Concept 1, the Courage of Australia,* etc...

The future was now for hot rodders across America, including Brent Fanning, who, due to the screwy economics of Jimmy Carter's America, couldn't afford a nitro Funny Car but could afford a rocket (!).

"I got to see a rocket car run and got to studyin' 'em and stuff. I thought, 'Them things can't tear up hardly,' y'know? 'We got to make money somehow, enough money to get a nitro Funny Car'—that's what I always wanted. So we ran a lot of match races with that rocket car. The first year we ran the (hydrogen) peroxide car, it would cost me $250 a run for fuel. When we quit four years later, it would cost $1200 a run. The last year we ran, I bought more hydrogen peroxide from FMC (Food Machinery Corporation, the manufacturer and distributor) than the U.S. Government. They had doubled the price. Basically, that put us out of business. It was only good for a flower pot so I gave it away and took a tax write-off."

One of the finishing strokes for Brent's career as a Mad! Rocket Scientist was when the NHRA tech daddies vetoed some of Brent's ideas for propulsion enhancement. "Since I had a really weak rocket," he clarifies, "I was actually going to try to inject a little nitro in it to increase the specific impulse on it—NHRA wouldn't let ya'. I can't blame them; it would have made it a little more... unstable."

(*Excerpted from INFINITY OVER ZERO*)

top fuel wormhole

PART THREE: COLLAPSE

THE PASSING OF STEVE COLLISON AND THE DEATH OF DRAG STRIP JOURNALISM

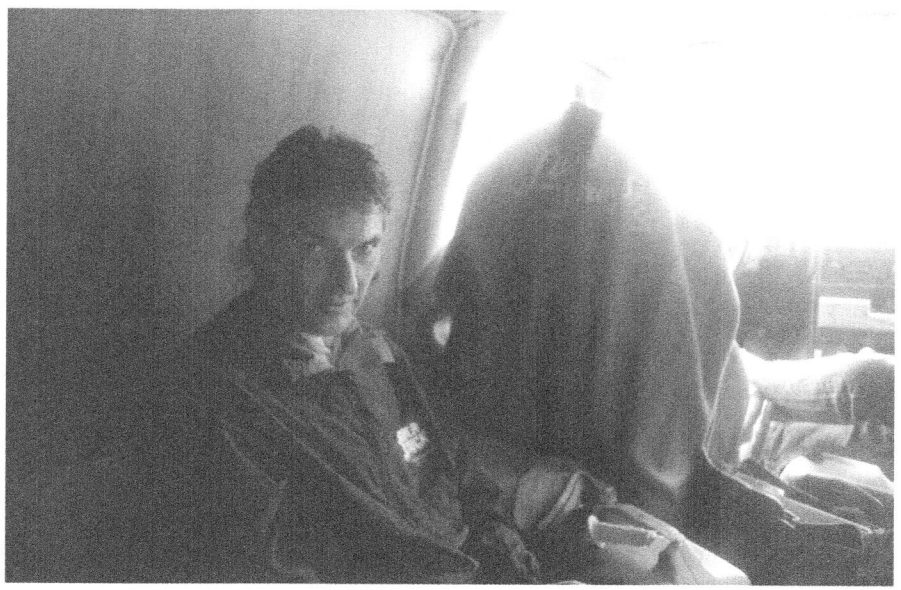

Steve Collison died last Thursday and I am very unhappy about that. I considered him my friend as well as a compatriot and I will miss our discourse.

Out of the Bataan Death March for Drag Racers what was Y2K, Steve's death has hit me harder than any of the others...

Steve was on the masthead of a variety of high performance magazines, usually as an editor. He was very good at what he did.

That being said, something else died with Steve. Drag racing magazines as an art form.

I am sad because I have known Steve since 1994. I have known drag racing magazines since I could read. I miss them both.

top fuel wormhole

At one time drag racing magazines were as cool as drag racing itself. They were two of the greatest things on the planet. One was hot, loud and overwhelmed the senses. The other was cool, introspective and static. But they were both art forms unto themselves.

Drag News, Drag World, Hot Rod, Car Craft, The Wally, Super Stock & Drag Illustrated, Drag Cartoons, Ralph Guldahl's Drag Racing, Drag Racing USA, Petersen's Drag Racing... Whether waiting in my mailbox or at the newsstand or at a swap meet, all of these rags raised the temperature in my heart and cranked up my id. (This list is by no means all-inclusive; this is just the list I came up with off of the top of my head...)

Life has little meaning if there are no pleasures to look forward to, but what a pleasure drag-racing magazines were: when any of these publications were in a groove, they were bigger than the photos, captions, text and pull quotes contained therein. There was a definite gestalt happening with these publications. They were a weird slice of American pop culture, and they were written, photographed and edited by enthusiasts for enthusiasts.

Which, again, brings me to Steve Collison: he was the last true drag racing enthusiast left in the drag racing publishing world. He was the last guy to say what he felt and what he knew, because he couldn't lie about something he cared about, which is what I thought the whole idea behind journalism was in the first place.

You take your rarefied pantheon of drag strip journalists and they have all bailed out of the print world. Ralph Guldahl (*Drag News, Drag Racing, Hot Rod*, etc.) retired almost thirty years ago. Dave Densmore (a newspaper reporter whose love for the digs led to gigs with *SS&DI* among others) is now Force's flack and for penance work he does critical analysis for a couple of websites. Dave Wallace, Jr. (who or what hasn't he written for?) works as an agent for manufacturers in the high-performance sector. Terry Cook (*Car Craft*) ripcorded a long time ago... I dunno' what he is doing these days; John Raffa (*Car Craft, Nat'l Dragster*) makes jewelry and plays with filters in Photoshop (last I heard). Chris Martin (*ND* and author of *Top Fuel Handbook*) and Jeff Burk (*SS&DI* and many others) morphed their creative bent toward the web more or less full-time, establishing a year ago what they mistakenly believe is the first drag-racing e-zine (a canard they have repeated in both print ads and in editorials, a fallacy that underscores how the web has become a haven for print-media stringers, even those who don't understand the Internet's scope nor its history); Rick Vogelin (*Car Craft*) cranks out press releases for Warren Johnson and the IRL; Ro McGonegal (*Car Craft's* prodigal poet) is now at the rudder of *Hot Rod*, but besides its proprietary coverage of the muscle-car circuit, it has only a tenuous connection to the drag strip nowadays...

These guys were the hitters of drag strip journalism—its Studs Terkels, its Jimmy Breslins, its Ring Lardners, its Woodwards and its Bernsteins—the writers who transcended the genre—and they have all bailed. The well is polluted, all of these guys are cognizant of how foul the water is and all of them have decided to cut their losses and if not get mercenary, they at least sought out different scenery.

And nobody can blame them. They had their run and they left quite a body of work. (cf. Raffa's entire editorial direction at *Car Craft* and at the *Wally*, underscored by any number of McGonegal pieces under Raffa's tutelage, any of Guldahl's Lions Drag Strip coverage from the pages of *Drag News* in the 1960s; Vogelin's "White Line Fever" in *CC*; just about everything Martin had ever written before he decided to pontificate about his year-old e-zine's status as the industry's first "real" publication in cyberspace; Burk's *SS&DI* editorial whereupon he revealed the NHRA's Dun & Bradstreet numbers; Densmore's did-he-or-didn't-he exposé of nitrous oxide use cum mindfuck by Don Prudhomme at Indy years ago in *SS&DI*; Wallace's 1996 feature on Clayton Harris for *SS&DI* (the genius of which is that Wallace basically transcribed Harris' quotes verbatim and ran that... Wallace barely wrote a word himself... he knew that Harris' story was so epic that anything interjected by the writer would disturb the flow of an amazing oratory by one of the sport's more ingenious yet tragic figures; Wallace wrote a boxcar's worth of editorial and race coverage elsewhere, whereupon he used his voice to jarring-yet-karmically-correct effect, the Jimmy Nix obit in *SS&DI* particularly haunting yet efficacious); and there are other examples of stylin' drag strip journalism, but these are the ones that come to my cranium after a couple of drinks on a Tuesday night...

Collison's talent and enthusiasm were/are equal to anybody in that group. (My grammar is correct: Steve is gone, yet art is always referred to in the present tense.) But Collison was never able to execute an exit strategy out of drag-racing journalism in the print world...

And this is all borne out by the fact that as often as not, the magazine that Steve Collison was last hired to edit wouldn't run his editorials.

Occasionally he would shovel some of these to the *Nitronic Research* website and we'd run it (cf. "If I Were the King of Drag Racing," which was mothballed in the print world because of its content and its perceived adversarial and antagonistic tone towards the NHRA; ironically enough, it's tamer itself and less controversial than *Nat'l Dragster* editor Phil Burgess's obit of Collison on the nhra.com website).

Steve Collison was the last man in the room—and he knew it.

The last guy to leave a room is supposed to turn out the light on his way out. Instead, I maintain it was the other way around. And as much as I don't care about drag-racing magazines anymore, Steve Collison deserved a better fate than dying while looking for photographs of a bracket car for an industry that didn't care about what made Collison such a pearl of a journalist.

Bless you, Steve Collison. **–30-**

*****

STEVE COLLISON FUN FACTS:

Favorite Class: Competition Eliminator.

What Sucked Him Into Drag Racing Permanently: Watching Jr. Fuel cars under the lights at Lions Drags Strip.

The People Who Feared Him Most: Probably not the NHRA. Probably rental car agencies.

(*Originally published in* Nitronic Research)

'I've got you m.f.s.'

"VIVA LA NITRO!"
HOW THE SON OF A TIRE TORCHIN' TACO TASTER SET THE FUNNY CAR WORLD ON FIRE

Las Vegas Motor Speedway, October 26th. As the sun sets on Vegas, the top two Funny Car drivers on earth prepare for a final drag race, a four second shoot-'em-up that will settle who is the baddest hombre in a fire suit in this, the Proverbial Year of Our Lord, 2003. Aww, Funny Cars: The motors have nitromethane—a poor man's rocket fuel—coursing through the fuel lines. The drivers have ice water flowing through their veins. If all goes well, the drag racers will follow this timeline to victory: 0 to 100 mph in less than a second. 0 to 250 mph in 3 seconds. 0 to over 320 mph in 4 seconds. The first guy to cover a quarter-mile wins.

To the east, the skies darken precipitously, the winds blow the moon around, and to the west, behind the drag strip and down Vegas Boulevard, Lost Wages cranks up its foot-candles. But the point of singularity is the starting line of the drag strip. There, in an absurdly hot-rodded and amped-up carbon fiber mutation of a Dodge Stratus, Whit Bazemore, a towheaded, brown-eyed Lance Armstrong-doppelganger of a speed maven, sits behind a 7000 horsepower (!) engine and lets his crew guys cinch the fighter pilot-strength seat belts to a taught tension that will somehow withstand an instant gravitational pull five times that of Bazemore's body weight—and yet somehow not crush Whit's ribs.

In the opposite lane, Chicano drag racer Tony Pedregon and his crew guys go through a similar drill in a bastardized simulation of a Ford Mustang. Pedregon, by his own account, acknowledges it a quirk of fate that he is here, a quarter-mile away from claiming the Funny Car Title of the Universe. Tony is the hired gun slash "second shoe" for the dynasty known as John Force Racing. John Force has driven his way to 11 of the last 12 Funny Car Points Titles.

"I used to drive a truck in this town, and my buddies would say, 'Force, c'mon back and drive a truck and tell stories because you aren't going to win any drag races," -- John Force, *'I Saw Elvis at a Thousand Feet.'*

Aww, John Force, the Lonesome Rhodes of Drag Racing. A hobo truck driver who had a dream and quit his day job, went nitro Funny Car racing and then set himself on fire so often that he burned his niggling, begged, borrowed and stolen inventory to the ground, whereupon he parlayed people's sympathy and generosity with his own gumption and desire into a drag-racing empire that would make Colonel Tom Parker, Charles Foster Kane and Wal-Mart blink. The funny car driver who said, "I want that Elvis Presley following. When they bury me, buddy, I want the fans to come by and see me." Notoriously loquacious and stream-of-consciousness-esque, Force is a crew cab of a man and a frothy anthropomorphic run-on sentence who has single-handedly gathered a brain trust of engineers, mechanics and aerodynamicists whose talents rivals any space program and whose sole function is to install Force into the Winner's Circle race after race after race.

And with all of that talent, including his own, for over a decade, Force has crushed, dominated, demoralized and shocked-and-awed his opponents with the relentless and ruthless precision of Marco Polo, Attila the Hun, Babe Ruth's New York Yankees and Napoleon.

But a funny thing happened on the way to the Waterloo known as Las Vegas, 2003: For the first time in over a decade, Force is not in contention for the National Hot Rod Association's Funny Car Title. Eight years ago Force hires Tony Pedregon to run a second car, a "research and development" Funny Car, whose *raison d'être* is to test avant-garde technologies that will push the teams' competitive envelope. It is a win-win for Force: If the new equipment—say, an experimental camshaft "grind," or an aerodynamic approach or a trick fuel pump—fails, it fails on Tony's car and he loses the drag race and the precious title points, not Force. And if the new piece of kit works better than what the competition is using, it is immediately installed on Force's Mustang.

The second function of Pedregon's racing entry is to eliminate the competition, which is to say any of the other race teams who have the potential to unseat John Force as the Ultimate Funny Car Driver of the Year. And, when it comes to the moment when teammates Force and Pedregon have to square off in a race, well, let's just say that all-of-a-sudden-like, some of that experimental gear on Tony's funny car may find a way to not work all that well... In boxing, this is known as "going in the tank." In drag racing, it is known by the same denigration.

Tony Pedregon had been hired as a ringer. And as a racer, it has been tearing his heart out. For eight years. In 2003, Force had an uncharacteristically sub-par year and was out of contention for the Points Title. Ergo, at Vegas, Pedregon ain't a' takin' a dive no mo'.

*****

"We don't have any egos on this team, except for mine," -- John Force.

The only driver to dent John Force's brutal domination over the NHRA Funny Car Points Title is Tony's oldest brother, Cruz Pedregon, who won the tournament in 1992. In the scope of history, it is a small victory, as Force won consecutive Championships from 1993 until 2002, and as late as September, pundits maintained Force had a chance of rallying and thwarting the aspirations of Tony Pedregon and nemesis Whit Bazemore.

The Pedregon Brothers. At the Vegas race, rumors swirl like a casino ashtray about Tony Pedregon joining his brother Cruz—and maybe even their middle brother Frankie, who is also a Funny Car driver—in establishing a two- or three-car "dream team," that will challenge the hegemony of John Force and squash the title hopes of other super teams, including that of Bazemore's.

On Saturday, the day before the Bazemore/Pedregon showdown, Tony's brother Cruz takes a time trial in his Pontiac Firebird funny car that lands him in the hospital: Cruz approaches the finish line at a maximum velocity of nearly 300 mph and everything goes Space Shuttles Columbia and Challenger. Faster than you can say "Christa McAuliffe," Cruz's motor's supercharger explodes when parts break from stress and nitromethane flows simultaneously into both the intake and exhaust ports of the never-more-aptly-named combustion chambers of the cylinder heads. KA-BOOM. The entire Firebird makes like a bad day in the Middle East, and is shredded into taco meat. What was once a race car is now a swing set on wheels, out of control, on fire and with the braking parachutes swirling in the wind. Momentarily blinded by flames and oil and valiantly trying to stop what is left of the car, Cruz shoots across both lanes of the drag strip like Mr. Magoo and POW! punches into a safety retaining wall, further deconstructing his steed. After that impact, the car mercifully bounces to a halt. Miraculously, after a brief stop at what drag racers call "the White Sheet Hotel" for evaluation, the doctors conclude that Cruz's biggest injury is to his hearing.

The crash only cranks up the chatter about the Pedregon Brothers racing as a team in 2004. And two weeks later Cruz is back in a Funny Car at Pomona Raceway for the NHRA Series Finale.

*****

San Fernando Raceway, 1966. A primitive drag strip—nowadays an outdoor flea market—buttresses and runs perpendicular to Glenoaks and Foothill Boulevards. A concrete flood control channel flanks the western edge of the track. At the end of the track, the only safety barrier separating the racing surface from the drainage ditch is a chain link fence.

On a Sunday afternoon typical of the era, "Flamin' Frank" Pedregon is racing "Wild Bill" Alexander in a Top Fuel dragster match, when chaos and providence provide Pedregon with an opportunity to exercise his twisted and macabre sense of humor.

As the dragsters cross the finish line, "Wild Bill" pulls his parachutes, but in the other lane Pedregon's *Taco Taster* dragster veers left, hits the chain link and disappears into the concrete ravine. Alexander, the track owner, and a coterie of grease monkeys give chase. Upon arrival at where the dragster had finally stopped tumbling, they are accosted by a grisly sight: Pedregon is lying dead still a couple of yards from the crash site, face down with his arms spread like a post-crucifixion still life and as the track workers and ambulance workers climb through the tangled fencing, "Flamin' Frank's" wife drives up in a station wagon with three young boys in the back seats. Nobody can tell if Pedregon is still breathing.

Amidst the pandemonium, as they reach Frank he leaps to his feet and begins pointing, laughing and howling, "I FOOLED YOU! I FOOLED YOU! I'M OKAY! I'M OKAY!"

Tony Pedregon is in diapers and is one of the kids in the station wagon. Frankie and Cruz are the others. Almost forty years later I am in Tony's trailer at the drag races in Pomona and he tells me about that day. "It was just the sense of humor my dad had. When the other driver and the ambulance people showed up, my old man just stood up and said, 'I've got you m.f.s.' And I don't think m.f.s stood for 'my friends.'"

*****

"Flamin' Frank." "The Taco Taster." "The World's Fastest Mexican." A dashing, mustachioed ladies' man and a fearless dare devil, Frank Pedregon is absolutely legendary in vintage drag racing "bench race" circles, where tales of his bravery, insanity and swagger—stories of faking his death, setting his rear tires on fire for the spectacle of it, inadvertently gathering unsuspecting rattlesnakes in parachutes, etc.—cloud the ether thick as the quarks in a bowl of menudo. I recently asked a group of old time drag racers if they had any Frank Pedregon anecdotes. One graybeard told me, "At Beeline Raceway in Tucson we were warming the car up and changing oil and so on, when Frank pointed to a pile of oil cans on the ground and turned and said to me, 'Where did all of those Mess-a-cans come from?'"

About Pedregon's playfulness with his taxonomy, the racer remembers, "Frank always used to say, 'When I see green-go'…"

Another retired drag racer, Wayne "the Peregrine" King is loaded with sentiment: "In '69 Frank was racing at Fresno, doing his flaming tire deal," he recalls. "Frank was making a pass and was blinded by the flames. He veered off the track, with lots of dust and tumbleweeds flying. Frank's wife and the family were terrified that he had crashed. They raced down the track, stopped at the pavement's edge, all four doors of the station wagon flew open and the whole Pedregon family ran to the crash site. Frank was fine. The only injury was to his wife. She stepped into a gopher hole and broke her leg. They held up the race until the ambulance came back from taking her to the hospital."

But wait there's more...

"Another time, while sitting in a tavern in Spokane back in 1964 in walks Frank," "the Peregrine" continues. "He had just pulled into town and the first stop was the tavern. We had a few beers and bench raced a while, then Frank really got wound up, telling of his crash at a track in Canada. He said the promoters didn't want to pay him his money. Said he didn't put on a good show. Frank went into detail of what happened during the crash—of course we all had to go out and see the damage. Under the lights the coupe looked like a scorpion ready to strike. The front wheels were over the driver's compartment. I am sure that car was never repaired."

*****

I ask Tony Pedregon what he remembers about his childhood. "Our first house was in Chino," he says. "My dad nicknamed one of his race cars the 'Chicken Coupe' because we had chickens in the backyard. When the car wasn't running, chickens lived in it."

Later the family moved in among the scrap yards of Gardena, adjoining Compton. "I was raised in an environment where I heard the sirens and the gunshots. We used to sleep three in a room. I know Cruz's feet very well. It was a one bedroom house, and that is what a lot of Hispanic people here are up against."

Tony remember his Mom as being "fundamental but understated, and to this day mild-mannered and supportive" and Dad as being incredibly resourceful and scrappy. "My dad would fabricate everything in his race car, from the chassis to the motor. He'd get other guys' junk—stuff they literally would throw in the trash—and he'd go run faster than they would."

"He wrote on his car, 'The World's Fastest Mexican.' My dad was one of the few guys who said, 'Hey, I'm Mexican.' He also put on the back of his car, 'Adios Amigo.' That was a statement. And if you messed with him, you probably had to fist fight him."

*****

We are talking about Tony's two-toned Latino and Caucasian coalition of a fan following. As we talk, I am struck by Tony's movie star countenance and an extemporaneous playfulness with the language, with a delivery not unlike Oscar de La Hoya sparring in the gym. I ask him specifically about his Hispanic fans, and he says they bring him as much inspiration and adulation as the other way around...

"La Raza has become more important to me," he says. "The people have made that more important to me. After we moved to Torrance, I wound up at some private school. And hey, that's parenting; you always want what was best for your kids. And because of that, I thought this (image of a) very mild-mannered, very proper person who wanted to do absolutely everything that the sponsors and John Force Racing wanted him to do (was the way to go). But that only goes so far. I found out over the years the true person comes out. I really have a passion for people of my ethnic background and heritage. I mean, I like people in general, but I've found out that I have inspired them in some way to fulfill some of their needs too."

Tony takes a breath, like a bell rang. Then he says, "I don't lay out in the sun to get the tan. I speak the language. This is the way that I am."

For example?

"AAA has this program, Youth in Education. They send me into high schools and middle schools in Pomona, Rancho Cucamonga, all the way to Texas. We're going to a school that is 99 percent Hispanic and that is really where I come from. I go in with Gary Densham (John Force Racing's third team driver, and who happens to be Caucasian) and I don't care what his credentials are, you want to get their attention? Who you going to send? I told 'em you guys want to send Densham in there (to the barrio), send him with me and he'll be okay."

*****

"I think my dad's personality was split into thirds," Tony says. "Cruz inherited the temperament. The impatience. I got the artistic side. Frank does his own thing, like my dad. I mean, we came from a broken home and he has..."

"A wandering eye?"

"Yeah."

By the mid 1970s, "Flamin' Frank" had hung up his fire suit and began concentrating on his trucking business. His connections ran from Texas to California and into Mexico, and he had taken use of a private propeller-driven plane to facilitate overseeing various transactions. On a trip into Mexico, he got visually disoriented and crashed near a highway that led into a sleepy villa. That crash had severed an arm and he bled profusely, yet he managed to make it to the highway, whereupon he had to make a decision that Robert Frost once wrote about. Unfortunately, in his confusion, Frank Pedregon took the road less traveled by, and walked away from any possible medical help from denizens of the nearby town. This time he didn't fake his death.

Tony says, "I remember I was at a race and Frankie and Cruz showed up. My dad had been missing, as he ran into some weather and I just knew."

Tony drops a little history on me. He tells about how he and Cruz raced each other in Texas a few years back. He says, "Cruz and I were the first brothers to race in an NHRA final. The starter said he looked up to the sky as we staged the cars and said, 'You'd be proud of these guys.'"

*****

Tony is confirming the rumors about leaving John Force Racing. There will be an announcement at an automotive trade show later in the year as to who his sponsor will be, but once he is satisfied that this story will not run before a televised awards banquet where he will be ceremoniously crowned as NHRA PowerAde Funny Car Champ, he tells me he is teaming up with Cruz and leaving the most successful dynasty in the history of drag racing. He cites his Dad's legend as one of the factors…

"My dad was a leader and not a follower. My dad was about doing things on your own. That's one of the reasons I'm stepping out. For me to accomplish some of the things I want to do, I need to be in control. To continue that legacy is important."

I ask him how he got this far. La Raza is kicking into high gear…

"We did it the hard way. Everything that Cruz did, he did it on talent. He got in the car and he performed. And of course, now it has evolved into corporate America. Are you a good spokesperson? Can you deal with the media? Are we good representatives to the companies that have invested money in us? And that's how you make it in this business we're in.

"But I'm not trying to live up to anybody's expectations. When I was in Houston, parts of my interviews were in Spanish. Because I was at home. I won the Atlanta race the day before Cinco de Mayo. I gave my interview in Spanish there, too. The sponsors said, 'We don't know what you said, but it was great.'"

Tony is on a journey. I am trying to figure how much of it is Don Quixote, how much is Cesar Chavez and how much is Tony Robbins. He voices a desire for the community to "have better things for their kids. To live a better life. Maybe my dad wasn't around long enough to say, 'You don't have to chase women like I did and do what I did.' I learned that and he never really told me, but I learned that."

He then says he has been hired by his new sponsor to appeal to the purchasing power of his people. "What they're interested in is going to where their market share is down. In Southern California, in Texas, in Florida—these are big Hispanic markets."

For Tony Pedregon, the son of a taco taster, there is cultural pride and then there is personal pride also.

"Maybe part of the reason I'm leaving is that I am in John's shadow."

*****

I ask Tony to tell me about this final-round race over Bazemore in Vegas, the heat that decided the Season's Points Title. He laughs.

"Before I got in the car, I went up and shook Whit's hand. I said to him, 'Let's just get out of this alive.'"

From a spectator's vantage point, the race was utterly spectacular. The starting lights went green, and both drivers stomped on the throttle. At half-track, Tony's tires began spinning furiously and futilely and Bazemore started putting car lengths ahead of Pedregon. Tony remembers the moment well.

"The last thing I thought it would do was smoke the tires (lose traction). Probably out of fear, I got lucky and reacted to what the car did at that moment.

top fuel wormhole

When the car got loose the first time, I rolled out of it and then floored it again. I hit the first one just right, but I knew it was losing traction because I heard the motor coming unglued."

Uncannily, Bazemore began experiencing problems also. His car was also making too much horsepower; more than a cold track surface could process and he began to spins the tires like Tony. Pedregon smelled blood.

"'I don't care if this car is on fire,' I thought. The car made a move and it fishtailed. The sidewalls started to rock, and it wasn't stable. Again, I rolled out the throttle and rolled back into it. I knew the motor was going south. I saw that win light and let out years of frustration."

As Tony won the drag race and the 2003 Funny Car Championship, his motor exploded and created a pyrotechnics display as he crossed the finish line in victory. If it isn't hardwired into his genetic code, seeing his dad crash when Tony was still in diapers has made him afraid of nothing, not even the unknown. "I got so excited. I forgot to pull the parachutes. I was screaming. I was yelling. That (emergency) sand trap is coming and I saw the sand traps coming. The car was on fire, but I didn't care."

Our interview is done. I'm taking pictures of Tony greeting his fans. A prepubescent little curtain climber makes his way through the legs of the teeming masses of nitro-addled and beer-besotted race fans and approaches Tony for an autograph, clutching a copy of *National Dragster*, whose cover is a collage of images depicting Tony's triumph at Las Vegas.

Tony scrawls across the picture of his mug with the Sharpie and answers the youngster's question about winning the race against Bazemore.

The boy points to a shot of Tony, crouching on his knees, overcome with emotion and burying his head into his fire gloves.

"Why were you crying?"

Pedregon goes all WC Fields on the lad: "How do you know I was crying? We were in the desert and there was sand blowing all over the place. How do you know I don't have something in my eye?"

Tony looks up from the boy and shakes his head.

"That was years of tears waiting to come out."

(*Originally published in* LA CityBeat)

FRYING THE BALONEYS OFF OF DANICA PATRICK AT THE SMOG CUTTER

My friend Myron and I were sipping good, smoky whiskey at the Smog Cutter in the Thai Town section of East Hollywood, while listening to various Burmese chanteuses chirp out ballads on the jukebox. We began the night by bench racing, but ended it by arguing about IndyCar sensation Danica Patrick and female race-car drivers.

Myron is a drag racing writer and is a geeky, greasy-haired academic type with Clark Kent-type cheaters. His goofball nerdiness is mitigated by a penchant for pop-art t-shirts. Tonight he was wearing a white cotton t-shirt featuring a photo of a vintage Barracuda Funny Car doing a burnout. Through the copious clouds of smoke, the garment is emblazoned with the motto: "I'd Rather Be Frying the Baloneys."

I asked Sunshine, the brunette Asian bar wench and part owner of the Smog Cutter, who was singing on the jukebox.

"That 'Hwa Hwa and Bell.'" Sunshine said in broken English. "Famous hit single 'Oh Oh Oh' Big seller in Bangkok."

Myron was unimpressed with Hwa Hwa and Bell and their record sales. For a nerdy gearhead, he can exhibit a real mean streak that surfaces after a couple of belts of the hard stuff, and tonight was going to be one of those nights.

"I can't get a buzz and sing along to this crap, Sunshine" Myron complained. "You got any Kitty Wells or Patsy Cline on that jukebox of yours?"

"Kitty Wells? This no cowboy bar, John Wayne. This Thailand bar. You want redneck girls singing about handjob in pick-up truck, you go to cowboy bar in North Hollywood. Smog Cutter just play music from Thailand."

"Hey, speaking of Thailand, I hear you can get a virgin for seven dollars over there," Myron reported. "Or two for twelve."

Sunshine stuck out her tongue. "You funny guy, *Crark* Kent."

I ordered another round of Bushmills. During a lull in the libation and conversation, I looked over my shoulder at the smattering of elderly Thai gents smoking cigarettes and playing pai gow poker with a couple of Vietnam bets. Meanwhile, Myron began thumbing through the new Sports Illustrated and he had had enough.

"*Hay-sus Chreest-o,*" he blathered. "Can't I get a friggin' drink in a hole in the wall in a godforsaken section of town where nobody speaks any English without having to read about Danica freaking Patrick?"

"I'm with you, dude," I concurred. "You can't get away from Danica-fever and all the cheesecake photos of her. Apparently, this week she was googled on the Internet more often than Lindsay Lohan, Pamela Anderson and Britney Spears, and was out-googled only by Paris Hilton."

"Lindsay Lohan? Pamela Anderson? Britney Spears? Paris Hilton? What a litany of trust-funders and clothes-horses who have done their entire gender a disservice," Myron spluttered. "Just like Danica. Danica is all style and no substance. She finished fourth in the Indy 500 only because she spun out on a caution lap and caused four other cars to crash! Give me a break."

"Dude, I have to play devil's advocate. Crash under the yellow flag aside, Danica led a couple of laps in the Indy 500. No chickee has ever done that before. And she's a rookie."

I then told Myron about the time I went to Pole Day for the Indianapolis 500 a couple of years ago. That year the fairer sex was represented on the speedway by Lyn St. James, who qualified at the back of the pack. Just to show that the race fans were behind her efforts, some of the bleacher rats hung a banner that read: "Atta' Boy, Lyn!"

As I finished that anecdote, "Heart of Glass" by Blondie began to spin on the jukebox.

"Hey Sunshine," Myron yelled. "I thought you only had Thai music on the jukebox."

"Blondie popular all over the world. Besides, Debbie Harry and Blondie good for karaoke night."

"Finally," Myron whispered dreamily as he basked in Debbie Harry's crooning and ran his dirty fingernails through his unkempt hair. "A woman in the mix who has earned her stripes."

"Listen, dude," I interrupted. "You are wrong about Danica Patrick and you are wrong about Blondie. Debbie Harry was a no-talent blank slate for a team of songwriters and record producers. Her voice is as thin as a reed and is as torturous as said bamboo shoot up the fingernails."

The pai gow poker players heard the bit about the "bamboo shoots," put down their cards and cigarettes and looked at Myron and me.

Myron was oblivious to their actions and fired back at me. "I think your low regard of Ms. Harry as a so-called 'blank slate' is mebbee' a little bit too simple and is possibly sexist."

"Wait a minute, 'Mr. Two Virgins for Twelve Dollars.' You're calling *me* sexist?"

"Yes, I am. Your take on Ms. Harry was kinda reductive and painted with a real broad stroke of the brush, no doubt about it."

I felt compelled to explain myself. "I don't think that being a 'blank slate' is necessarily a bad thing," I said. "For example: Some of the finest pop music ever made only happened because some kind of egomaniacal freak went apeshit in the recording studio with some glorified blow-up doll of a singer. Like Blondie. Or like Phil Spector's catalogue: the Teddy Bears, the Ronettes, etc. My point is someone has to be the mastermind and SOMEONE has to be the blow-up doll."

"Are you calling Blondie and Danica Patrick blow-up dolls?" Myron asked as he tossed the copy of *Sports Illustrated* down the bar.

"I am saying that Blondie is a blow-up doll, but that Danica Patrick can actually drive a race car. But even so, there is a tradition of no-talents of the fairer sex making waves in popular culture, whether it is with a race car or a microphone. I am saying that regardless of talent, brazen sexuality trumps substance and makes headlines."

This caught Sunshine's ear.

"Danica Patrick may be bigger than Britney Spears blow-up doll," she said. "But she no Hwa Hwa and Bell."

Myron got up and put some money in the jukebox.

(Originally published in Drag Racing Online*)*

top fuel wormhole

DRAG PRINCESS

"A supercharger blew up in my face at 240 mph. There was a flash of fire that singed my eyebrows, and there was all of this hot, burning oil in my face, and I couldn't see snot." -- Mendy Fry, the nitro-burning CPA

With all the hoopla surrounding 23-year-old Indy Car phenom Danica Patrick and her fourth-place finish at this year's Indy 500 and Sports Illustrated cover (d'oh!), you'd think a girl had never put on a fire suit before. Meet Mendy Fry, a fresh young face from San Diego who says she is "29-ish" and acknowledges that she has been driving at speeds of over 200 mph since she was a teenager. Yes, like Patrick, Mendy is a veteran racer, but also a rookie—this is her first full year as a "hot shoe" driving an AA/Fuel Dragster, arguably the gnarliest contraption that relies on internal combustion for propulsion. And unlike Patrick's methanol-powered Indy Car, Fry's dragster runs on nitromethane, a chemical the feds consider to be a Class A Explosive.

"I'm going to be mixing fuel now." Thus beckons Fry with a mocking and self-effacing nod to Norma Desmond and the histrionics of show business, as if she, Mendy, were ready for her close-up. But this ain't *Sunset Boulevard*—it's Bakersfield, and Fry is more like a star on the rise.

We are in the "hot pits" of a racetrack located about one and a half beers north of the honky-tonk where Buck Owens sings to drunken cowpokes every Friday night. Here, Fry is competing in an annual drag race run at an abandoned Air Force base, and she's busy helping prep her race car for competition. "We can talk while I cut 20 gallons of 100 percent nitro," she says.

Adjourning to her dragster's trailer, a romper room of tires, tools and exotic metallic engine parts, she mixes expensive combustible chemicals in a makeshift laboratory. On orders from her crew chief, her assignment is to come up with a cocktail consisting of 94 percent nitromethane, cut with 6 percent alcohol. The alcohol will calm down the explosive effects of the liquid nitro, like vermouth to gin.

I ask Fry about the metaphysics of working with what, in essence, is a rocket fuel.

"The job of mixing fuel gives me a better understanding of what makes the car haul ass," she says. "And it does make me feel more connected with my team. It's a very simple, yet precise, job that helps me focus."

Ah yes, nitromethane. CH_3NO_2. The stuff that drag racers have torched for over 50 years, as an elixir guaranteed to transform a hot-rodded engine into a beastly leviathan. When it burns for six seconds, it will send Fry down the drag strip at 250 mph, with a *Sturm und Drang* that makes the observer wonder if the sky is tearing itself apart and the Hand of Doom is reaching into hyperspace to pull out the Big Bang's moment of singularity, only to dump the whole heapin', smolderin' enchilada in Fry's lap. (Ten years ago, convicted terrorist Timothy McVeigh laced his fertilizer bomb with nitromethane and then carved a hole into Oklahoma City and the nation.)

Fry's means are far more benign, of course. Still, it was kind of disconcerting to hear her ruminate about the most explosive of fuels.

"I just learned how to mix nitro yesterday," Fry grunts, struggling with the heft of a 5-gallon plastic jug loaded with the Armageddon juice. "I really don't want to spill any on the car right now . . ."

It's her first day? That's slightly incongruous because her press kit says she has been around the sport of drag racing since she was born. In fact, under her dad's tutelage, she drove her first race at age four. 4. F-O-U-R.

"I was my father's only boy," Fry explains, wiping her brow. "He was an engine and chassis builder and wanted a son. He got me instead, so he cut his losses and introduced me to racing. I started racing quarter-midgets before I was in kindergarten. My family did not take vacations, we went to the races." Fry continues multitasking, her gaze focused on a "hydrometer," a glass beaker that holds a sample of the volatile mixture she will pour into the tank of the *Mastercam/Plaza Hotel* AA/Fuel Dragster, owned by a 60-something SoCal drag-racing legend who answers to the *drag de plume* "Root Beer."

She is quiet for a second, staring at the mixture and the glass tube floating in the concoction. "I don't know the technical terms, but the gauge is off 3 percent on Root Beer's hydrometer, so I have to do the math in my head and make up the difference."

"Well," I say, "they split the atom and landed on the moon using punch cards, so a little adding and subtracting shouldn't make your race car blow up, should it?" The question is rhetorical.

"That's funny—but the measurements have to be dead on," Fry says, not laughing. She's been on the receiving end of a catastrophic engine explosion once or twice.

"Last year I had a supercharger blow up in my face at almost 240 mph. There was a flash of fire that singed my eyebrows and there was all of this hot, burning oil in my face, and I couldn't see snot. Imagine roller-skating down a hill in San Francisco and suddenly someone puts a paper bag over your head. The lights go out, and I am reaching for the brake and the parachute and just have to trust that the car is still going straight, that the end of the track isn't too close, that the other car didn't come into my lane. And then I had to unpucker my ass from the seat when I tried to get out of the car."

That was one of her first rides down the drag strip in a Top Fueler. But the misfires (if you will) have been offset by the triumphs. Earlier on the same day as the explosive oil fire, Fry made history as the first female driver to turn a five-second clocking in a nitro-burning AA/Fuel Dragster, recording a time of 5.87 seconds. On the same trip down the drag strip, she earned passage into the exclusive AA/Fuel Dragster "250 Mile Per Hour Club"—only its sixth member. All of this after a mere handful of passes in an AA/Fueler.

Fry continues her personal story: "I worked in my dad's chassis shop in the Bay Area as a teenager, answering phones, placing orders, paying the bills, etc., and then building race-car bodies. I moved to San Diego when I was 19 and built dragster bodies and components while going to college."

While she was at San Diego State, Fry's father died suddenly, and everything changed. She got away from racing and concentrated on her studies, graduated, and then became a wife and a certified public accountant. But drag racing kept re-appearing in her rearview mirror, an apparition of her past that would wormhole itself into her future.

"I was the San Diego Chapter president of the American Women's Society of CPAs for the year 2000," she notes proudly, while wrestling with the container of nitro, but that same year, she revisited the drag strip.

"I was absolutely blown away by the evolution of the sport and the fact that a lot of people remembered me and even missed me."

She was back. But this racing stuff does not come without a human cost.

"In high school, my first serious boyfriend told me that I would have to 'grow out of this' because he wasn't going to put up with it. He had to go very soon after that. Racing definitely put a strain on my marriage, too, which ended a year and a half ago. But the positives certainly outweigh the negatives. I have met and forged strong friendships with so many people because of drag racing."

Sloshing around the nitro and alcohol, she tells me about her relationship to nitromethane.

"It's definitely an adversarial relationship. I have been chasing this explosive fuel almost all of my life. And y'know, I may have been brought up around this sport and worked my ass off for and in it, but I'm not one of drag racing's elite. I'm not one of its guaranteed heirs. I'm a member of its blue-collar work force." She stops and catches her breath. "And nitro weighs a lot more than alcohol—Jesus, this stuff is really heavy!"

I laugh.

"Sometimes I have to wonder," says Fry, "is the girl mixing the nitro or is the nitro mixing the girl?"

Fry pours another sample into her beaker and examines it as I get behind her, stepping out of her light.

"Are you looking at the crack of my ass?"

I assure her that no, I am just watching a hard-working woman sweat out a nasty job. Does she have the right mixture yet?

"Oh, I am definitely doing the math—do you smell smoke? It's dangerous for me to think around nitro because there are sparks coming out of my ears."

The next day, eventual winner Howard Haight would beat Fry when her car's engine produced more horsepower than the tires could actually process and control. And in her next race, at Sears Point, Fry was crossing the finish line at over 200 mph when her engine exploded. Except for singed eyelashes and eyebrows, she climbed out of the dragster's cockpit unscathed.

(*Originally published in* LA Weekly)

"They're gonna put me in the movies..."

BUCK OWENS, TOP FUEL & THE DEATH OF THE BAKERSFIELD SOUND

"They're gonna put me in the movies/They're gonna make a big star out of me We'll make a film about a man that's sad and lonely/And all I have to do is act naturally" – John Bright Russell, Voni Morrison, "Act Naturally"

Bakersfield California is one of a handful of place on the planet where a purist can hear the aggressive roar of supercharged drag racing machines burn unlimited percentages of nitromethane in an internal combustion engine.

Last month on a Sunday morn in a vineyard, I sat in wooden grandstands and absorbed the Sounds of Bakersfield.

I listened to Vintage Top Fuel cars on bodacious loads of nitro as they rumbled, cackled and *ack-ack-acked*, and beat their chests thermodynamically with a vicious, beastly aplomb.

After they ran the first round of Top Fuel, three gas coupes crashed in two tries. The sun was coming out after it had rained for two weeks in a row and water seeped up through the asphalt and made the drag strip too slippery to traverse. The race was cancelled.

I drove home through the back roads of Famoso and Oildale, and went by country music star Buck Owens' ranch.

I grabbed Highway 99 South by the old Rain for Rent billboard and motored through town, catching a glimpse of the Crystal Palace, Buck's personal-yet-public shrine to the heritage of West Coast Country Music, as well as a restaurant/night club for local shit-kickers and boot-scooters.

*****

Country music has been the called the white man's soul music or the honky's rhythm and blues, and that is hard to argue with. Unfortunately, like soul music, the form of country music has been corrupted and mummified, and has become a doddering replication of itself.

A few folks argue that country was kaput when Ernest Tubb allowed a snare drum on a Grand Ol' Opry radio broadcast over 50 years ago. But that would overlook some tremendous performances by a coterie of crucial country artists, including the work of some pivotal California pickers and grinners, musicians like Red Simpson, Merle Haggard, and Buck Owens, all of whom made names for themselves as Bakersfield troubadours whose bands were often made up of the sons and daughters of migrant dirt farmers, who had escaped the Dust Bowl of Oklahoma.

Like the Dust Bowl topsoil, the sound of Bakersfield is just about gone with the wind, despite Buck Owens' attempt to keep it stoked at his Crystal Palace.

On damn near every Friday night for the last ten years or so, it was a recurring meta-media moment that manifested itself every time Buck Owens, its owner and star attraction, strode onto the stage.

I went to see this for myself, five or six years ago, with a couple of drag racers, after the opening day of the March Meet.

There were five or six of us getting seated for dinner, and we entered a narrow fuselage of a hallway that leads past the side of the stage and opens up into a dance floor, a bar and a dining area.

As we sat down, I commented on the first disturbing sign.

"Did anybody notice that gal in the wings with a Macintosh PowerBook?"

I was talking about Buck's teleprompter operator.

The prompter screens were mounted on silver metal stands, transparent and unobtrusive and invisible to the typical hard-partying patron. This set-up was the modern equivalent of cue cards and the same devices used by Presidents during State of the Union addresses. But this was not about any State of the Union. This was so Buck never forgot his own lyrics...

Before Buck took to the stage, an opening micro-set by his modern Buckaroos drowned out any attempt to place an order. A massive, booming drum kit went *DOO-DUH-DOO... DOOO-DOOO* as the drummer completed a roll that served more as a salvo than any time-keeping device.

This was the Sound of Bakersfield? As performed by field hands and cowboys?

After an aural assault that lasted for a half-dozen songs or so, a tall sparkling figure sauntered across the lip of the stage and commandeered a microphone. It was Buck. Immediately, there were signs of chinks in the armor.

"Is that a real person? Or a hologram?" somebody asked.

It was hard to tell. If it was a hologram, its movements were animatronic, and jerky as a home movie. If it was a human being, it could just be drunk.

Whatever it was, the voice was the same as the first wave of Bakersfield Sound. But Buck was trying to make himself heard against the sonic armada of a generic rock band as he struggled to read the lyrics off of a screen.

"They're gonna put me in the movies..."

A conservative estimate is that Buck Owens has performed "Act Naturally," his signature song, 4800 times since he first recorded it in 1963 and a British rock and roll band known as the Beatles appropriated it on their *Yesterday and Today* elpee. And he can't remember the words to the one song that made him more money than his Oildale mineral rights?

It was difficult to tell what we were seeing exactly. But it was easy to know when it was over.

Buck exited stage right and the band played a *chunka-chunka* overture to his departure.

"There's not going to be any encore," I observed.

"What makes you think that?"

"The chick with the laptop packed up her gear and went home."

The Buckaroos kept on pounding away for a few more generic modern country songs, embracing the sonic elements that makes modern country music far more bombastic, yet much less believable. And just like his teleprompter operator, Bucks Owens had left the building.

A couple of weeks ago, he died on his ranch, downwind of where the aforementioned vintage Top Fuel cars rumble like thunder on fat loads of nitro. Except when it rains.

(*Originally published in* Drag Racing Online)

top fuel wormhole

I'm thinking lemons beget Lemonade

TOMMY JOHNSON'S DIPPITY-DO & A MODEST PROPOSAL TO SPIKE DRAG RACING'S BAD HAIR DAY

It's no secret that things are bad in big-time professional drag racing. Television ratings are in the toilet. The NHRA's "Countdown" playoff system—a contrivance designed to correct plummeting ratings—imploded with indifference and, ironically, facilitated a further decline in ratings rather than stanching the broadcast bloodletting. Apparently, funny-car chassis are unsafe at any speed and the mandated 11th hour fixes are worse than the problem. Meanwhile, the prime patrons of the sport—General Motors, Ford, and Mopar—are hanging on by their teeth, nails and talons as their stock prices plummet and are jettisoning marketing dollars across the board, the draconian measures making the mavens of motorsport wonder: Is drag racing next? And when it comes to whatever discretionary foldin' money is lying around, some hillbilly Howard Hughes with a MySpace account promised two dozen race entries barrelfuls of free money and then became the mother of all Injun' givers, canceling checks quicker than Ken Lay on crank, leaving dozens of professional racers in the lurch and in search of non-existent corporate coin, all the while scratchin' their noggins with the furiousity of a fleeced WorldCom employee. Worse yet, the contract of broadcast anchor Paul Page—the mastodon of the malapropism—was renewed.

But Paul Page or no Paul Page, the most punishing blow to Big Time Drag Racing is the high-finance hanky panky of something called HD Partners—the publicly-owned tax dodge that was supposed to buy the professional divisions of the NHRA and four of its drag strips at fire-sale prices. Instead, HDP pulled the plug on the deal that was hawked as "taking drag racing to the next level," quicker than Alan Greenspan can mutter "irrational exuberance."

In the words of Paddy Chayefsky (as voiced by Howard Beale): "I know things are bad. Things are bad everywhere. It's a depression." Well, if drag racing ain't in a depression, it is certainly in a sub-prime mortgage crisis.

All of which leads us to PowerAde and funny car racer Tommy Johnson Jr.'s spiky haircut.

With Rome burning and Nero sawing away on horsehair, the most pressing drag-racing dilemma has naught to do with countdowns but couture; not with HDP but with hair gel…

To wit: after visiting Tommy Johnson's blog on the NHRA website and an accompanying photo showcasing the driver's latest hairdo, a friend alerted this scribe to a real conundrum. He wrote: "How does Tommy Johnson Jr. fix his hair back up after putting on his helmet? If he goes four rounds in one day does he have to fix his hair with 'product' four times daily as well? That's my biggest question going into this new season…"

His concerns are grave and valid, of course. But I am thinking the Tommy Johnson dilemma engenders solutions… In other words, as per bad hair days at the drag strip, I'm thinking lemons beget Lemonade. Or more specifically, PowerAde. i.e., if TJ Jr. "goes rounds" this year, afterwards, while being interviewed by Gary Gerould on national teevee, he can kill two birds with one magic marketing bullet by spiking his hair with PowerAde. This gesture opens up some promotional angles for CocaColaCorp (PA's parent company), who can reposition and re-focus the PowerAde brand to a broader and less-athletic demographic.

As it stands now, in advertising, when trying to make the rather pushed comparison between Tony Schumacher's 6500 hp Top Fuel car and "extreme" amateur athletes (who supposedly drink this stuff, yet none of whom know a dragster from a doughnut and are too busy surfing a lava flow or riding a bicycle up Mt. Kilimanjaro to sit still and watch drag racing), the PowerAde disclaimer has to read: "PowerAde does not increase strength. It provides carbohydrate fuel."

That means PowerAde is colored sugar water—which is behind only egg whites and Torco Oil in effectively manipulating human follicles to stand up like porcupine quills. I say TJ Jr. should shill in some new non-athletic, pompadour-centric marketing campaign, with new promotional spots that can read: "PowerAde: For Helmet Hair." Or "PowerAde: The Drag Racer's Dippity-Do." No disclaimer needed.

My guess is AquaNet's sales will plummet as motorheads flock to the new en vogue sticky stuff, and that this will logarithmically increase PowerAde's Return On Investment and may very well inspire CocaColaCorp to spend more dough on our sport and thus save NHRA drag racing.

Who needs HDP?

(*Originally published in* Drag Racing Online)

SMOKIN' DON SCHUMACHER'S, INTERNET WORM FOOD AND WHO KILLED MARK TWAIN?

Sample dialogue once overheard in a grandstand, Anytown Raceway, USA:

"Hey man, can I bum a choke?"

"Well, I'd like to lend you one, but I can't because we both smoke the same brand of cigarettes – O.P.'s."

"O.P.'s?"

"Other People's."

It began plaintively enough a couple of Saturdays ago with a post on "Nitroland," an online drag racing bulletin board. It seems "aj," a possibly pseudononymous poster wrote that: *"I would love to be able to go back into the old Header Flames' Archives and read again, that post by the late Cole Coonce one more time regarding opm. It was the only post by Mr. Coonce I ever understood and then only after it was explained to me................"*

"Opm" is not a phrase I coined. I am not sure who explained to "aj" that the abbreviation "opm" is an abbreviation for "Other People's Money." But Chris Martin, *DRO's* editor-at-large emeritus and a man who drinks more O.P.s than anybody, will tell you that the language is malleable and can twist, bend and flex like the chassis of a Top Fuel car with too much front wing, and that "opm" now stands for "Don Schumacher Racing." Or Something.

On the good ol' Internet, the language grows more distorted than even in meatspace, excepting maybe John Force trying to pronounce "PowerAde" with a mouthful of crackers, or new ESPN talking head Paul Page trying to pronounce the silent "c" in "Gary Scelzi." Which is to say that on the Nitroland forum, 'aj' was experiencing pronoun trouble and subject/adjective agreement when he referred to "Cole Coonce" as being late. (For the record: This column is late. I am alive. And even after having missed a reasonable deadline.)

What "aj" meant was that the Header Flames forum was "late," or more accurately defunct. Because Header Flames degenerated from a reasonable resource of racing knowledge circa 1995 into a cesspool of disinformation and a sleeper cell of personal attacks by the craven keyboard Attas of the Internet circa 2003, it was mothballed. By me.

When I read about my own death on a drag racing forum, I felt vindicated in shuttering the old Header Flames forum. Nothing proves a point like reading about your own death, I reckon...

Anyway, the next comment in this thread about my death was posted anonymously and read: *"cole coonce is worm food now? since when?"*

And the game was *on*. E-mails began trickling in, inquiring about my health and the eternal dirt nap. The phone rang and rang and I changed my outgoing message to: "I'm too busy being dead to come to the phone right now, but if you'd like to leave a message..."

It rang again and I picked up. It was Wrenchski. He asked me what it was like pushing up daisies on the Internet, and I told him it was kind of an out-of-body-experience, but that there was no brilliant white light, just the same blue glow off of the computer screen. But I did tell him that dying in cyberspace is kind of neat, because you get to see who your friends are, and if anybody has anything nice to say about you, you get to hear it. He mentioned that maybe I would want to stop the rumors, but I responded that I only write on the Internet if there is OPM involved. So I said that he could quell the rumors if he wanted or he could go ahead and write an obit, if he felt like it.

So he did. It reads as follows:

NAME: Ski
(Wrenchski@aol.com)
SUBJECT: Semi-famous author/scenester dies in mulholland rally...
DATE: - Saturday, May 27, 2006 at 14:31:00 (EDT)

NEWSFLASH — Noted author/musician/raconteur COLE COONCE died in a fiery wreck during the running of yesterday's Mulholland Rally... navigating for slightly more famous author Mickey Spillane, Team Hyundai's lead driver. Coonce's last words were rumored to be: "NOOOOOO... DUUUUUUDE... YOUR *OTHER* LEFT."

*****

Bruce Springsteen once sang that it ain't no sin to be glad you're alive. Mark Twain once wrote that the news of his death as being greatly exaggerated. Noted pianist/hypochondriac Oscar Levant's tombstone reads, "I told you I was sick." I kinda know how they all feel...

But when I do take the dirt nap, please mark my gravestone with an epitaph liberated from the Internet: "Cole Coonce is worm food." And the Reverend Wrenchski can read, *"Ashes to ashes, dust to dust, binary code to binary code..."*

(*Originally published in* Drag Racing Online)

THE DAY OF THE DELUGE AND SURVIVAL OF THE UNFITTEST

They say the definition of a "drag race promoter" is that he is the guy that bets it ain't gonna rain. At the Winternationals in Pomona, there was no second meaning.

It is not just a sour economy that is knocking drag racing's dick in the dirt. Here the weather seemed to conspire against this event: On the heated heels of the mother of all California Indian Summers—January was more searing than Hugh Hefner's hot tub—dark clouds gathered ominously and bunched up like puppies in a cardboard box and for five days it rained and rained and rained. This was no mere drag race. It was the modern Day of The Deluge.

Yes, Noah should've parked his rig here and gathered specimens, if only to ensure drag racing survives.

Because it is going to need it...

*****

Before the flood, due to a miserable economy, the car count at Pomona was sparse. Nobody expected otherwise.

Then the weather turned foul and the bleacher bums stayed home in droves. Race fans—casual and fanatical—seemingly avoided this race like the Plague.

Is it just the economy and the weather? Or is part of the problem that those nitromaniacs who once lived for Top Fuel have found less and less to relate to? In the interest of safety when it comes to Top Fuel dragsters and Funny Cars, there has been a neutering of nitro percentages the last few years and now an emasculation of the distance of the drag strip from 1/4 mile to 1000 feet.

Take the one session of qualifying that was run here. It's been raining all day Saturday; between cloudbursts the Safety Safari diligently dries and re-dries the track, then finally that evening the call for Top Fuel goes out. If you've endured the weather and now you're sitting at 900', trying to figure out what a 1000' run actually looks like or means.

To some of us, we don't know what's good, bad or ugly when it comes to the new drag racing distance.

The whole qualifying experience didn't help.

Apparent to anybody who could see the scoreboards mounted 320 feet beyond the finish, the left lane displayed spurious speeds. It credited Funny Car racer Jim Head with a 1000' elapsed time of 4.26 seconds, coupled with a top end speed of, uhh, 21 mph. Del Worsham went even quicker (4.03), and showed a Top End Speed of all of 24 mph. Mr. Magoo could see the whole thing was bollixed. Then the clocks stopped showing any mph at all…

Rumors began to manifest about the possibility of the computer tracking the first mph light as the second light, and vice-versa. Who knows what was wrong?

It got worse. Top Fuel came up. Then everything went Dixie.

Four pair of dragsters into the session, Arley Langlo and the *Titan Xpress* fired their engine. Apparently, the team forgot to fasten a throttle stop, Arley rolled through the water box, stepped on the throttle and the rpm went to the moon and POOF!—a flash of fire and the burst panel pops like a frozen beer can.

The parachute follows suit, dumping unceremoniously in the rear. As a denouement to what has become a series of sight gags, Arley engages his reverse gear and backs over his flaccid parachute. The cloth canopy is now in front of the dragster…

Somebody in the Pomona pressroom uttered, "Darwin was wrong. It ain't survival of the fittest that will ensure perpetuation of the species; if anything, it is survival of the unfittest."

Meaning what? "Meaning that NHRA once banned these guys from racing. It had plenty of entries that could make a pass and not scatter part and oil all over the drag strip. The economy took care of that… Hillary Will, Dave

Grubnic, Hot Rod Fuller, etc. They are all gone this year. Now NHRA needs the leakers. It needs Top Fuel entries who were once banned and who can't do a burnout without sneezing the blower. It doesn't matter. NHRA Top Fuel is like the statue of liberty: 'Bring us your poor, your tired…'"

To dispel such drag strip demagoguery, in subsequent passes Antron Brown and Joe Hartley roared down the racetrack and posted career best numbers. At 3.70, Brown's was the quickest 1000' pass in the sport's history. Or was it? These benchmarks transpired in the dubious left lane.

The rains came again, and somebody ran the numbers and Brown's and Hartley's times were dismissed as popcorn, if not poppycock.

As CompetitionPlus.com reported that night re the rotten recordings, "The NHRA made a decision to race ahead instead of halting action, which would have likely forced postponement due to rain.

"In checking the incremental elapsed times of low qualifier Antron Brown and Joe Hartley, the NHRA decided their runs, although obviously quick, could not be counted as legit runs."

NHRA itself acknowledged something was awry: "NHRA is confident that the two cars in question were among the sixteen quickest cars, but because it's impossible to assign times, the ladder will remain intact. Also, NHRA will not be awarding qualifying points for this race to Top Fuel drivers."

What their release didn't address is that the whole situation is bongoed. Moreover, it is even salvageable?

What times really mattered? Is this competition or isn't it? As much as one may enjoy both horseshoes and hand grenades, there is a lot to be said for competition that is not fuzzy, but is dead nuts precise to as much as a $10/1000^{th}$ of a second. Drag racers have DIED trying to squeeze out an extra 100th of a second out of their machine's elapsed time. Or an extra mile-an-hour. And now such pursuit means nothing at all? It is as if, "If you appear to be quick enough, that's good enough for us."

"A new low," somebody muttered.

Perhaps. But if drag racing hasn't stepped on its dork, it has at least backed up over its own parachute.

(*Originally published on* Drag Racing Online)

ABOUT THE AUTHOR

Cole Coonce immigrated to California in the grease bucket of a Studebaker wagon in the 1840s. Since he could not afford passage at the time, he was given to stow away. As a young hobo on the road in America, Coonce picked up many Native American languages and social mannerisms. (Most of which had to be sold for rent money in Los Angeles.)

Coonce now pioneers Goodyear drag-slick tire melting & air intake research for blower explosions. His final countdown looms in this torrid display of straightline tarmac wizardry.

Arden Treader — *Boston Post Beanery*

Made in the USA
Monee, IL
10 January 2021